SAMPLE
NOT FOR SALE

INVESTMENT ATLAS II

USING HISTORY AS A FINANCIAL TOOL

Kenneth G. Winans

STRATTON
—PRESS—
Publishing Life

Investment Atlas II
Copyright © 2018 **Kenneth G. Winans**

Stratton Press, LLC
1603 Capitol Ave, Suite 310,
Cheyenne, WY 82001
www.stratton-press.com
1-888-323-7009

ISBN (Paperback): 978-1-948654-43-2
ISBN (Ebook): 978-1-64345-232-6

Printed in the United States of America

TABLE OF CONTENTS

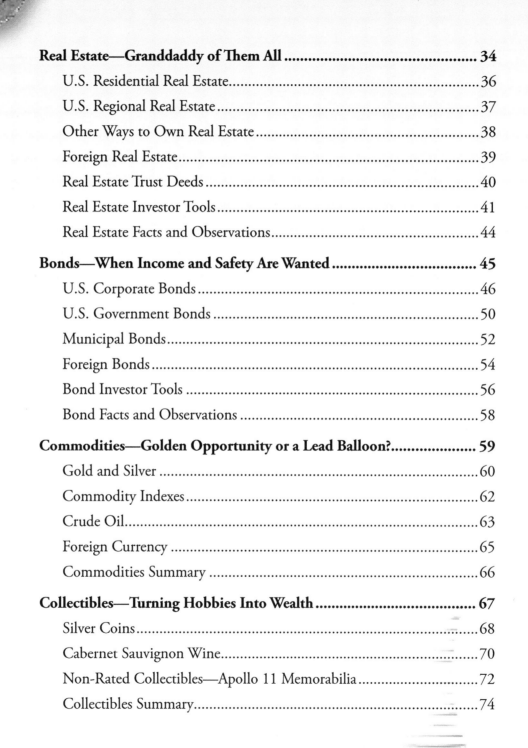

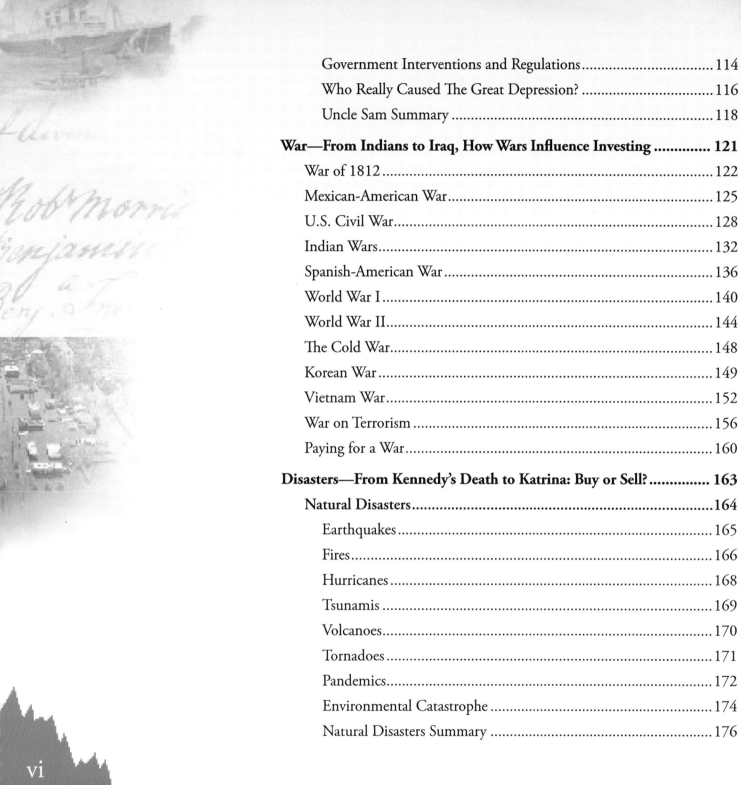

ACKNOWLEDGMENTS

No author ever writes a book by himself or herself, and with an illustrated reference book, it is especially true. A special thank you to the following:

Winans Investments Staff
    Marc Edwards
    Justin Gularte
    Kathleen Cuenco
    Priscilla Armstrong
    Karen Blair

FitchInk Staff
    William P. Barrett
    Joseph Colitto
    Stephane Fitch
    Erik Kobayashi-Solomon
    Samantha Shaddock

Global Financial Data
    Bryan Taylor

Museum of American Finance
    SG&A Productions
    Renee Robinson
    Rik Rice
    John Mayberry

DEDICATION

This is my fourth book since 2006. The hundreds of hours of intense work required to construct a book take a toll on a person both physically and mentally. More importantly, it requires sacrifices by the author's family.

This book is dedicated to my wife and soul mate, Debbie Wreyford. While it would take me writing another book to express my gratitude for her encouragement as I accomplish my life's important tasks, I want to simply thank her for supporting my ambitions and dreams.

Deb, let's go on vacation!

Love,
Ken

PREFACE and QUOTES FROM DISTINGUISHED READERS

What should a reader gain from *Investment Atlas II*? A logical assumption is that this is merely a reprint of the 2009 award-winning book *Investment Atlas*.

This is incorrect!

Investment Atlas was written before the Great Recession of 2008, and with stocks, bonds, and housing near record highs, it seems like a good time to revalidate the importance of using financial history within the investment process. Unfortunately, investor memories fade and fear recedes in long-running bull markets as "buy and hold" investors actively promote the success of their so-called strategy.

In *Investment Atlas II*, quotes from veteran investors/traders of a century ago such as Henry Clews, Edwin Lefèvre (a.k.a. Jesse Livermore), and W. P. Hamilton are used throughout the book to remind us of the need to protect ourselves from financial calamity in future bear markets in stocks, bonds, real estate, and commodities. I'm convinced that if they were alive today, these old pros would think the widely promoted global asset allocation strategy of today's investors being 100% invested, 100% of the time is absurd.

Remember the Great Depression.

As proof of the success of historically based market analysis, many of the time-tested research tools presented in *Investment Atlas* performed brilliantly on signaling a new bear market had arrived in January 2008 in stocks, bonds, and real estate, and the new bull market in common and preferred stocks in April 2009.

Investment Atlas II not only updates this past research but also several new market indices, such as the Winans-GFD International Housing Index and the Winans Legacy Stock Index, are presented. These valuable tools add insight to global real estate markets, new ways for calculating stock market valuations, as well as improved benchmarks for portfolio management.

The foreword of *Investment Atlas* sums up what the reader should ultimately learn in this book: "Like any atlas, the goal is to help the investor find out where they are going." Enjoy the book!

—Kenneth G. Winans, MBA, CMT

I have spent half a century studying two plus centuries of American financial history and using history's lessons in making financial decisions. Ken Winans's *Investment Atlas II* makes it possible for the reader to learn much of what I've learned, and some new things I learned from it, in a week, or even a long weekend. The books lavish and thoughtful illustrations make it a treat for the eyes as well as the mind.

—Richard Sylla, PhD,
Henry Kaufman professor of financial institutions and markets,
NYU chairman, Board of Trustees, Museum of American Finance

I am also a history buff and love all if your historic references and pictures. Price is a fact, earnings are an estimate. Charts truly represent the visualization of data both fundamental, economic and technical, incorporating all of investors' knowledge, emotions, experiences and biases. Read and enjoy this wonderful book and remember, "He who doesn't learn from the past is condemned to repeat it."

—Ralph Acampora,
CMT senior managing director,
Altaira Investment Solutions cofounder, Market Technicians Association

Ken Winans has written a book that will fascinate anyone interested in the financial markets and their history and will hopefully convince everyone else of the important of studying our financial past.

—Bryan Taylor, PhD,
president and chief economist, Global Financial Data

INTRODUCTION
IT'S DIFFERENT THIS TIME?

We have all heard the phrase "History repeats itself." Yet very few people apply long-term history to the art and science of investing.

There is no better example of this than how the majority of modern investors, the most knowledgeable and technologically advanced in history, mishandled the 50% stock market corrections during the dot-com busts of the early 2000s and the Great Recession starting in 2007. Throughout the preceding bull markets, the phrase "It's different this time!" was used over and over again by Wall Street's top gurus. Yet investors kept buying stocks and mutual funds in 1999 and 2007 without ever realizing their odds of success would be considered long in Las Vegas. In fact, they weren't even taking a CliffsNotes "glance" at the behavior of past bull market tops.

Does this sound familiar? "The Federal Reserve is much blamed because it made money easy" and "The real fault is that too many people are eager to grab something for nothing." No, these weren't written in 1999 about tech stocks, nor in 2007 about real estate securities. These words appeared in a business publication in January 1929!

The lunacy of twenty-first century "easy-money" mania might have been avoided if the investing public had realized that the stock market's advance over the previous years had far exceeded the return of the great bull market of the Roaring Twenties. With that knowledge, would they have been so eager to buy another "new age" stock with no earnings that was being managed by a twenty-five-year-old kid?

At the other end of the spectrum, the terror attacks of September 11, 2001, were compared to the Pearl Harbor disaster. Panicked investors didn't even consider that the market would act in a similar wartime way as they dumped their stocks with no plans to reinvest their money. The time-tested knowledge that investments go up, not down, in war cost them dearly as the 2003 US-led invasion of Iraq kicked off a four-year bull market in stocks, bonds, real estate, and commodities.

Historical ignorance isn't limited to stock investors. Throughout the 2000s, many real estate investors bought overpriced investment properties with nothing down, using adjustable rate mortgages based on the myth that real estate never loses value. It might have been wise for them to study how rising interest rates sent housing into a nosedive in the late 1960s and early 1980s.

Clearly, the constant barrage of news, earnings projections, economic reports, and advice from respected professionals streaming in over the web twenty-four hours a day hasn't helped investors separate the forest from the trees and tackle the age-old problems of successful investing.

Cartoon, 1882

HISTORY IS AN IMPORTANT KEY TO PROFITABILITY!

Though personal experience is an important teacher, learning to correctly interpret and apply history's lessons is a more important factor in successful investing. Remember, the names and faces are different, but the basic investment game hasn't changed in the past 150 years!

This reference book has been designed to help an investor build and maintain a strong foundation based on financial facts—a sort of investment history playbook—that an investor can refer to during a future calamity or to find out the performance record of a certain type of investment over the past two hundred years.

This book is divided into five sections. The first section, There's Gold in Them Financial Hills!, examines the amazing growth of the US economy and key developments of investing in America.

The Time-Tested Investments section studies the basic characteristics of six different types of investments since 1800. Unlike many investment books that view only one type of investment in a vacuum, this section includes stocks, real estate, bonds, commodities, collectibles, and cash in combined studies. The reader will realize that each type of investment has a different personality, and just like dealing with people, investors either learn to deal with the different types or avoid the ones they can't get along with. Though investors don't have to invest in every type of investment studied in this book, it is important that they follow the historical trends and know the advantages and disadvantages of these investments to determine which are the best investments for them.

Section 3, Market Cycles: From Easy Money to Crash Landings, examines the major bull and bear markets in stocks and real estate since 1800 and demonstrates how some of the tools outlined in Section 2 can provide the reader with clues as to the market's overall health.

Historical Events: Does Wall Street Care? studies the reactions of stocks, housing, and interest rates to various factors and scenarios that have continually confronted investors throughout history, such as wars, disasters (natural and man-made), and the never-ending government actions (i.e., interest rates, taxes, and regulations) in reaction to these situations.

The last section, Investing the Historic Way, demonstrates practical ways to use historical information in establishing a disciplined investment strategy, which involves setting reasonable goals, dealing with taxes, and finding proper ways to monitor an investment portfolio's progress. This section demonstrates that a successful investor doesn't need to be a genius or well educated but does need to study major issues and events that have affected investments through the ages and have the discipline to stay the historical course and not emotionally follow the herd to the financial slaughterhouse during future bear markets in stocks, bonds, and real estate.

The knowledge in this book is also a good BS detector in screening investment professionals and should help you find the elite investment advisors, wealth managers, financial planners, and brokers who are worth hiring. In other words, if they don't know the information in this book, don't waste your time and money working with them.

This book's emphasis is not to pick market tops and bottoms with a secret indicator but rather to identify investment scenarios that have been historically good times to make money in and warning signs to help preserve those hard-won profits as the investment climate becomes turbulent. In other words, this book helps you determine when you should be a "bull" or a "bear" for the right time-proven reasons. Simply put, only investors knowledgeable of history's trends can successfully navigate the investment world over time.

> **It has been my lot to discuss these Dow averages in print for many years past…It might not be becoming to say how constantly helpful the analysis of price movement proved.**
>
> **—W. P. Hamilton, editor of *The Wall Street Journal*, 1922**

WHAT IS NEEDED TO STUDY INVESTMENT HISTORY?

Three items are required to conduct the proper historical analysis of investments:

Reliable Investment Indexes

The invention of the Dow Jones Industrial Average (DJIA) marked an important milestone in the history of investing because it provided a common reference point of current stock market activity as well as a means to track its past performance. The index has been so successful that it has spawned the development of other investment indexes and products such as index funds and market derivatives, just to name a few.

But not all areas of investing are as well-indexed, and many investors have had to develop their own indexes. Take preferred stocks, one of the oldest and most reliable exchange-listed income investments in existence. Until the Winans Preferred Stock Index™ (WIPSI™) was introduced in 2005, there hadn't been a reliable index tracking this investment medium since the early 1900s.

DJIA's first day

Charles Dow's autograph, 1891

Financial Archaeology

One of the greatest problems in conducting long-term investment analysis is getting reliable data. Because of this, most investors and Wall Street professionals don't take their studies far enough back in time to be useful for long-term historical comparisons.

A great amount of time and effort went into amassing and compiling data needed to construct studies for this book. In fact, much of the data are from hard-to-find sources or required physically going into the library stacks to find the information.

Furthermore, to have continuous, usable charts and tables over a long time frame, many different indexes' percentage movements had to be combined. In other words, the focus in constructing charts used in this book is on percentage change of various indexes, not the indexes' values. For example, US common stock studies in this book came from many sources, such as Smith and Cole Studies (1800–1870), Cowles Commission Studies (1871–1895), Dow Jones Industrial Average (1896–1927), and S&P 500 Stock Index™ (1928–present), with volume figures from the New York Stock Exchange (1871–present).

Charts: The Maps of Investment History

We have all heard the phrase "A picture tells a thousand words." The pictures in this book are primarily charts of past investment activity. As you will see, these are an effective way to identify historical investment trends. Just as a traveler uses a road atlas to determine time and distance for a trip, charts of past market conditions help determine the overall direction and make historical comparisons with other types of investments. As the examples show, it is much faster and easier to determine the overall direction of the market with a chart than with a table of numbers.

I started writing the first edition of this book on a beach in Puerto Vallarta, Mexico. I was struck by how much the study of investment history resembles the movement of ocean waves. It was easy to see that the size and shape of no two waves were identical, yet the forces and factors that created them are the same.

INVESTMENT CHARTS

US PREFERRED STOCK YIELDS (SINCE 1900)

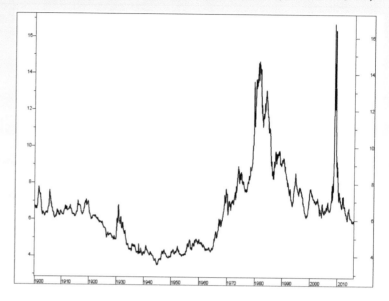

PREFERRED STOCK PRICE (SINCE 1900)

INVESTMENT CHARTS

Winans Investments Preferred Stock Index

Date	Yield	Price	Date	Yield	Price	Date	Yield	Price	Date	Yield	Price
1909	6.36%	7.17%	1936	4.42%	3.72%	1964	4.32%	3.10%	1991	9.12%	12.42%
1910	6.06%	-6.51%	1937	4.26%	-4.26%	1965	4.21%	-6.26%	1992	8.09%	4.80%
1911	6.38%	0.37%	1938	4.45%	7.25%	1966	4.48%	-14.25%	1993	7.69%	9.88%
1912	6.36%	-0.45%	1939	4.15%	0.95%	1967	5.24%	-11.82%	1994	6.97%	-16.43%
1913	6.39%	-3.74%	1940	4.11%	4.34%	1968	6.00%	-1.27%	1995	8.58%	16.06%
1914	6.64%	0.19%	1941	3.94%	-5.29%	1969	5.92%	-15.99%	1996	7.49%	-0.14%
1915	6.62%	6.15%	1942	4.15%	-0.95%	1970	7.32%	3.58%	1997	7.50%	14.77%
1916	6.24%	1.61%	1943	4.19%	1.92%	1971	6.86%	1.88%	1998	6.69%	9.87%
1917	6.14%	-12.20%	1944	4.16%	7.06%	1972	6.83%	-2.04%	1999	6.23%	-14.74%
1918	6.99%	6.89%	1945	3.87%	8.14%	1973	6.89%	-12.28%	2000	7.43%	2.11%
1919	6.54%	1.96%	1946	3.57%	-5.08%	1974	7.82%	-10.83%	2001	7.34%	11.54%
1920	6.42%	-8.98%	1947	3.75%	-8.30%	1975	8.78%	4.42%	2002	6.97%	6.90%
1921	7.05%	7.95%	1948	4.04%	-0.99%	1976	8.50%	13.21%	2003	6.98%	9.78%
1922	6.53%	8.31%	1949	4.14%	7.02%	1977	7.65%	-4.26%	2004	6.32%	4.76%
1923	6.03%	-2.33%	1950	3.87%	-0.88%	1978	7.84%	-11.32%	2005	6.32%	-4.35%
1924	6.17%	3.26%	1951	3.90%	-9.95%	1979	8.91%	-13.43%	2006	6.59%	1.98%
1925	5.98%	2.31%	1952	4.29%	5.00%	1980	10.14%	-17.08%	2007	6.44%	-17.46%
1926	5.84%	3.17%	1953	4.11%	-1.94%	1981	13.78%	-6.56%	2008	7.90%	-25.33%
1927	5.66%	4.93%	1954	4.22%	6.60%	1982	14.78%	20.27%	2009	12.15%	26.76%
1928	5.40%	5.63%	1955	3.92%	-3.15%	1983	12.36%	-0.04%	2010	8.39%	21.37%
1929	5.11%	1.02%	1956	4.05%	-7.96%	1984	12.46%	3.01%	2011	7.03%	-0.73%
1930	5.06%	0.58%	1957	4.62%	-0.13%	1985	12.18%	13.51%	2012	7.30%	9.60%
1931	5.03%	-15.88%	1958	4.44%	-4.24%	1986	10.65%	30.26%	2013	6.29%	-10.67%
1932	5.98%	2.39%	1959	4.62%	-5.81%	1987	8.69%	-10.63%	2014	6.66%	11.02%
1933	5.84%	1.00%	1960	4.89%	2.11%	1988	9.76%	-0.96%	2015	5.93%	0.44%
1934	5.78%	16.76%	1961	4.85%	3.50%	1989	9.76%	9.64%	2016	5.90%	-2.87%
1935	4.95%	12.02%	1963	4.42%	1.64%	1990	8.96%	-2.04%	2017	5.59%	2.42%

Look at the front cover of this book. Isn't it amazing how much the stock market trends of the three great bull markets shown resemble one another? In other words, when charts of an investment, from the same scenario in two different time frames, are compared, the patterns are not usually identical, and yet the direction of the trend is. This is because the economic forces that move the investment in a certain direction are the same in the long term.

Ultimately, people's emotions (i.e., greed and fear) about money and investing haven't changed much over time, and their actions typically resemble those of previous investors. The critics of this type of analysis will tell you that investment prices don't trend and, instead, move randomly through time. Their unrealistic answer to investing is to "buy all the time." As you study the following pages, it will soon become obvious that investment prices do trend over long periods of time.

This information, coupled with the tools outlined in the Time-Proven Investments section, can help investors make important investment decisions. As stated before, this book is not about attempting to pick market tops and bottoms with a magic formula. Rather, it uses history to keep you on the right side of the tracks in major bull or bear markets.

THE WINANS COLLECTION

Throughout my education and career, I have read many useful yet incredibly boring books on economics, finance, and investing, whose important messages are lost on less-than-enthusiastic readers. To ensure this book does not fall into that infamous category, the best parts of investment, history, and art books are combined. Useful yet beautiful!

As a serious collector of antique financial documents, photographs, and publications (many on display in the Museum of American Finance), I have used pieces of this collection, some dating back to the 1600s, to decorate this book and help bring historical events back to life.

As a final note, I am a twelfth-generation American whose Dutch family first arrived and established colonies in New York and New Jersey. They became some of this nation's first multimillionaires. My mother's Swedish family immigrated to California in the 1850s and soon became leaders in science, architecture, agriculture, and business.

An epiphany hit me as I began working on this book: "My ancestors experienced everything I'm writing about—the wars, depressions, natural disasters—all of it!" To honor their achievements, I also have accented their investment experiences throughout this text.

Enjoy the journey!

"**The most influential financier in this country's history, J. P. Morgan, was also a voracious collector throughout his life. He bought on an astonishing scale, collecting art objects in virtually every medium, including the rare books, manuscripts, drawings, prints, and ancient artifacts.**"

—**The Morgan Library & Museum website**

First edition of *The Wall Street Journal*, July 8, 1889, from the author's collection, on display at the Museum of American Finance in New York City

Nieuw Amsterdam onlanx Nieuw jorck genaemt,
en nu hernomen by de Nederlandere op den 24 Aug 1673.

Von Eisenbletter family crest, 1600s

New York Stock Exchange during the panic of 1914

Remember, successful investing is timeless!

Winans coat of arms, 1100s

The bubbles burst, but Bulls and Bears still exist in full vigour.

—Thomas Mortimer, *Every Man His Own Broker*, 1791

THERE'S GOLD IN THEM FINANCIAL HILLS!

During the 1849 California Gold Rush, crowds of people ran up and down San Francisco's dusty streets yelling, "Gold found near Sacramento!" as evidenced by the return of the first miners with sacks of gold nuggets.

Without hesitation, many people abandoned their jobs, spent their life savings on mining tools, and headed into the wilderness with dreams of easy money. The plan was simple: just dig—something's bound to show up!

The outcome was predictable; only a handful of miners ever found enough gold to be rich. After a few years, many unsuccessful miners returned from the goldfields angry and bitter from the experience. Most blamed their misfortune on the businessmen who made their fortunes by selling equipment and supplies to them while filling their heads with fantasies that the easy riches were just another shovelful of dirt away.

Modern financial bull markets conjure up similar dreams of easy riches that are just a computer keystroke away for anybody and everybody with an internet brokerage account!

Yet during the bear markets that follow, many novice investors blame the financial community for their economic demise, claiming the stock market is just another casino, and that only Wall Street makes money through the fees and commissions they charge investors.

Is there really gold in them financial hills, or is it a deception created by Wall Street to sell investment products?

In this section, it can be seen that the path to financial success has been, and continues to be, alive and well for disciplined, knowledgeable investors.

Regardless of their professional standing, the vast majority of investors underperform the markets. Emotions easily overwhelmed reasoning when money is at stake. When times are good, investors take them for granted and do not prepare for risks.

—Richard Peterson, *Inside the Investor's Brain*, 2007

U.S. ECONOMY

Long-term investing can be successful only within a healthy economic environment of solid growth and mild inflationary pressures.

As can be seen, the US economy has grown to be $19.4 trillion in 2017. This is a 4.2 million percent increase since 1800.

The second chart shows that economic growth isn't a straight line. The cycle from a recession low point to the top of the following economic expansion has happened thirty-nine times in the past 217 years, and averages 5.7 years in duration, with future growth generally making up lost financial ground quickly.

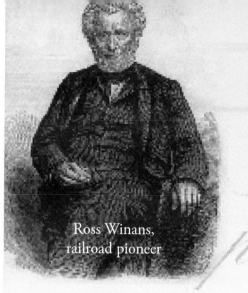

Ross Winans,
railroad pioneer

US GROSS DOMESTIC PRODUCT (SINCE 1800)

Current level: $19.4 trillion

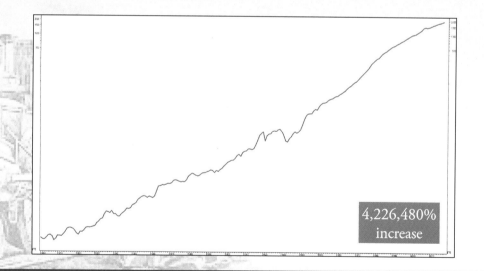

4,226,480% increase

ECONOMIC EXPANSIONS AND RECESSIONS

with US Stocks (since 1800)

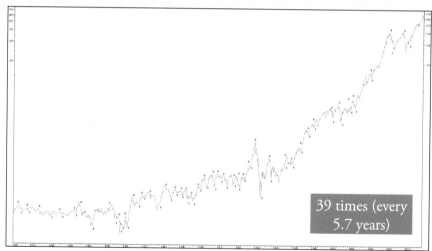

39 times (every 5.7 years)

From 1869 onward, the United States evolved from a preponderantly agricultural setting, in which it depended on and was oriented toward foreign commerce, into a growing industrial and service-oriented economy with a vast and expanding domestic market at its disposal.

—Nicolas Spulber, *The American Economy*, 1995

INFLATION

Inflation is the erosion in the value of money mainly caused by government policies that overproduce the amount of their currency held by the public in light of the limited availability of goods and services for consumption. Simply put, a dollar today doesn't buy the same goods and services as yesterday. History has repeatedly shown that unchecked inflation has led to worthless money and global conflicts.

As seen in this chart, over the past 217 years, the annual US inflation rate has been as high as 25% (1864), deflation as low as -16% (1802), and has averaged 4.2%. Inflation rates are significantly higher during wars than during peacetime. Since 1859, the average annual inflation rate has been 2.2%. During the seven wars since that time, the average inflation rate has been 5.3% while the peacetime rate was only 1.2%.

Article on inflation, *The Magazine of Wall Street*, 1934

US INFLATION RATE (SINCE 1800)

Current level: 2.1%

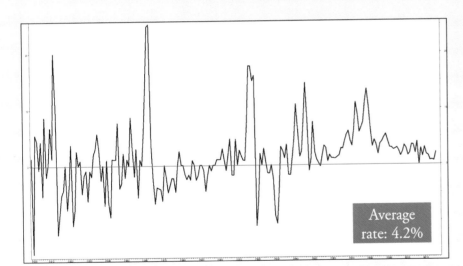

Average rate: 4.2%

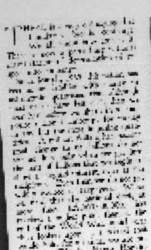

After World War II the Federal Reserve System continued to increase the quantity of money rapidly, thereby feeding the inflation.

—Milton and Rose Friedman, *Free to Choose: A Personal Statement*, 1979

INVESTMENT LIQUIDITY

To effectively invest, you have to have systems of exchange to buy and sell investments efficiently. In world history, no country has done this better than the United States, where the financial industry has been able to keep pace with the ever-growing demand for stocks, bonds, and real estate.

NYSE SHARE VOLUME (SINCE 1874)

Current monthly level: 20.7 billion shares

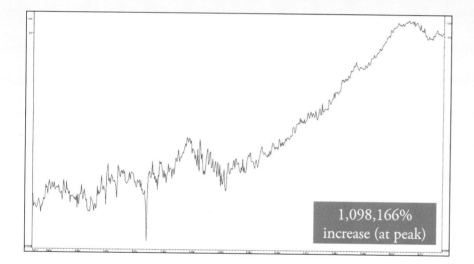

1,098,166% increase (at peak)

NYSE CORPORATE BOND VOLUME (SINCE 1900)

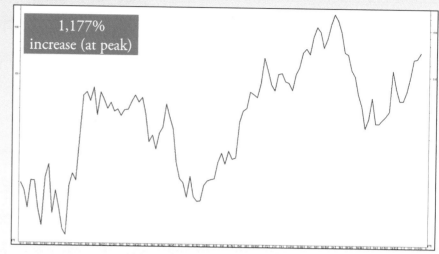

1,177% increase (at peak)

US HOME SALES (SINCE 1964)

Current monthly level: 65,000 homes

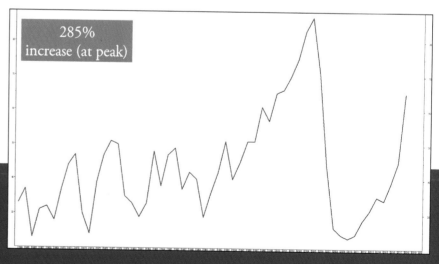

285% increase (at peak)

The Stock Exchange or Bourse in its present use is a modern creation.

—Samuel Armstrong Nelson,
The ABC of Stock Speculation, 1903

INVESTMENT INVENTIONS

INDIVIDUAL RETIREMENT ACCOUNTS (SINCE 1962)

Current level: $726 billion

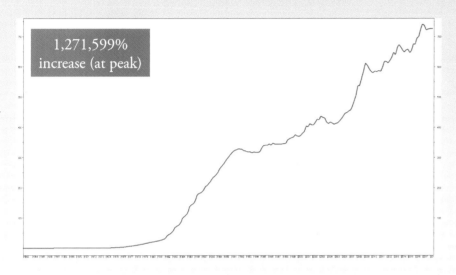

1,271,599% increase (at peak)

Modern investors have a wide assortment of products that allow them to tax-effectively invest in stocks, real estate, bonds, commodities, collectibles, and cash-equivalent investments.

Two of Wall Street's most popular inventions are mutual funds and tax-deferred individual retirement accounts. In fact, both of these products have significantly increased the participation of smaller investors in stocks and bonds.

Summary

Yes, there is definitely still gold in them financial hills! The following sections of this book will show what is reasonable to expect from an investment in the next bull or bear market as well as how investors have typically reacted to historical events.

By learning history, you shouldn't end up like most miners of the 1800s or the majority of investors today, who bank too much on luck and thus repeat the same financial mistakes that others made in the past.

MUTUAL FUNDS (SINCE 1940)

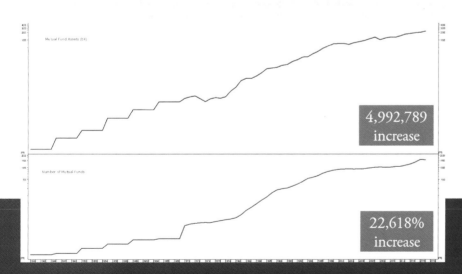

Mutual Fund Assets ($B)

4,992,789 increase

Number of Mutual Funds

22,618% increase

How Investment Trusts are Meeting the Depression

Mutual fund article, 1932

There are over two hundred mutual funds, some of enormous size. Mutual funds are merely co-ops, and they can be started by anyone in any way.

—Ellen Williamson, *Wall Street Made Easy*, 1962

Which nation is best at creating economic growth from its national savings? US capital markets—that is, much maligned Wall Street—are tops in the world!

—*Investor's Business Daily*, February 6, 2016

TIME-TESTED INVESTMENTS

With all the colorful vocabulary produced by the financial community, it's interesting to note that all investments basically come down to two types. Investors either own or loan, and neither kind constitutes a "perfect" investment for everybody. Sorry, there is no holy grail of investments!

Undoubtedly, owning is the best way to create wealth over the long term (i.e., capital appreciation), but it can be volatile in the short term and, if done stupidly, can cause significant, often devastating, losses.

On the other hand, loaning can provide a predictable rate of return and produce income to meet an investor's regular cash needs without the need to sell or borrow against investments. Unfortunately, many investors confuse low risk of default with market volatility that can cause surprising swings in market value throughout the life of income investments.

Simply put, every investment has its ups and downs!

This section examines the long-term characteristics of stocks, real estate, bonds, commodities, collectibles, and cash-equivalent investments.

Though the results might be a bit surprising and quite possibly contradict your own limited experiences, this long-term research should help investors better identify the best investments for their individual needs and know what is reasonable to expect, good and bad, from different types of investments over time.

WHY IS LONG-TERM INVESTMENT ANALYSIS IMPORTANT?

Investment analysis is often done backward, with an overemphasis on short-term results. Long-term statistics are commonly presented as unimportant, curious facts. Ironically, most of the investing public consider themselves "long-term investors," yet they focus on the short-term value fluctuations of their investments.

We all enjoy pictures sent back from outer space that show the earth from a distance. They show us weather patterns and topographical formations that seem random at ground level.

Long-range investment analysis can be seen in the same light. If an investor starts from a high or long historical vantage point, then the investor should gain a broader prospective of his/her investment's overall trends and performance characteristics. The wise investor hopes that when the next market panic erupts, he/she will be less likely to overreact to short-term events and the media's perspective on them.

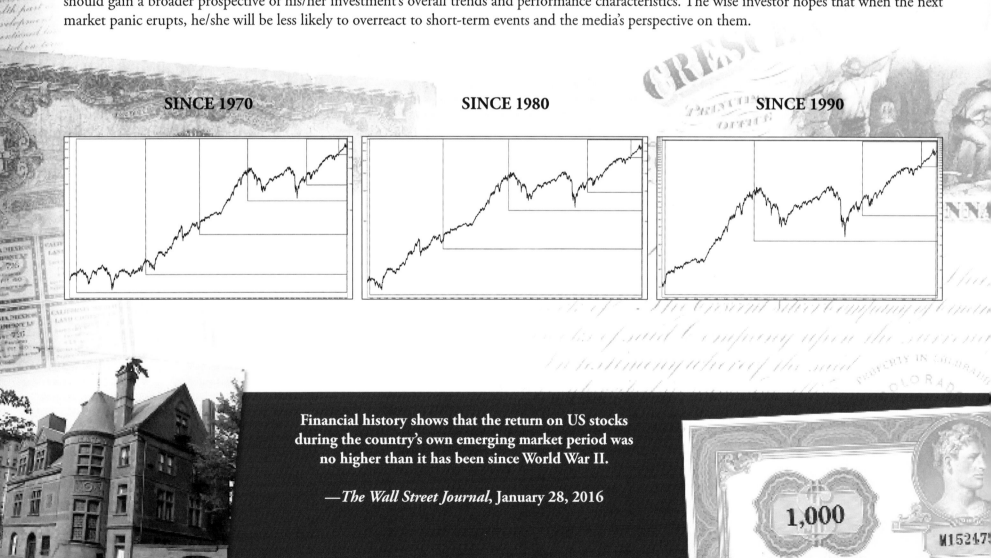

SINCE 1970   **SINCE 1980**   **SINCE 1990**

Financial history shows that the return on US stocks
during the country's own emerging market period was
no higher than it has been since World War II.

—*The Wall Street Journal,* January 28, 2016

ANSWER: EARLY DETECTION OF A SIGNIFICANT CHANGE IN THE MARKET'S DIRECTION

Look at these charts of US common stocks from different time frames:

1. Since 1970
2. Since 1980
3. Since 1990
4. Since 2000
5. Since 2010
6. Since 2016

A picture (or chart) really does tell a thousand words! Though a trader focusing on short-term volatility could have easily sold stocks investments in 2015, investors need to be aware that the longer-term charts show the stock market's uptrend possibly changing course.

SINCE 2000　　　　**SINCE 2010**　　　　**SINCE 2016**

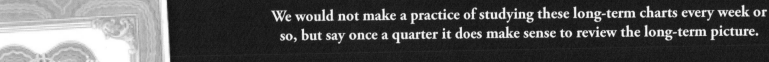

We would not make a practice of studying these long-term charts every week or so, but say once a quarter it does make sense to review the long-term picture.

—Martin Pring, *Technical Analysis Explained*, 2002

1,000

This stock transaction receipt from the bear market of
1906 and 1907 belongs to legendary collector and scientist
Dr. Gustav Eisen, the author's great-great-great uncle.

STOCKS — SIMPLY THE BEST!

The invention of the corporation in the 1600s has transformed the world in ways that even Adam Smith, the father of modern economics, would have had trouble imagining. It is ironic that his classic work *The Wealth of Nations* was written in 1776, the year America was born, because no country has embraced the corporation more passionately than the United States as it has amassed wealth at a rate never seen before in world history.

Every year, leading magazines list the richest people in America, and the vast majority of these individuals made the bulk of their fortune through various business (i.e., stock) investments, thus proving their value as the premier wealth producers.

But it is not "easy money" at the push of a button on a brokerage website. With billions of shares traded daily in the US alone, stock investing is fast-moving and volatile, where strong companies can suddenly lose a year's worth of gain in seconds from events they did not necessarily cause. It's also worth noting that every single past generation has gone through serious multiyear stock bear markets (1906–1907, 1929–1932, 1973–1974, 2000–2002) where losses exceeded 40%, and the financial devastation is well remembered with fear and anger.

THE GREATEST SECURITIES MARKET IN THE WORLD

Distrust of stocks was the prevailing American attitude throughout the 1950s and into the 1960s, when the market tripled and then doubled again.

—Peter Lynch, *One Up on Wall Street*, 1989

U.S. COMMON STOCKS

Below are charts showing the prices and dividends of US common stocks since the early 1800s, as well as the total return (annual price change and dividends combined) adjusted for inflation since 1850.

Common Stocks Since 1850		
Average Annual Total Return	11.2%	
Inflation Adjusted Total Return	8.9%	
Highest Total Return	88%	in 1915
Lowest Total Return	-42%	in 1931
Negative Returns	27%	
Consecutive Negative Returns	7%	

US COMMON STOCKS PRICES

with dividend yield (since 1800)

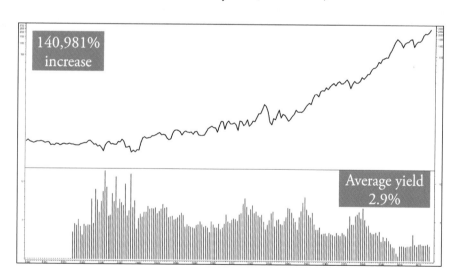

140,981% increase

Average yield 2.9%

US COMMON STOCKS TOTAL RETURN

with inflation-adjusted return (since 1850)

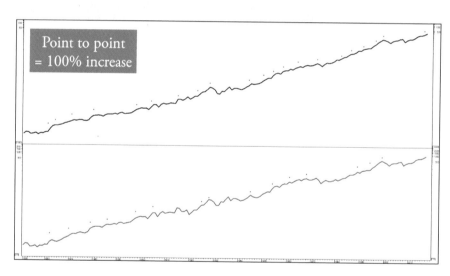

Point to point = 100% increase

Common stock is more often a speculative or semi-speculative security than preferred stocks or bonds. In many cases common stocks have never received dividends and probably never will. Their chief value is measured partly by their voting power and partly by the fluctuating value of the equity in the property of which they are shares.

—John Moody, *The Art of Wall Street Investing*, 1906

US stocks come in many sizes. Wall Street has long indexed and evaluated their performance by the market capitalization of the companies within groups of similar-size corporations.

Which group performs best?

Since 1927	Total Returns	Negative Years	Consecutive Neg Years	Returns Extremes		Outperform Large Cap
				< 20%	>(20%)	
Large-Cap Stocks						
Cumulative	324,099%	27%	9%	35%	6%	na
Ave	12%					
Median	13%					
High	53%					
Low	-44%					
Midcap Stocks						
Cumulative	1,758,921%	28%	9%	36%	7%	56%
Ave	14%					
Median	16%					
High	102%					
Low	-46%					
Small-Cap Stocks						
Cumulative	702,803%	34%	9%	39%	10%	56%
Ave	14%					
Median	18%					
High	120%					
Low	-50%					

This chart shows large, medium, and small stock performance since 1927. They look nearly identical, and yet by far, the best-performing group is mid-cap stocks. These securities have produced a higher cumulative return due to having fewer negative years than either small- or large-cap stocks.

Simply put, bigger does not mean better!

US COMMON STOCKS

by market capitalization (since 1927)

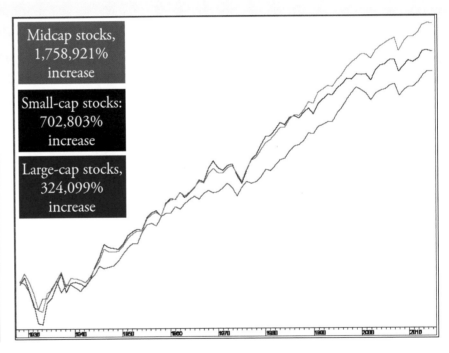

Midcap stocks, 1,758,921% increase

Small-cap stocks: 702,803% increase

Large-cap stocks, 324,099% increase

Higher returns are associated with higher risk. If there is a trade-off between risk and reward, medium capitalization stocks theoretically should track between the large-cap and the small-cap over the long run.

—S&P MidCap 400 Directory, 2006

GOING LONG

Besides its superior long-term performance, stock investing is multidimensional. Through the use of margin, short sales, and stock options, even a small investor can increase his or her gains during bull markets and make profits in bear markets.

Margin loans are backed by the assets held in a brokerage account. This allows investors to access their account equity by either withdrawing funds from the account or buying additional stocks without having to deposit more funds. It also allows aggressive investors to increase the return on investments in large, conservative companies whose shares are more liquid than smaller companies' shares.

NYSE MARGIN USE (SINCE 1918)

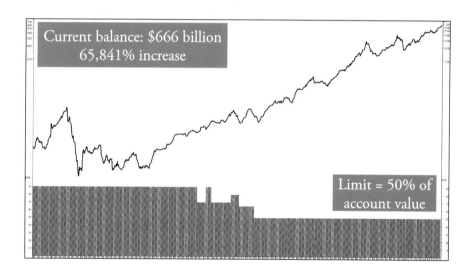

Current balance: $666 billion
65,841% increase

Limit = 50% of account value

CBOE STOCK CALL OPTIONS (SINCE 1989)

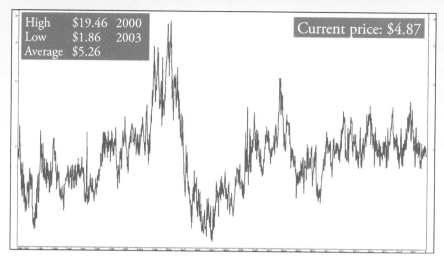

High	$19.46	2000
Low	$1.86	2003
Average	$5.26	

Current price: $4.87

An investor can make money in stocks without even owning them. For a small price paid to the stock owner, a stock option gives its holder the right to buy (call) or sell (put) shares in the stock for a limited period of time at a set price. If the holder of the option has correctly judged the future direction of the stock's price within the option's limited life, then the option should greatly appreciate in price far more than the stock itself.

Remember that leverage is a two-edged sword, and investment mistakes are very painful. Margin loans need to be paid back with after-tax dollars regardless of the account's current value, and options often expire worthless. Both add significant volatility to a stock portfolio in both bull and bear markets.

Trading in put and call options is known to involve financial risks, but it is sometimes physically dangerous to trade options. Or at least it was in the 19th century, before organized option exchanges were developed. Before 1973, when the Chicago Board Options Exchange opened its doors, put and call options were primarily a matter between the buyer and the seller.

GOING SHORT

An aggressive stock investor can make money on stocks in bull markets by owning long for upward appreciation and short selling during bear market declines.

    This is done by borrowing another investor's stock held at a brokerage house with interest, selling the shares at the current price, with the objective of buying the shares back at a lower price in the future and returning the shares to the original owner. Remember, as with any margin loan, the shares borrowed for the short sale need to be paid back in the future at the brokerage house's discretion!

NYSE SHORT SELLING (SINCE 1931)

Short interest sales

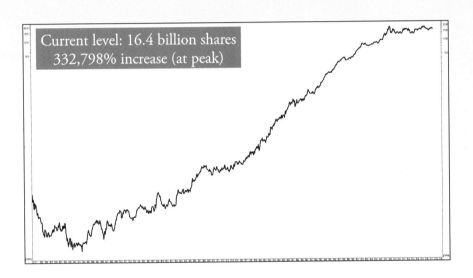

Current level: 16.4 billion shares
332,798% increase (at peak)

CBOE STOCK PUT OPTIONS (SINCE 1989)

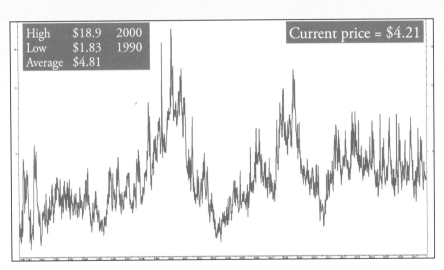

High	$18.9	2000
Low	$1.83	1990
Average	$4.81	

Current price = $4.21

Short selling is not a short cut to fortune. You might be right on the general market but go short on some stock that rises against the trend and suffers enormous losses.

—*The Magazine of Wall Street,* September 19, 1931

Prudence suggests that investors have an adequate idea of stock-market history, in terms particularly of the major fluctuations in its price level and of the varying relationships between stock prices as a whole and their earnings and dividends.

—Benjamin Graham, *The Intelligent Investor*, 1973

Philadelphia and Lancaster Turnpike Road, 1795
This is one of the first stock certificates to add artwork (vignettes) to the face of the certificate. The back of the certificate lists all its owners until its retirement in 1900.

What has been done will be done again. Such examples fortify the doubts and misgivings which possess the mind during the first stages of a bull market, and stimulate the hardihood and pride that goeth before a fall.

—William Fowler, *Ten Years in Wall Street*, 1870

United Artists Theatre Circuit, Inc.

COMMON STOCK

Buffett himself once said that growth investing and value investing are aspects of the same thing.

—John Train, *The Midas Touch*, 1987

Warren Buffett

This is a stock issued to Mr. Buffett in 1961.

The most successful stock investor of all time is Warren Buffett, who has amassed $71 billion in assets since 1951 and is currently ranked the third richest person in the world.

The essence of Warren Buffett's thinking is that the business world is divided into a tiny number of wonderful businesses—well worth investing in at any price, and a huge number of bad or mediocre businesses that are not attractive as long-term investments…Bonds are often better investments than stocks of bad or mediocre businesses.

—John Train, *The Money Masters*, 1980

FOREIGN COMMON STOCKS

Investing in foreign equities is not new to Wall Street. Since colonial times, there has been active free flow of investments, with American investors buying foreign stocks and foreign investors buying American stocks. In fact, foreign stocks have been traded on US stock exchanges since the late 1800s.

Below are charts listing foreign investment activity and prices since 1958, and they clearly show that as the post-World War II world economy expanded, so did the trading of stocks globally.

It is commonly believed that foreign stocks outperform domestic stocks and provide better protection against a bear market in US stocks. This is not necessarily true. As can be seen in the charts and tables below, mid-cap US stocks have outperformed world markets overall, and both mid-cap and small-cap US stocks provide better diversification against a sell-off in large US stocks than international stocks. It should also be noted that many investors confuse investment performance of a foreign stock with changes in the value of the US dollar versus the home currency of the foreign company. This analysis was done in US dollars.

GLOBAL STOCK TRANSACTIONS (SINCE 1958)

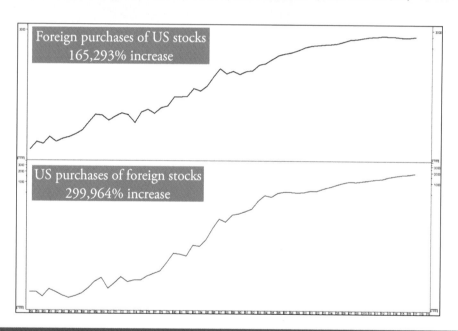

Foreign purchases of US stocks
165,293% increase

US purchases of foreign stocks
299,964% increase

From the standpoint of US investors, the benefits of global diversification tend to decline just when they are needed most (in bear markets).

—International Monetary Fund Report, 2007

FOREIGN STOCKS VERSUS US STOCKS (SINCE 1927)

Market capitalization

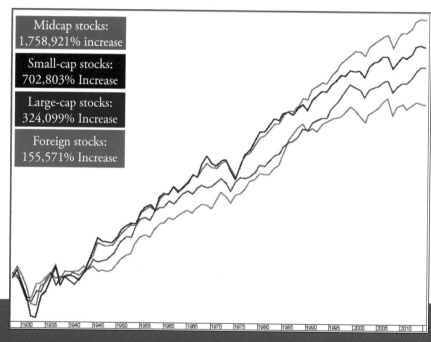

Midcap stocks:
1,758,921% increase

Small-cap stocks:
702,803% Increase

Large-cap stocks:
324,099% Increase

Foreign stocks:
155,571% Increase

Emerging markets aren't lucrative investments just because they are 'emerging.' They deliver higher returns only after they have been battered.

—The Wall Street Journal, January 28, 2016

COMMON STOCK FACTS and OBSERVATIONS

Since 1900

Positives

- US common stocks have produced a 63,427% cumulative gain (a 12.0% average annual return).
- $1 invested in stocks in December of 1899 is worth $71,039 today ($2,074 after inflation)!
- They have doubled in value 15 times (every 8 years on average).
- 36% of the total return was from dividend income.
- The best annual return was 87.5% in 1915.

Negatives

- US common stocks have posted negative years 29% of the time.
- Multiyear bear markets occur 8% of the time.
- The average loss in a negative year is -13.1%
- The worst annual return was -42% in 1931.

Since 1927

When stocks are separated by size (i.e., market capitalization), US mid-cap stocks have produced the best overall returns (1,758,921% cumulative, 14% average annual returns). They also have fewer negative years than small-cap stocks.

Since 1958

When US stocks are compared to world markets, US mid-cap stocks have produced better overall returns and offer better diversification against a sell-off in large US stocks than a basket of foreign markets in general.

Ads, 1929

Since 1958	Total Returns	Negative Years	Consecutive Neg Years	= Large Cap Neg Years	Returns Extremes < 20%	Returns Extremes > (20%)	Outperform Large Cap
US Large-Cap Stocks							
Cumulative	21,053%	21%	5%	NA	30%	4%	na
Ave	11%						
Median	13%						
High	38%						
Low	-35%						
US Midcap Stocks							
Cumulative	112,505%	25%	5%	42%	33%	4%	58%
Ave	15%						
Median	16%						
High	57%						
Low	-37%						
US Small-Cap Stocks							
Cumulative	45,399%	32%	4%	42%	33%	9%	56%
Ave	14%						
Median	18%						
High	64%						
Low	-35%						
World ex US (in USD)							
Cumulative	40,436%	28%	5%	67%	30%	4%	54%
Ave	11%						
Median	12%						
High	70%						
Low	-46%						

NYSE listed the Mexican Telephone Company, 1899

U.S. PREFERRED STOCKS

These investments have been called Wall Street Orphans and are often overlooked for the high returns of common stocks and the promised interest payments of bonds. In reality, these income investments offer several key advantages: they pay a high fixed-rate dividend indefinitely, unpaid dividends usually accumulate, many issues can be convertible at any time into the company's common stock, and they can qualify for lower taxes than bonds. Most importantly, history has shown that preferred stocks have generally outperformed corporate and municipal bonds over the past 117 years, and that they could be included in investment portfolios for overall better returns. Simply put, they are Wall Street's best-kept secret in income investing!

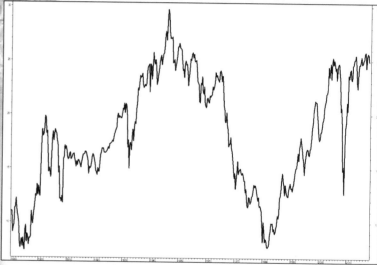

WINANS PREFERRED STOCK INDEX™ (SINCE 1890)

Preferred stock issued to Thomas A. Edison, the Edison Portland Cement Company, 1906

As between the comparatively low yields on good bonds and the uncertainty in connection with common stocks, investors are paying more attention to the attractive return and security obtainable in the preferred share market.

—*The Magazine of Wall Street,* September 29, 1923

PREFERRED STOCK FACTS and OBSERVATIONS

Since 1900

Positives

- US preferred stocks have produced a 2,919% cumulative gain (a 7.7% average annual return).
- $1 invested in stocks in December of 1899 is worth $3,040 today ($85 after inflation)!
- They have doubled in value 11 times (every 10.6 years on average).
- 86% of the total return was from dividend income.
- The best annual return was 40.9% in 1986.

Negatives

- Preferred stocks have posted negative years 24% of the time.
- Multiyear bear markets occur 7% of the time.
- The average loss in a negative year is -6.4%
- The worst annual return was -22.5% in 1907.

WINANS PREFERRED STOCK INDEX (WIPSI) YIELD (1890–2017)

Investors are showing a renewed interest in, if not a preference for, preferred stock.

—*The Wall Street Journal*, June 16, 2005

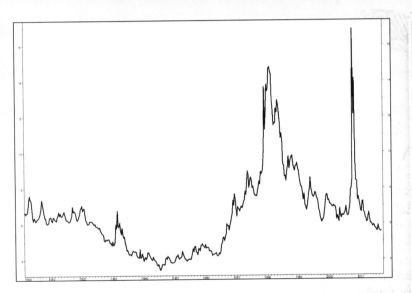

Preferred stock issued by legendary stock speculator Russell Sage, 1866

While preferred shares are listed on major stock exchanges, they aren't widely followed or understood— so there's a chance to unlock hidden value.

—*The Wall Street Journal*, August 6, 2006

STOCK INVESTOR TOOLS
Some Things Never Change

Stock investing has always been a curious mixture of old and new. Every day, hundreds of billions of dollars in stock transactions travel the globe through electronic transfers by the marvels of modern technology, yet the basic tools used by earlier investors such as financial news, corporate annual reports, brokerage house statements, and charts of stock market barometers are as important today as they were in the 1800s.

As you review the following analysis, remember that successful stock investing is as much about identifying the overall stock market's trends (i.e., when to buy or sell) as it is selecting individual investments (i.e., what to buy or sell). Unfortunately, it is hard to conduct long-term analysis on individual stocks, because very few companies have continuously traded over a long time frame.

An almost infinite number of fundamental and technical tools are used by market analysts to determine market trends and to measure the market's strength. On the following pages are market indicators every stock investor should monitor.

In 1904 there was begun the pioneering work of keeping investors informed on fundamental conditions and on specific issues in which they might be interested. The need was urgent, for too many people were making investments blindly, not really knowing whether a security fitted their needs, nor whether it was a proper time to buy or sell.

—Roger Babson, *Investment Fundamentals*, 1930

The simple and effective way to use the following tools is to remember the technical indicators should be moving in the same direction as market prices. When these indicators are moving in the opposite direction to market price (called a divergence), there is a strong possibility of a change in market direction.

In the Market Cycles section later in this book, these tools will be further examined to show that they proved useful in past bull and bear markets in providing investors advanced warnings that things were changing for better or worse.

200-DAY MOVING AVERAGE OF MARKET INDEXES

Used as a filter to determine overall price trend. When price is above the moving average, the trend is up. When price is below the moving average, the trend is down. If a moving average is flat, the trend is sideways—better known as a trading market.

NYSE ADVANCING VOLUME/ DECLINING VOLUME LINE

Used to measure the strength of the market's price movement. Weaker levels of volume are usually present near bull market tops and bear market bottoms. It uses the 200-day moving average similar to the previous chart.

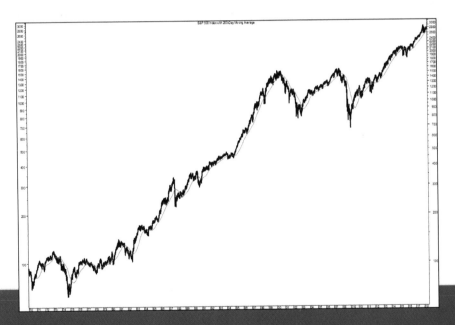

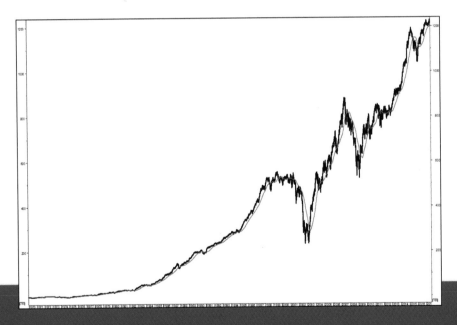

The moving average is one of the most versatile and widely used of all technical indicators.

A profitable synergy can be produced by blending together an analysis of market indices with individual securities.

—John Murphy, *Technical Analysis of the Financial Markets*, 1993

—Ken Winans, *Preferred Stocks*, 2007

Technical Indicators

NYSE ADVANCING/DECLINING STOCK PRICE LINE

This measures the number of individual stocks where prices are moving up versus down. It uses the two-hundred-day moving average similar to the previous charts.

NYSE TWELVE-MONTH NEW HIGH/ NEW LOW PRICE LINE

This measures the number of individual stocks making twelve-month highs versus twelve-month lows. It uses the two-hundred-day moving average similar to the previous charts.

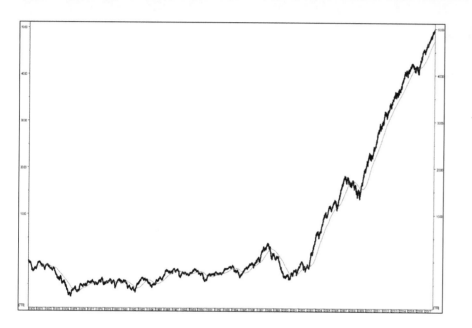

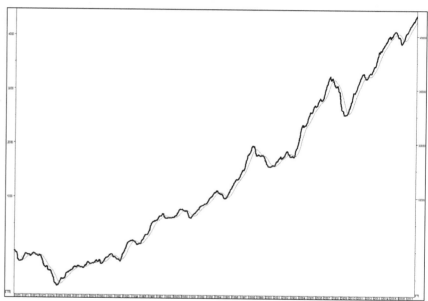

The Trend is Your Friend! The Advance/Decline Indicator is one of two ingredients that, when combined, have an outstanding record in calling bull market advances.

—Martin Zweig, *Winning on Wall Street*, 1986

Fundamental Measures

WINANS LEGACY STOCK INDEX (WILSI)

Price-to-Sales and Price-to-Earnings Ratios (since 1970)

Measures common share value in relation to revenues and earnings: A P/S ratio above 1.6 or a P/E ratio above 20 occur near major market peaks. A P/S ratio below 1.0 or a P/E ratio below 13 indicate an undervalued stock market.

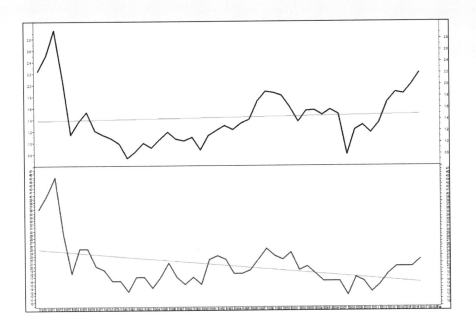

WINANS LEGACY STOCK INDEX (WILSI)

Dividend Yields (since 1970)

Measures common share value in relation to cash dividends: A dividend yield below 2.1% indicates the market is pricey. A dividend yield above 4% indicates an undervalued stock market.

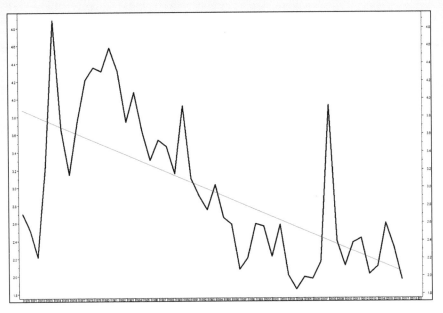

The security analyst should compare the price with earnings, dividends, asset value, and with sales.

—Benjamin Graham and David Dodd, *Security Analysis*, 1934

British real estate deed, 1737

Real estate itself is one of the oldest forms of investment and has come to be an absolute essential of life under the present established form of civilization. Real estate is also a form of investment which ordinarily does not become worthless in periods of drastic financial readjustments... One thing about real estate, however, is that it is not always readily saleable on short notice.

—Roger Babson, *Investment Fundamentals*, 1930

House of Ross Winans (author's ancestor) as it appeared in *American Architect and Building News*, April 30, 1887. Photo by Maryland Historical Society.

With shelter of primal concern to all people, real estate is one of mankind's oldest types of investments and has been one of the most effective ways to amass wealth and power in all past civilizations. Today, home ownership is called the "American Dream" and is the largest asset owned by most investors.

Winans Mansion, Baltimore, Maryland, 2006

Many people who traditionally invest in real estate didn't really understand—or trust—the stock market, while most people who invest in stocks were uncomfortable with, or had little understanding of, real estate.

—Ralph Block, *Investing in REITS*, 2006

35

U.S. RESIDENTIAL REAL ESTATE

Unlike the fast-paced world of stocks, where market values are accessed every second in organized exchanges worldwide, real estate's slower pace is conducted through loose networks of brokers centered on publications and websites that post listings of properties for sale. This decentralized transaction structure, where a typical sale takes thirty to ninety days to complete (due to the high amount of mortgage debt used in most purchases), makes it one of the hardest investments to analyze, and only a handful of indexes track home prices over the long term.

The Winans Real Estate Index® (WIREI®) shows the price of new US homes since 1830. As can be seen in these charts, residential real estate was more volatile before 1950, with dramatic swings in value during the 1930s and the late 1800s. Even though home price appreciation since 1950 looks like endless profitability, there were rough times in the 1970s, 1980s, early 1990s, and 2008 when excessive leverage wiped out many homeowners.

US NEW HOME PRICES (SINCE 1830)
Winans Real Estate Index (WIREI)

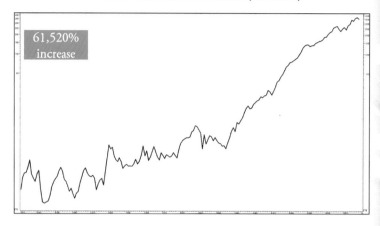

61,520% increase

US HOME PRICES TOTAL RETURN (SINCE 1850)
(Inflation adjusted)

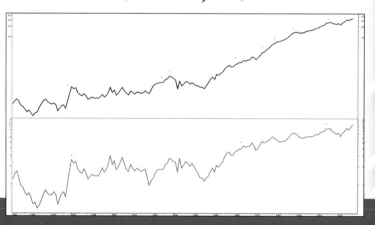

US Homes (New)—Since 1850		
	No Mortgage Debt	
Average Total Return	4.9%	
Inflation Adjusted Total Return	2.6%	
Highest Return	67%	in 1933
Worst Return	-44%	in 1932
Negative Years	36%	
Consecutive Negative Years	16%	

The stock market is the consumer-confidence barometer of the upper-end real estate buyers.

—*The Wall Street Journal*, January 18, 2016

U.S. REGIONAL REAL ESTATE

California Mexico Land Company, 1888

This was a deed to Southern California property. It was printed in both English and French because France occupied Mexico in the 1860s.

TOTAL RETURN BY REGION (SINCE 1974)

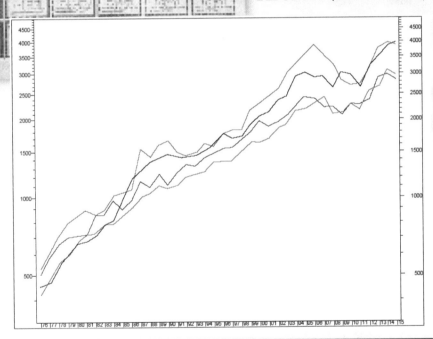

Though it is important to follow the overall trend of the US real estate market, an investor also needs to follow the regional differences of home values. US housing has long been divided into four geographic areas for local comparison: Northeast, South, Midwest, and West.

As can be seen below, the Northeastern region has had the best overall performance since 1974, followed closely by the West.

But the steadiest performance came from the South, with negative years occurring only 9% of the time. This is especially astounding when you consider the number of major hurricanes and tornados to have ravaged this region since 1974.

New Home Prices				
	Total Returns	Negative Years	Consecutive Neg Years	Annual Outperformed US New Homes
9 Northeast States		21%	9.0%	63%
Current Price	$589,850			
Cumulative	1192%			
Average	6.6%			
Median	5.6%			
High	31%			
Low	-21%			
17 Southern States		9%	0%	49%
Current Price	$303,950			
Cumulative	755%			
Average	5.3%			
Median	4.9%			
High	17%			
Low	-13%			
12 Midwest States		23%	7%	51%
Current Price	$299,950			
Cumulative	715%			
Average	5.2%			
Median	5.8%			
High	21%			
Low	-9%			
13 Western States		21%	9.0%	53%
Current Price	$387,150			
Cumulative	1010%			
Average	5.9%			
Median	5.1%			
High	30%			
Low	-13%			

I heard countless times that what matters most in real estate is location, location, location. I don't dispute the validity of this mantra, but location in and of itself cannot protect an investor buying at the top of a cycle and taking a loss on the way down.

—Craig Hall, *Timing the Real Estate Market*, 2004

OTHER WAYS TO OWN REAL ESTATE

Which is the best way to own real estate: direct ownership in properties or exchange-traded investments that focus on real estate?

Traditional investors believe that owning brick and mortar is the best way to play the real estate game and that the time spent dealing with the problems surrounding the four *T*s of investment property ownership (tenants, taxes, toilets, and termites) is the price paid for success.

But Wall Street offers investors another route to successful real estate investing: real estate investment trusts (REITs), pools of numerous residential, commercial, and industrial properties throughout the nation, and stocks in home-building companies.

All have produced solid price appreciation (not including rents and dividends). Since 1974, REITs have risen 797%, home building stocks have appreciated 4,132%, and the average for US homes was 801%. Though direct home ownership offers the use of higher levels of leverage (margin on stocks and REITs is limited to 50% of value), real estate investment trusts and homebuilding equities are more liquid and cheaper to buy and sell because they trade on major stock exchanges.

Today's real estate investors could take advantage of both types of investments to maximize performance and liquidity while minimizing transaction costs.

Florida Gables ad, 1929

HOME BUILDER STOCKS (SINCE 1965)

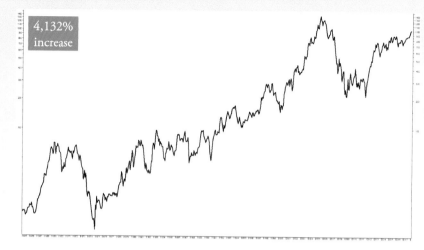

4,132% increase

REAL ESTATE INVESTMENT TRUSTS (REIT) (SINCE 1974)

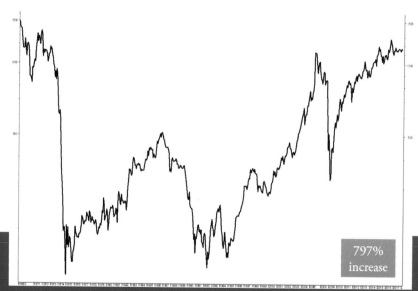

797% increase

GLOBAL HOUSING MARKET (SINCE 1970)

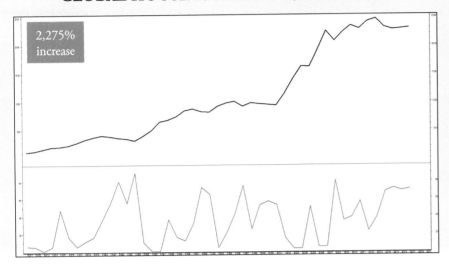

2,275% increase

Index Components	
Africa	Morocco, South Africa
America	Brazil, Canada, Chile, Colombia, Mexico, Peru, USA
Asia	China, Hong Kong, Japan, South Korea
Europe	Austria, Belgium, Czech Republic, Denmark, Finland, France, Germany, Greece, Hungary, Ireland, Italy, Netherlands, Norway, Poland, Portugal, Romania, Slovakia, Spain, Sweden, Switzerland, Thailand, UK
Middle East	Israel, Turkey
Pacific Region	Australia, Indonesia, Malaysia, New Zealand, Philippines, Singapore, Thailand
Other	Russia

As with most types of investments, there are opportunities outside the United States. The chart tracks the global housing market in forty-four countries since 1970 (in US dollars). While the overall trend in prices is positive (black line), the index's A/D line clearly display periods of time where the annual performance in individual countries' housing markets varied widely (red line).

China's economy has become the second largest in the world, but its rapid growth may have created the largest housing bubble in history.

—CBS News, March 3, 2013

Italian land deed, 1600s. It was written in Latin and had to be notarized.

REAL ESTATE TRUST DEEDS

Trust deeds are property loans made directly between an investor and the homeowner. These illiquid, high-fee investments are issued at yields significantly higher than thirty-year mortgages. Like any home loan, they are secured by the value of the real estate itself, and if a payment default occurs, the property can be sold to repay the investor after the primary mortgage is made whole.

THIRTY-YEAR FIXED RATE MORTGAGES (SINCE 1990)

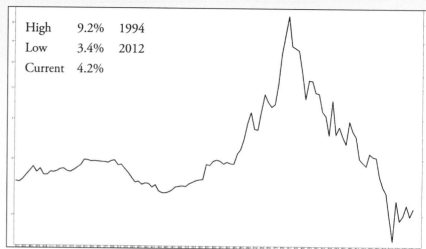

High	9.2%	1994
Low	3.4%	2012
Current	4.2%	

Kansas land mortgage investments, 1887

FIRST TRUST DEED YIELDS (SINCE 1990)

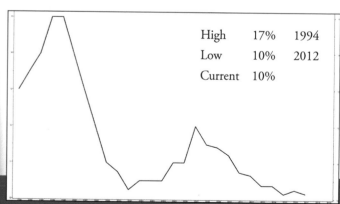

High	17%	1994
Low	10%	2012
Current	10%	

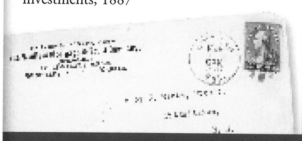

Speculators in real estate often borrowed of the United States Bank for speculative purposes, sums as high as $250,000.

—Matthew Smith, *Bulls and Bears of New York*, 1875

REAL ESTATE INVESTOR TOOLS

Successful real estate investing is as much about identifying the overall real estate trends
(i.e., when to buy or sell) as it is selecting individual investments (i.e., what to buy or sell).
Listed are several tools that investors can use to monitor the real estate market.

Moving Average of Home Prices

Moving averages are effective in identifying the overall trend of a market. If the index and sales levels are above the moving average, then the market is in a bullish uptrend, and vice versa means real estate is in a bear market.

US New Home Prices Adjusted for Square Feet

The size of the average US home has increased 55% since 1974. To make apples-to-apples price comparisons to new houses in the past, prices should be adjusted to size.

WINANS REAL ESTATE INDEX AND
FIFTEEN-MONTH MOVING AVERAGE
with monthly new home sales volume (since 1990)

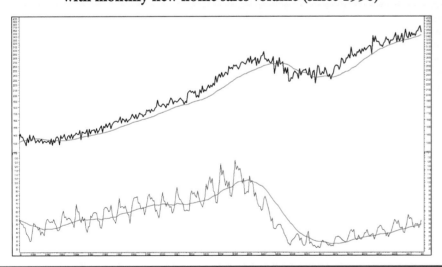

US HOME PRICES ADJUSTED
FOR SIZE (SINCE 1974)

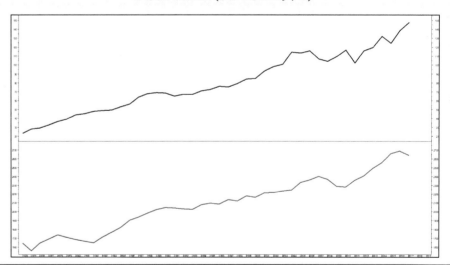

**While many people think low mortgage rates will cause a housing rebound, there are other
indicators to watch, such as home prices, new home sales and months for sale.**

—Financial History Magazine, summer 2011

New Homes Listed and Inventory (with regression line)

These indicators measure the number of new houses listed for sale and the number of months it would take to sell this at the current sales rate. Generally speaking, prices trend upward when the number of listings and inventory levels are low.

Sales and Months on Market (with regression line)

Similar to stock trading volume, these indicators measure the number of new houses sold and the number of months they were on the market. Generally speaking, declines in sales volume coincide with a dramatic rise in the time (from 4–8 months) it takes to sell a house.

US NEW HOME LISTINGS WITH MONTHS OF INVENTORY (SINCE 1963)
(with regression lines in blue)

Current monthly level: 294,000

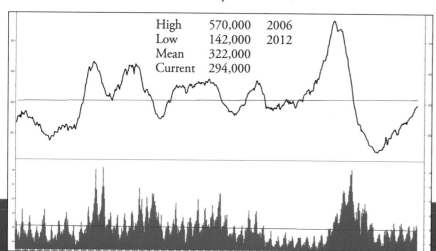

High	570,000	2006
Low	142,000	2012
Mean	322,000	
Current	294,000	

US NEW HOME SALES WITH MONTHS UNTIL SOLD (SINCE 1963)
(with regression lines in blue)

Current monthly level: 48,000

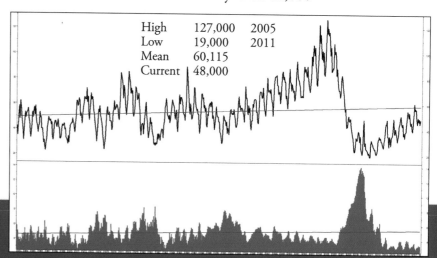

High	127,000	2005
Low	19,000	2011
Mean	60,115	
Current	48,000	

Needy people will always offer premiums in proportion to their distress; therefore, mortgages may be had at five percent when money is worth only four.

—Thomas Mortimer, *Every Man His Own Broker*, 1791

Mortgage Rates

Because leverage is heavily used in real estate investing, the level and direction of interest rates are key to performance. Generally speaking, high or rising interest rates should be viewed with caution by real estate investors.

Mortgage Rate Spreads

Since 1981, the difference between the interest rate a thirty-year fixed-rate loan and a one-year adjustable-rate mortgage has ranged between 3.3% and -0.47%. Since high levels of debt are often used, real estate investors need to closely evaluate the differences between the rates on various types of loans in order to find the best deals for a new purchase and/or refinancing.

US MORTGAGE RATES SPREAD (SINCE 1981)

(thirty-year fixed rate minus one-year adjustable)

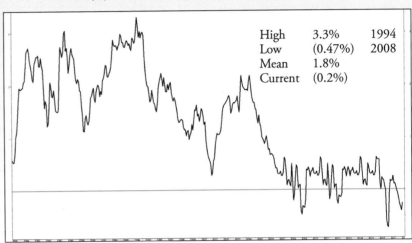

High	3.3%	1994
Low	(0.47%)	2008
Mean	1.8%	
Current	(0.2%)	

US MORTGAGE RATES (SINCE 1900)

(thirty-year fixed rate)

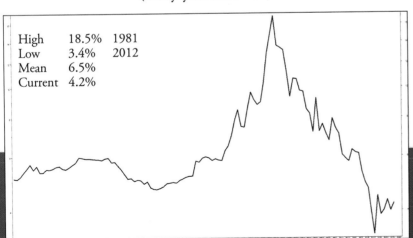

High	18.5%	1981
Low	3.4%	2012
Mean	6.5%	
Current	4.2%	

US MORTGAGE RATES (SINCE 1980)

(one-year adjustable)

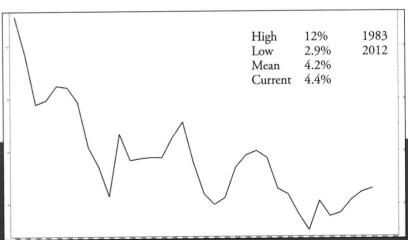

High	12%	1983
Low	2.9%	2012
Mean	4.2%	
Current	4.4%	

REAL ESTATE FACTS and OBSERVATIONS

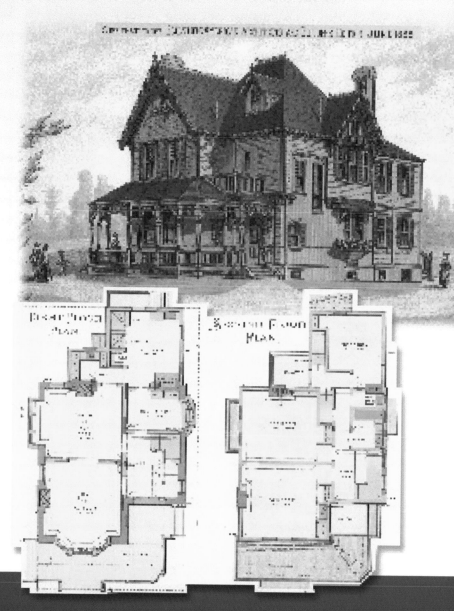

Since 1900

Positives
- US residential real estate has produced a 105% cumulative gain (a 5.2% average annual return).
- $1 invested in housing in December of 1899 is worth $117 today ($3.84 after inflation).
- Homes have doubled in value 7 times (every 16 years on average).
- The best annual return was 67% in 1933.
- Since 1974, the homes in the Northeast and West posted the best price appreciation.

Negatives
- US new homes have posted negative years 30% of the time.
- Multiyear bear markets occur 13% of the time.
- The average loss in a negative year was 10%.
- The worst annual return was -44% in 1932.

This was a market phenomenon characterized by 30 years of house price growth with very few defaults.

—Financial Times, April 22, 2007

Sausalito, California is a place of half a dozen houses, once "destined" to be a great town; $150,000 lost there—city laid out, corner lots sold at enormous prices, "water fronts" still higher—a big city was bound to grow up there. The old California story—everybody bought land to rise in value, but no one built, no city grew there. Corner lots and water fronts are alike worthless.

—William Brewster, 1862

BONDS –
WHEN INCOME and SAFETY ARE WANTED

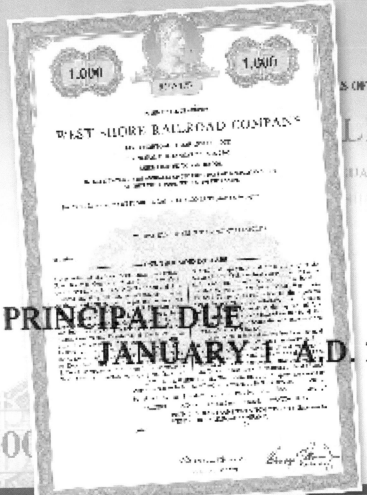

Many investors can't handle, or are wealthy enough that they don't need to deal with, the moderate to high level of investment risks associated with stocks and real estate. These investors value a greater certainty of return over the level of investment return and/or have income requirements that can't be met by common stock dividends.

Bonds are debts issued by corporations, governments, state and local municipalities. Interest rates vary, and maturities range from a few years to many decades. Because bonds provide a fixed income over a defined period of time, the near certainty of returns is their greatest advantage.

Recently, record numbers of consumers have been buying these little-understood investments, which many past investors considered to be downright boring. Regrettably, many of these seasoned stock and real estate investors rushing into this sector of investing have failed to learn the time-proven rules of bond investing.

—Ken Winans, *Preferreds: Wall Street's Best-Kept Income Secret*, 2007

U.S. CORPORATE BONDS

Below are charts showing the price and interest yields of US corporate bonds and the total return (annual price change and interest earned combined) adjusted for inflation since 1862.

Unlike common stocks, where most profits are made through increases in the value of the shares, the price of bonds oscillates around the maturity value (or par value) of $1,000 per bond, thus showing only a small change in bond values over the past 155 years.

The real profit power of bonds comes through the regular interest paid to the investor by the company that issued the bond. This has averaged 6.3% since 1862 for a total interest return of 969%.

Traditional corporate bonds have been steady performers where returns have doubled thirteen times since 1862 and have generally performed well against inflation.

US CORPORATE BOND PRICE AND YIELD (SINCE 1862)

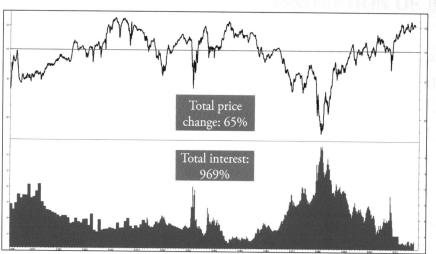

Total price change: 65%

Total interest: 969%

US CORPORATE BONDS TOTAL RETURN (SINCE 1862)
(Inflation adjusted)

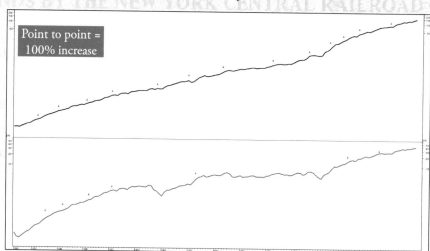

Point to point = 100% increase

Much of the research done when investing in corporate bonds is similar to that done for stock investing...Corporate bond values often track the health of a company that issued them even more than they are affected by interest rates.

—Sharon Wright, *Getting Started in Bonds*, 1999

Corporate income investments can be divided into bonds of high-quality companies, bonds in companies of lower standing, and preferred stocks (a type of stock that pays a high level of income to its investors and usually doesn't have a maturity date).

As can be seen in the charts on this page, while the levels of yield are different, the three types of corporate income investments look nearly identical. In fact, all had record-low yields in April 1946 and record high yields in late 1981.

US Corporate Bonds (Since 1863)		
Average Annual Total Return	6.6%	
Inflation Adjusted Total Return	4.4%	
Highest Total Return	39%	in 1982
Lowest Total Return	-14%	in 1931
Negative Returns	17%	
Consecutive Negative Returns	3%	

HIGH-QUALITY CORPORATE BOND
Yields (since 1900)

LOW-QUALITY CORPORATE BOND
Yields (since 1900)

PREFERRED STOCK DIVIDEND
Yields (since 1900)

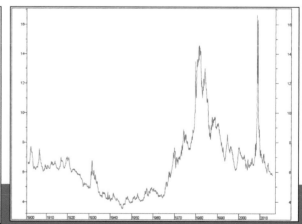

Low grade bonds, long and short term, can be judged more like stocks. It is better to look at them frankly for their appreciation possibilities.

—Gerald Loeb, *The Battle for Investment Survival*, 1936

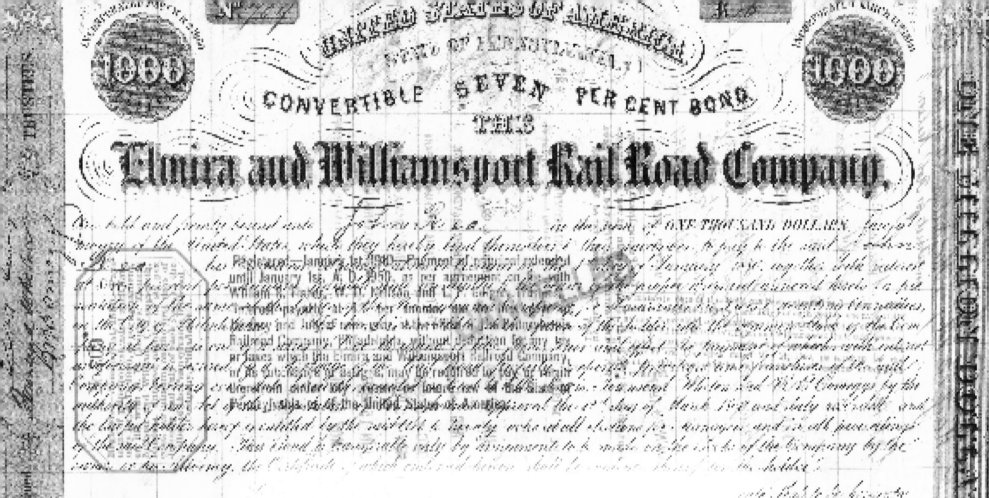

Elmira and Williamsport Railroad convertible bond, 1860

This is one of the earliest-known types of exotic bonds. It allowed its owner to convert (or trade) this bond for a specific number of the company's common stock at a specific price.

Industrial, finance, and real estate are the largest issuers of convertible bonds.

—**Frank Fabozzi,** *The Handbook of Fixed Income Securities,* 1983

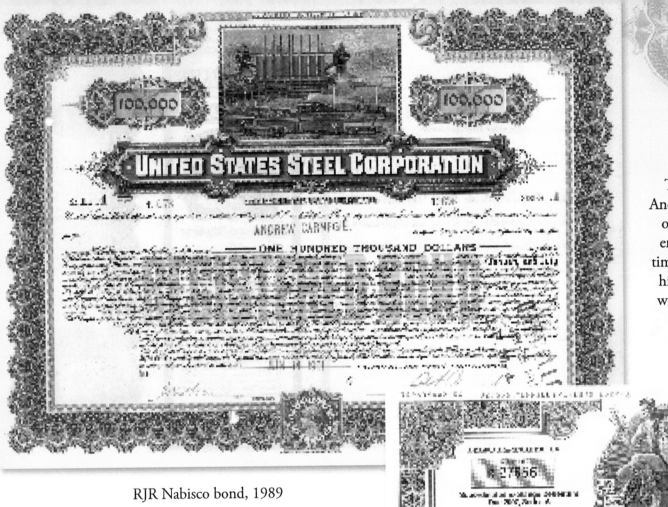

US steel bond, 1901

The owner of this bond was billionaire Andrew Carnegie. This investment was part of the proceeds from the sale of his steel empire to J. P. Morgan's US Steel. At the time, this was the biggest acquisition in US history, and it made Carnegie the second wealthiest person in world history (worth nearly $300 billion in today's dollars).

RJR Nabisco bond, 1989

The first of the great leveraged buyouts (LBOs) where debt was used to turn publicly traded companies into private enterprises. This bond was used in that $25 billion transaction.

U.S. GOVERNMENT BONDS

KNOW all Men by these Presents, That we, _____
_____ _____ _____ _____ _____
_____ _____ _____ _____ _____

are holden and firmly bound unto the Governor and Company of the
_____ _____ of _____, in New England, in the Sum of
Three Thousand Pounds, Lawful Money, to be paid to said Governor and Company; To the which Payment well and truly to
be made and done, we jointly and severally bind ourselves, our Heirs,
&c. by these Presents. Sealed and under Seals, this _____ Day of
_____ A.D. 1776.

THE Condition of the above Obligation is such, That whereas the
above bounden _____ _____ is appointed
Pay-Master to his own Company, now to be raised, to join the Con-
tinental Army in _____ _____ Now, if _____ said _____
—— shall faithfully and justly dispose of all the Monies he shall
receive out of the public Treasury, for the Purpose of clothing the Soldiers
by said Pay'g said Company, and shall account with the Committee
of the Pay-Table for the same, when thereto required, the above Obligation to be Void, otherwise to remain in full Force.

_____ _____

Signed, Sealed and Delivered,
in Presence of

_____ _____
_____ _____

Colonial government note issued
during the American Revolution, 1776

Government debt is always at the focal point of discussions about politics and business. The irony is that "we the people" have always owned the bulk of the US government's debt obligations, and our taxes are used to pay the interest on this debt.

Because the government owns a vast amount of assets and can collect taxes from its citizens, it is also the only investment that can legally be called "risk free" of default.

TEN-YEAR US TREASURY BOND YIELD (SINCE 1800)

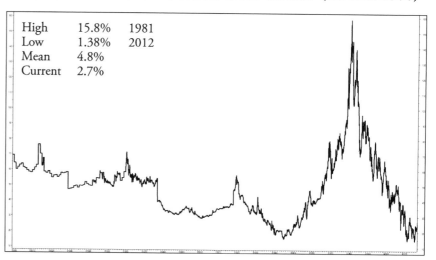

High	15.8%	1981
Low	1.38%	2012
Mean	4.8%	
Current	2.7%	

In scores of ways the US Treasury and Wall Street are brought into close contact.

—Sereno Pratt, *The Work of Wall Street*, 1906

Gazette of the United States.

PUBLISHED WEDNESDAYS AND SATURDAYS BY JOHN FENNO, No. 69, HIGH-STREET, BETWEEN ARCH AND THIRD STREETS, PHILADELPHIA.

[No. 9, of Vol. III.]   SATURDAY, MAY 28, 1791.   [Whole No. 217.]

Gazette of the United States, 1791.
This newspaper provided the first
price lists of government bonds.

THREE-MONTH US TREASURY BILLS (SINCE 1820)

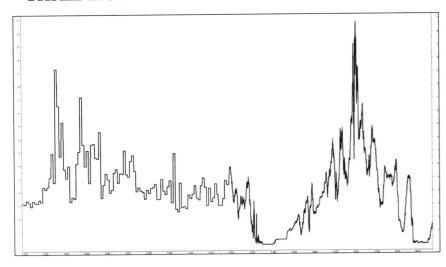

With credit quality assured, the investment focus shifts to maturity. For instance, during times of economic upheaval or high inflation, investors choose to buy Treasury debt with short maturities (usually under one year).

As can be seen, Treasury debt yields are hardly static! They have ranged from 17% in the late 1980s to 0.1% throughout the 1930s and since 2008.

PRICE CURRENT.— PUBLIC SECURITIES.
FUNDED DEBT.

> Through budget deficits, there will always be more than
> enough Treasury bonds to satisfy any and all buyers.

> —*Barron's,* February 5, 2007

MUNICIPAL BONDS

For anyone who doubts the power of taxes on investment decisions, you have to look no further than municipal bonds!

These low-yielding debts have been issued since Colonial times and have been a longtime favorite of investors. Why? Under constitutional law, interest earned on many municipal bonds cannot be taxed by the US government. Unfortunately, many investors are subject to different types of taxes (such as the alternative minimum tax) which can make "tax-free" muni bonds taxable to wealthy investors.

In the chart, you will notice that yields on municipal bonds have ranged from 13% in 1981 to 1.5% in 1945 and have generally had lower yields than Treasury or corporate bonds.

City and county of San Francisco bond, 1863

US MUNICIPAL BOND YIELDS (SINCE 1800)

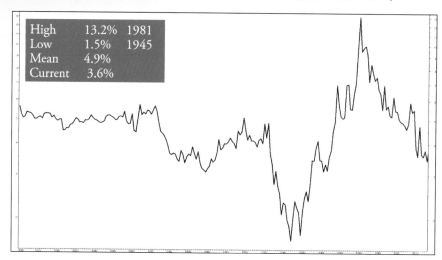

High	13.2%	1981
Low	1.5%	1945
Mean	4.9%	
Current	3.6%	

Although tax-exempt munis vary in the degree of credit strength backing them, and although there have been some famous defaults, their safety record has generally been excellent, earning them a place between Treasuries and high-grade corporate bonds.

—John Downes and Jordan Goodman, *Barron's Finance & Investment Handbook,* 1998

The divine doctrine of state sovereignty, which makes a State too dignified to be sued for its debts ought to make it also too respectable to cheat its creditors.

—Henry Clews, 1885

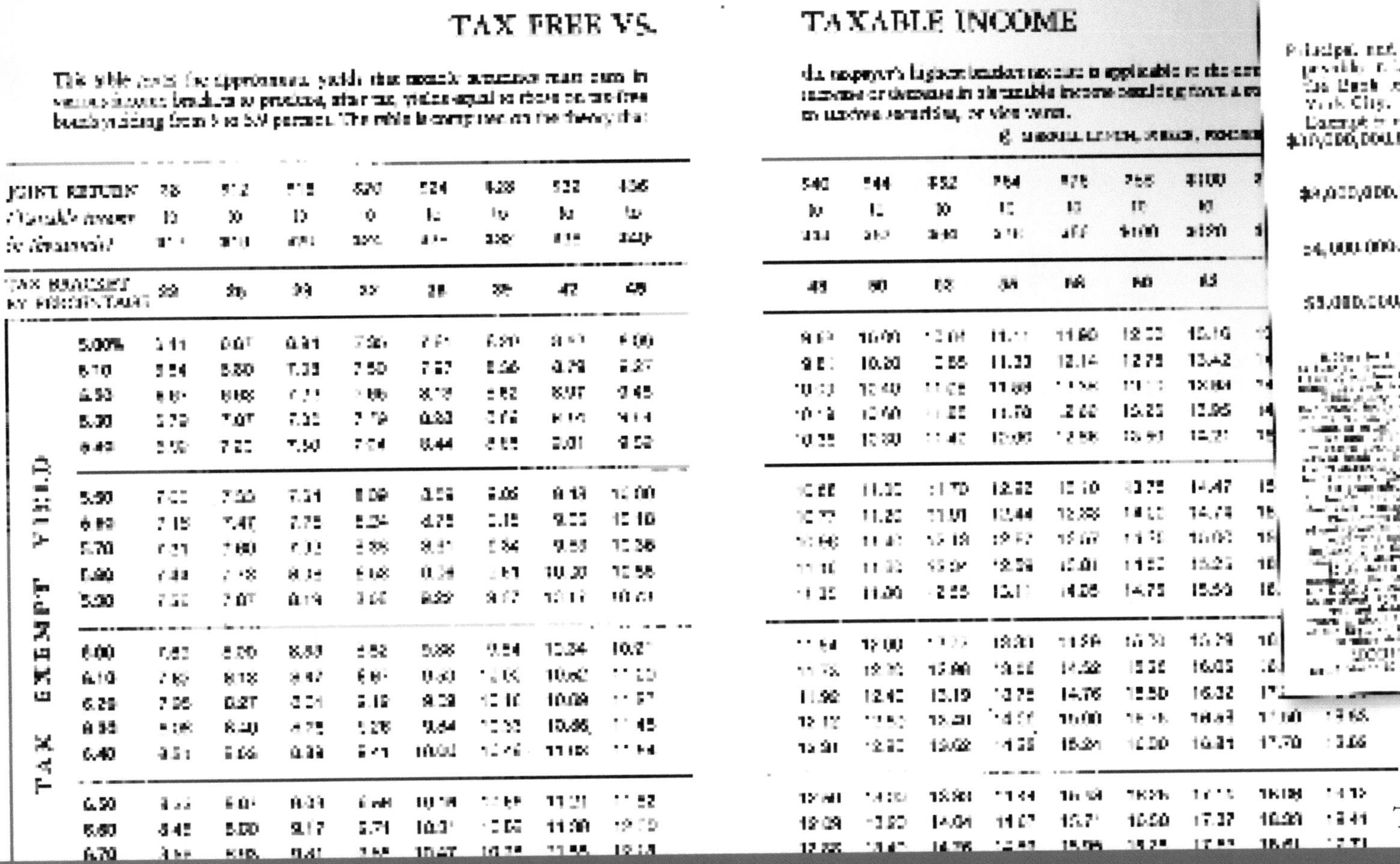

TAX FREE VS. TAXABLE INCOME

TAX EXEMPT YIELD

Tax equivalent yield table, 1974

The Comptroller of the State of New York

$50,000,000.00

State of New York

Muni bond ad, 1934

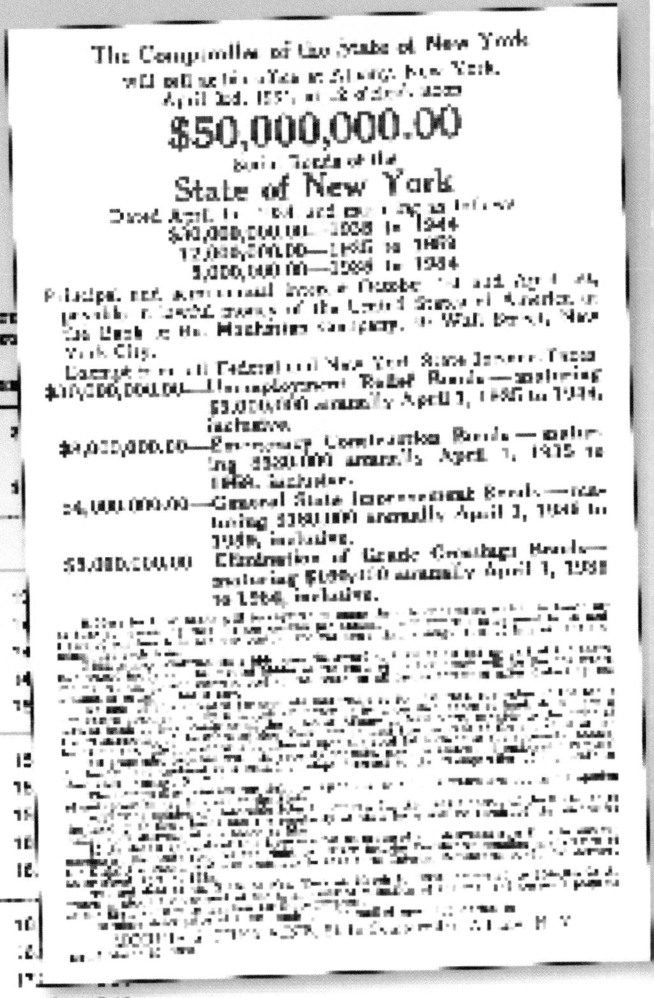

For tax reasons, municipal-bond investors often invest in the bonds of the city in which they reside, so they face double jeopardy. In the first place, if city officials are committing fraud, their bonds will turn out not to be so sound…The second risk is that they will have to pay higher taxes to cover shortfalls in their city's budget.

—*The Wall Street Journal*, November 27, 2006

FOREIGN BONDS

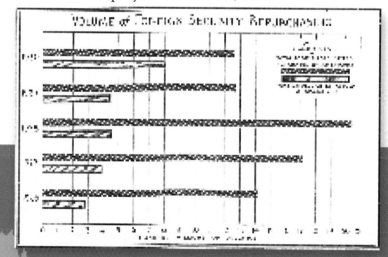

Ford Motor Company, Berlin division, 1929

Foreign investment chart, 1930

Americans have had a long love affair with international investing. Though stocks in foreign companies usually get most of the attention in the media, the bonds of foreign governments and international corporations have proven to be an especially good investment during times of declines in the value of the US dollar.

FOREIGN BONDS TOTAL RETURN (SINCE 1923)

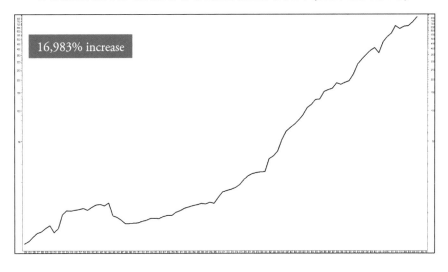

16,983% increase

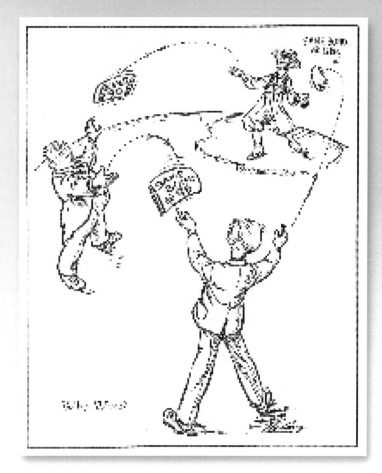

Foreign bond trading cartoon, 1932

In the chart on this page, you will notice that in the post-World War II era, there has been a continuous bull market in foreign corporate bonds when returns are adjusted in US dollars.

Since the United States has taken the position of a creditor nation,
it is becoming a great marketplace for foreign bonds.

—Roger Babson, *Investment Fundamentals*, 1930

BOND INVESTOR TOOLS

Though the yields of various types of bonds do seem to move in the same direction, they don't move to the same degree, and bond investors are constantly comparing yields in different bonds looking for the best deals. One of the tools that helps make these comparisons is yield spread charts.

These are built by simply subtracting the yield of one type of bond from another. The higher and lower numbers mark the extreme historical ranges between the two types of bonds and thus serve as reference points for future investments between corporate bonds and preferred stocks or Treasury versus municipal bonds.

Bond research, 1890

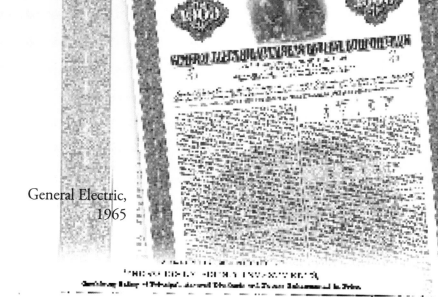

General Electric, 1965

Since the selection of high-grade bonds has been shown to be in good part a process of exclusion, it lends itself reasonably well to the application of definite rules and standards.

—Benjamin Graham and David Dodd, *Security Analysis*, 1962

Yield Spread Analysis

CORPORATE BONDS (HIGH-QUALITY)
versus low quality (since 1900)

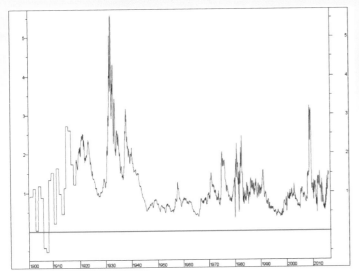

High	5.6%	1932
Low	(0.6%)	1907
Mean	.78%	
Current	3.0%	

CORPORATE BONDS (HIGH-QUALITY)
versus preferred stocks (since 1900)

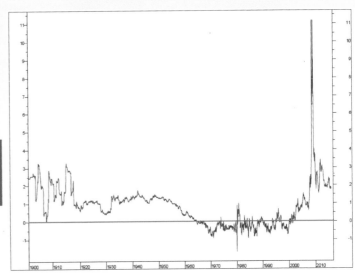

High	11.3%	2009
Low	(1.8%)	1980
Mean	1.4%	
Current	1.8%	

CORPORATE BONDS (HIGH-QUALITY)
versus ten-year treasury bonds (since 1900)

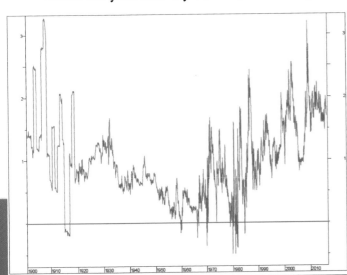

High	3.3%	1907
Low	(0.9%)	1979
Mean	1.1%	
Current	1.7%	

TEN-YEAR TREASURY BONDS
versus municipal bonds (since 1900)

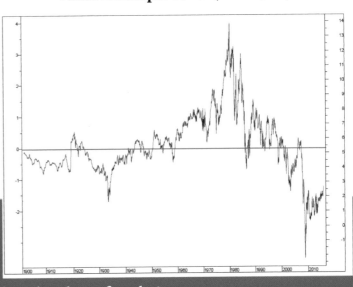

High	3.4%	1980
Low	(3.7%)	2008
Mean	0.3%	
Current	(1.3%)	

Bonds often act as a leading indicator of stocks…A technical analysis of stocks is incomplete without a corresponding analysis of the bond market.

—John Murphy, *Intermarket Technical Analysis*, 1991

BOND FACTS and OBSERVATIONS

US Corporate Bonds Since 1900

Positives

- Corporate bonds have produced a 806% cumulative gain (a 6.2% average annual return).
- $1 invested in housing in December of 1899 is worth $936 today ($26 after inflation)!
- They have doubled in value 9 times (every 13 years on average).
- The best annual return was 39% in 1982.
- 96% of the total return was interest income.
- The average yield is 6% and is significantly higher than Treasury and municipal bond yields.

Negatives

- Corporate bonds have posted negative years 21% of the time.
- Multiyear bear markets occur 3%.
- The average loss in a negative year was 3.3%.
- The worst annual return was -14% in 1931.

Ten-Year US Treasury Bonds Since 1900

- The highest yield was 15.8% in 1981.
- The lowest yield was 1.4% in 2012.
- The average yield was 4.6%.
- T-bond yields average 1.1% higher than 3-month T-bills.

Municipal Bonds Since 1900

- The highest yield was 13% in 1981.
- The lowest yield was 1.6% in 1945.
- The average yield was 4.5%.
- The tax-adjusted municipal bond yields are comparable to corporate bond yields.

Recent peak yields were far above the highest prime long-term rates reported in the United States since 1800, in England since 1700, or in Holland since 1600.

—Sidney Homer and Richard Salla,
A History of Interest Rates, 2005

Students of the bond market are constantly in danger of falling into the mental habit of thinking that the 'bond market' represents a single unified thing, which behaves in the same way throughout all its parts. A time like the present illustrates the highly composite nature of the bond market, and the variations in the responses of its different sections to the influences which affect it.

—*The Magazine of Wall Street*, September 29, 1923

It is perfectly possible to speculate in bonds, and periodically fortunes are made and lost in the bond markets. It is also perfectly possible to see a portfolio of high-grade bonds decline in value at a time when the majority of common stocks are climbing upward. Nevertheless there is a basic truth to the simile: of the vehicles available to investors, bonds are among the most conservative.

—Charles Rolo, *The Anatomy of Wall Street*, 1968

COMMODITIES
GOLDEN OPPORTUNITY OR A LEAD BALLOON?

He (Jesse Livermore) devised charts based upon a very careful and minute study of the behavior of prices in many markets stocks, bonds, grain, cotton, money and so on.
—Edwin Lefèvre, *Reminiscences of a Stock Operator*, 1923

GOLD and SILVER

GOLD AND SILVER BULLION IN BRITISH POUNDS (SINCE AD 1257)

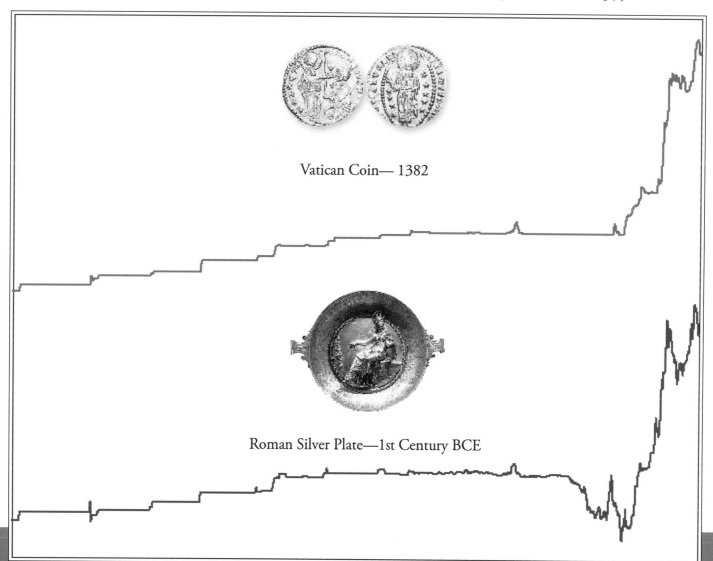

Vatican Coin— 1382

Roman Silver Plate—1st Century BCE

Caesar Augustus of Rome is the richest person of all time with personal wealth in today's money of $4.6 trillion.

—*Investor's Business Daily*, January 29, 2016

GOLD AND SILVER PER OUNCE IN US DOLLARS (SINCE 1800)

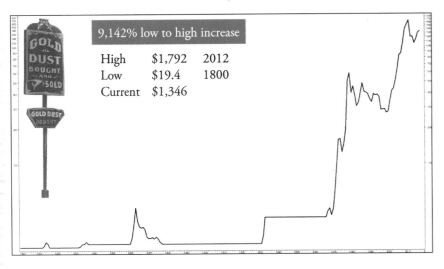

9,142% low to high increase

High	$1,792	2012
Low	$19.4	1800
Current	$1,346	

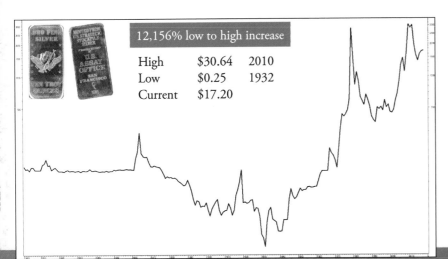

12,156% low to high increase

High	$30.64	2010
Low	$0.25	1932
Current	$17.20	

The conventional wisdom of the 1700s equated national wealth, and the power wealth could purchase, with stockpiles of gold and silver. British imperial policy sought to secure for the mother country as much precious metal as possible, even at the expense of Britain's colonies.

—Henry Brands, *The Age of Gold*, 2002

The turmoil in the stock market overflowed into the futures markets yesterday, sending livestock, cotton, grain plummeting. Precious metals futures meanwhile soared as investors sought safe havens for their money.

—*The New York Times*, October 20, 1987

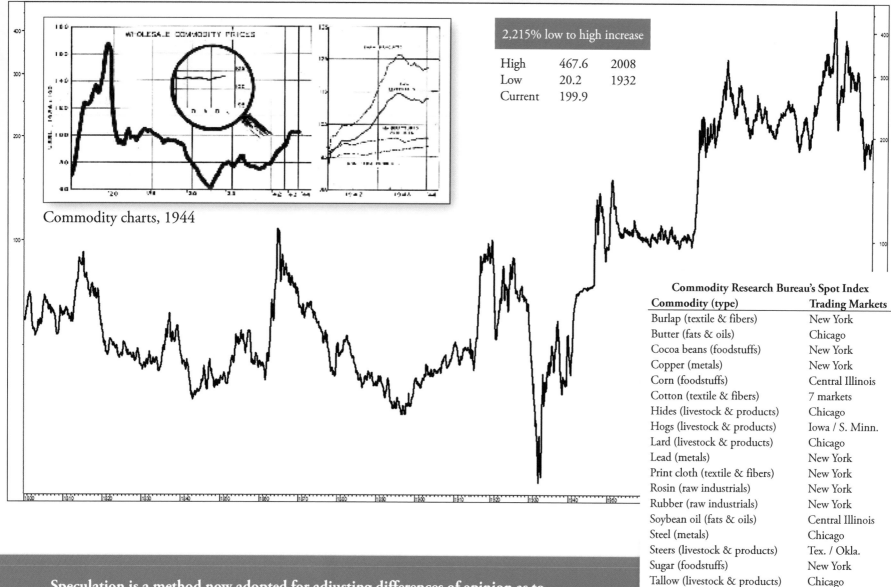

Commodity charts, 1944

2,215% low to high increase		
High	467.6	2008
Low	20.2	1932
Current	199.9	

Commodity Research Bureau's Spot Index

Commodity (type)	Trading Markets
Burlap (textile & fibers)	New York
Butter (fats & oils)	Chicago
Cocoa beans (foodstuffs)	New York
Copper (metals)	New York
Corn (foodstuffs)	Central Illinois
Cotton (textile & fibers)	7 markets
Hides (livestock & products)	Chicago
Hogs (livestock & products)	Iowa / S. Minn.
Lard (livestock & products)	Chicago
Lead (metals)	New York
Print cloth (textile & fibers)	New York
Rosin (raw industrials)	New York
Rubber (raw industrials)	New York
Soybean oil (fats & oils)	Central Illinois
Steel (metals)	Chicago
Steers (livestock & products)	Tex. / Okla.
Sugar (foodstuffs)	New York
Tallow (livestock & products)	Chicago
Tin (metals)	New York
Wheat (foodstuffs)	Minneapolis
Wheat (foodstuffs)	Kansas City
Wool tops (textiles & fibers)	Boston
Zinc (metals)	New York

Speculation is a method now adopted for adjusting differences of opinion as to future values, whether of products or securities. In former years the results of a crop were known only when it came to the market. Now almost everything affecting its future value is known with a fair degree of accuracy before the crop is harvested.

—Henry Clews, *Twenty-Eight Years in Wall Street*, 1887

CRUDE OIL or "BLACK GOLD"—Since 1860

US DOLLARS PER BARREL (SINCE 1860)

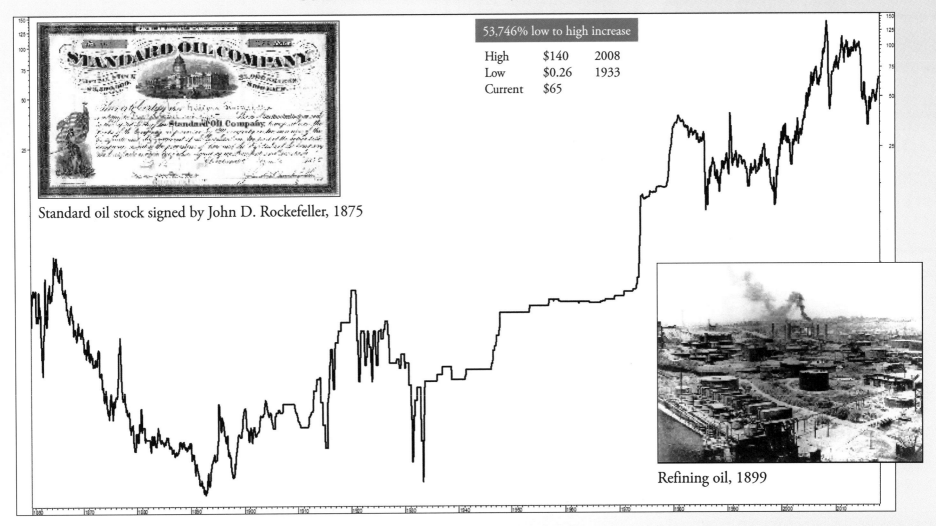

Standard oil stock signed by John D. Rockefeller, 1875

53,746% low to high increase

High	$140	2008
Low	$0.26	1933
Current	$65	

Refining oil, 1899

As Mr. Greenspan engineered low real interest rates in 2001–04, the prices of commodities, particularly oil and other minerals, started to climb in advance of a general price increase. Since commodity prices are determined by trading on fast-moving auction markets, they respond swiftly.

—*The Wall Street Journal,* September 20, 2004

British foreign currency table, 1830

The substitute of paper in the room of gold or silver money, replaces a very expensive instrument of commerce.

—Adam Smith, *Wealth of Nations*, 1776

FOREIGN CURRENCY

BRITISH POUND IN US DOLLARS (SINCE 1800)

(91%) high to low decrease

High	$12.8	1864
Low	$1.10	1985
Current	$1.41	

The world's major currencies have traded in a floating exchange rate regime ever since the Bretton-Woods international payments system broke down in 1971 when President Nixon broke the dollar's peg to gold.

—*The CRB Commodity Yearbook 2015*

COMMODITIES SUMMARY

Even in today's digital age, fast-moving, noisy trading pits for buying and selling all types of futures contracts are active in the world's financial centers. These exchanges evolved from the barter system of ancient times, when merchants exchanged goods and services directly without the use of a medium of exchange such as money.

Today's future markets trade everything, from carbon emission allowances to butter, with each contract (called cars) covering a specified price and amount of the commodity to be delivered at a specified date in the near future without the buyer and seller ever meeting each other. Traders can sell the contract before maturity or pay and physically take delivery of the commodity on maturity. Ironically, the vast majority of commodity contracts are "closed out" prior to the maturity date.

Futures provide investors a liquid, high-leveraged way to speculate in commodity bull markets (high demand and low supply) or bear markets (low demand and high supply). But high leverage is a two-edged sword! Because the purchaser of a futures contract is required to commit and maintain a cash deposit equal to exchange-imposed margin requirements as low as 10% (stock investments allow a maximum of 50% initial margin), volatile swings in the value of a futures account can occur in both directions quickly.

Commodity futures can be very profitable in the hands of disciplined traders who are equally skilled at handling bull and bear markets and are comfortable with the fact that most of their trades will result in a loss. But history has shown that they are not the best choice for investors who like to maintain only long positions with loose stop-loss orders.

Tools—Most of the tools used by practitioners of technical analysis (ranging from moving averages to advanced statistical models) have their roots in commodity trading, where hyper-monitoring of price action is required to prevent financial disaster.

Performance—Because commodities are not designed to be long-term investments, it is difficult to directly compare their long-term performance to growth investments such as stocks and real estate. Although history suggests that stocks, real estate, and bonds have produced superior "buy and hold" returns, the twenty-first century has produced record-setting bull and bear markets in gold, silver, oil, and foreign currencies where fortunes were made and lost.

Commodity	Contract Margin Requirements		2017 Spot Price	Since 1900 High	Low	Low to High	High to Low
	Initial	Maintenance					
Gold	$4,050	$2,500	$1,297	$1,792.00	$20.67	8570%	-99%
Silver	$6,075	$3,000	$17.01	$30.64	$0.25	12156%	-99%
CRB Index	$8,100	$5,400	$193.8	$467.60	$20.20	2215%	-96%
Crude Oil	$6,075	$4,500	$60.4	$140.00	$0.26	53746%	-100%
British Pound	$2,700	$2,000	$1.35	$493.00	$1.10	44718%	-100%
US Common Stocks			2,673.0	2,673.0	3.7	56585%	
Homes			373,100.0	373,100.0	2,183.0	15553%	

Tables and ads from early 1900s

66

COLLECTIBLES
TURNING HOBBIES INTO WEALTH

Almost everybody collects something at some point during his or her life. Children often collect sports trading cards, common coins (such as Lincoln pennies), and even rocks. The passion of collecting stays with many people throughout their lives as they acquire rare, expensive items through their increased financial capacity. The world's richest families have amassed large collections of artwork, books and manuscripts, and various types of antiques that are shared with the public through museum exhibits and publications (such as the display of antique financial documents used throughout this book).

Yet many investors perceive collectibles as a mere hobby and don't recognize the huge financial gains that are possible. As shown in the following table, several rare, vastly different items have had strong appreciation over the last twenty-five years.

Collectibles are broken into two general groups: (1) those graded by respected third parties (similar to the ratings applied to bond investments) such as coins, stamps, and vintage wine and (2) unique, nonrated items such as historical memorabilia and works of art.

Gathering long-term, reliable data on this subject is challenging, so the focus is on collectibles that are popular and actively acquired.

Morgan silver dollars and Beaulieu Vineyard's Georges de Latour Reserve Cabernet Sauvignon are studied as two extensively rated items that are collected in very different ways by investors. In the Wild West of unrated collectibles, we examine historical memorabilia tied to the Apollo 11 lunar landing in 1969. This fast-growing area is a favorite of baby boomers (who followed the space program as kids) and has annual "space" sales at major auction houses.

Collections Performance Overview Since 1990	
US Common Stocks	1,229%
US Homes	166%
Gold Bullion	228%
Morgan Silver Dollar (1883-S)	817%
Beaulieu Vineyard's Reserve Cabernet Sauvignon (1960)	790%
Apollo 11 Portrait (Crew Signed)	3,293%

With prices rising faster than ever, savvy collectors are shifting their strategies for nabbing deals.

—*The Wall Street Journal*, July 21, 2007

Falling oil prices, volatile stock market swings, and China's deepening economic woes are all taking their toll on the art collection market and spooking the world's wealthy.

—*The Wall Street Journal*, January 29, 2016

SILVER COINS

The Morgan silver dollar has an interesting history. It was born out of a politically scandalous legislation in 1878 that forced the US Treasury to buy more silver than it needed at premium prices from mines in Nevada and California. More than 378 million were produced by five mints across the country between 1878 and 1921. The silver dollar was headed for extinction when 282 million were melted down in 1918 and 1942 to help pay for both world wars. It is estimated that only 17% of all Morgans minted have survived, with certain years and mintages very hard to find.

In the complex world of coin investing, third parties (grading services) play a key role.

—*The Wall Street Journal,* November 25, 2006

MORGAN SILVER DOLLAR (ISSUED 1878–1921)

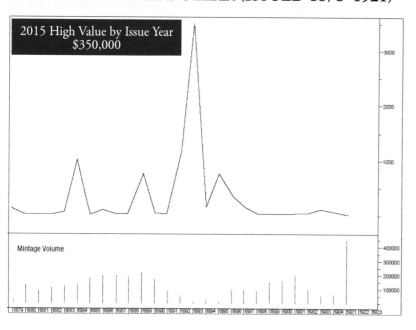

2015 High Value by Issue Year
$350,000

Mintage Volume

Today, it is one of the most popular collector coins and is an ideal coin for preliminary study of numismatics as an investment.

Two common mistakes are made in novice coin collectors' thinking: (1) older is more valuable and all coins with a high grade are valuable. Though the ANA grading given by respectable grading agencies (based on the condition of a coin) is more important than the coin's age; a coin's rarity is the most important determinant of value.

Caution is given that, before spending large sums of money on collectible coins, you should take the time to learn coin grading…Slight differences in grade can mean thousands of dollars in value.

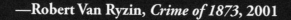

—Robert Van Ryzin, *Crime of 1873,* 2001

1893-S MORGAN DOLLAR (SINCE 1950)

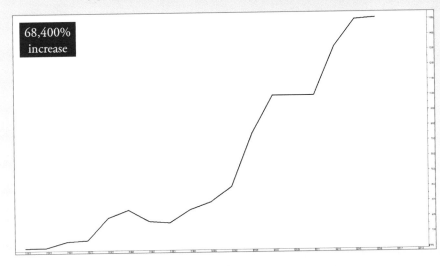

68,400% increase

1888-O MORGAN SILVER DOLLAR (SINCE 1950)

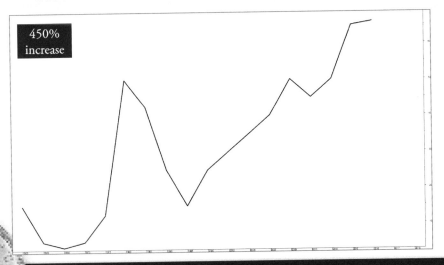

450% increase

On the previous page, the chart of the 2017 high values of mint state (MS) 64 Morgans from 1878 to 1921 shows that an 1893 coin is worth $350,000 while the older 1880 coin's highest value is $605.

In comparing the best and worst performances of various Morgan dollars with a MS-60 grade, it is seen that they have had wide-ranging returns since 1970. The best was the scarce 1883-S coin with a 1,425% cumulative return (32% per year). The worst was the 1888-O with a 1,100% cumulative return (24% per year).

While both coins significantly outperformed silver bullion (16% annualized), both had significant annual price declines, 11% of the time.

Though the Morgan silver dollar can be a great long-term investment, a collector needs to develop the expertise and dealer network to be successful in the end.

Morgan Silver Dollar (MS-60 Grade)				
Best and Worst Performance				
	1883-S	% Change	1888-O	% Change
1970	$5,250		$5.00	
1975	$20,000	281%	$12.50	150%
1980	$25,000	25%	$50.00	300%
1985	$17,500	-30%	$42.50	-15%
1990	$16,500	-6%	$25.00	-41%
1995	$25,000	52%	$15.00	-40%
2000	$30,000	20%	$25.00	67%
2002	$40,000	33%	$30.00	20%
2005	$75,000	88%	$35.00	17%
2007	$100,000	33%	$40.00	14%
2009	$110,000	10%	$50.00	25%
2011	$100,000	-9%	$45.00	-10%
2013	$90,000	-10%	$50.00	11%
2015	$80,000	-11%	$60.00	20%
2017	$95,000	19%	$62.00	3%

Coin prices rise when: (1) The economic trend is inflationary. The number of collectors increases, while coin supplies remain stationary or decrease through attrition or melting. (2) Dealers replace their stocks of coins only from collectors or other dealers, who expect a profit over what they originally paid. (3) Speculators buy large quantities. (4) Bullion gold and silver prices rise sharply.

—Richard Yeoman, A Guide Book of United States Coins, 2001

CABERNET SAUVIGNON WINE

Winemaking has been done in America since Colonial times, and the first vineyards in California have their roots in the 1849 Gold Rush. Although different types of California wines have come and gone, collectors have long preferred the cabernet sauvignon due to its long shelf life and great taste. In fact, wine collecting's key price index, the Wine Spectator Auction Index, lists eight California cabs out of the thirty-two wines used.

One of the oldest, continuously produced premium cabernet sauvignon wines is Beaulieu Vineyard's Georges de Latour Private Reserve. First produced in 1958 and named in honor of the vineyard's founder, it has a worldwide audience and is regularly listed with high rankings. In fact, a 1960s bottle of this hearty wine is still drinkable today.

Napa and Sonoma wine company, 1874.
Owned by Krug and Beringer.

Eisen Vineyard
1872-1926

Some of the best wines are made in ridiculously small quantities. We wouldn't say that quantity and quality are necessarily incompatible in winemaking, but at the very highest echelons of quality, there usually isn't much to go around.

—Ed McCarthy and Mary Ewing-Mulligan, *Wine for Dummies*, 2006

CABERNET SAUVIGNON WINE, BEALIEU VINEYARDS G. LATOUR RESERVE

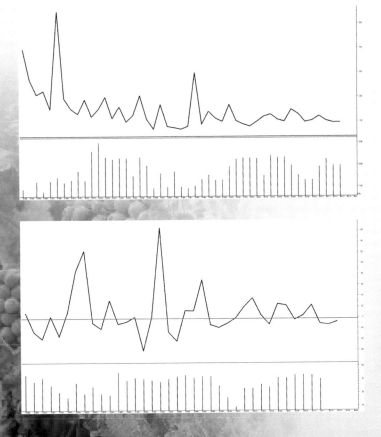

As can be seen in the first chart, this wine's current prices vary significantly between vintages. Last year, the 1968 vintage was most prized by collectors at $550 per bottle while the 1986 wine was a mere $69 per bottle. Both vintages had been made in limited quantities.

The second chart shows that though published rankings from respected third parties (such as *Wine Spectator* magazine) are important in determining the wine's quality, their influence on price appreciation isn't always clear-cut. Over the years, the lower ranked (WS 88) 1992 vintage had the largest price increase of 265% while the higher ranked 1990 (WS 90) actually declined -61% during this current wine bull market.

Apollo 12 astronaut Dick Gordon (middle) drinking the 1969 vintage

Wine Information Table					
Vintage	$ 2016	$ 2015	% Chg	Cases Produced	Wine Spectator Rank
1966	225	na		7,659	88
1967	150	149	1%	12,396	82
1968	550	506	9%	14,260	93
1969	195	265	-26%	11,830	88
1970	151	250	-40%	12,750	91
1971	131	129	2%	17,000	85
1972	190	289	-34%	12,680	80
1973	120	110	9%	26,000	76
1974	150	81	85%	29,900	87
1975	200	90	122%	23,390	79
1977	113	na		22,400	90
1978	161	179	-10%	23,000	84
1979	99	125	-21%	23,000	79
1981	125	95	32%	14,900	78
1984	206	na		23,350	81
1985	110	125	-12%	19,600	95
1986	69	75	-8%	9,230	89
1987	170	169	1%	16,000	91
1988	80	na		9,750	85
1989	75	na		16,800	87
1990	69	176	-61%	9,825	90
1991	80	80	0%	9,100	89
1992	299	82	265%	10,300	88
1993	88	120	-27%	13,300	90
1994	141	249	-43%	15,200	92
1995	113	100	13%	13,000	93
1996	100	89	12%	13,100	91
1997	169	100	69%	19,000	92
1998	103	119	-13%	21,000	92
1999	89	109	-18%	23,000	85
2000	80	90	-11%	23,000	76
2001	99	100	-1%	22,700	69
2002	120	100	20%	14,900	83
2003	129	95	36%	24,100	83
2004	108	103	5%	23,200	86
2005	100	115	-13%	23,350	84
2006	149	119	25%	19,600	91
2007	131	107	22%	15,200	91
2008	98	102	-4%	13,200	93
2009	104	100	4%	13,000	93
2010	122	99	23%	19,000	93
2011	104	117	-11%	22,400	na
2012	96	111	-14%	19,600	na

During the dot-com boom of the late 1990s, Napa Valley Cabernet Sauvignons—cult Cabernets in particular—enjoyed heady price increases, higher than those of all other regions...Then the NASDAQ plummeted, Silicon Valley hit hard times and cult Cabs saw a steep decline.

—*Wine Spectator*, November 30, 2007

NON-RATED COLLECTIBLES

APOLLO 11 MEMORABILIA

The raw capitalism of auctions for nonrated collectibles (artwork and historic artifacts) resembles the excitement on a casino floor when a one of-a-kind item is placed on the block and emotional bidding drives its price into the stratosphere.

When compared to the endless supply of sports, military, and political collectibles, space exploration memorabilia is the perfect picture of limited supply and rising demand. On the supply side, only twenty-four men traveled to the moon, and of those, only twelve walked on its surface from 1969–1972. On the demand side is a growing number of middle-aged collectors who enthusiastically watched these historical events unfold during their childhood.

Apollo 11 artifacts are the most popular space collectibles. They are regularly sold at auctions and command the best prices. Also because Neil Armstrong rarely signed autographs, it is easier to track the history of each item.

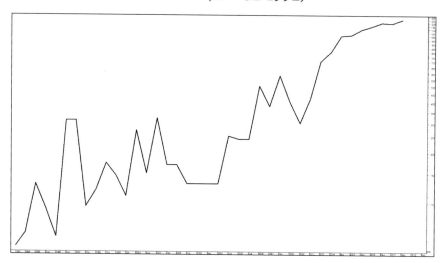

APOLLO 11 CREW AUTOGRAPHED PHOTO (SINCE 1992)

Three decades after the last moonwalk finally qualifies as one huge antique…objects that once whizzed overhead have finally acquired, for collectors, the mellow patina of Chippendale end tables.

—*Forbes*, November 27, 2000

APOLLO 11 CREW SIGNED ITEMS
(UNFLOWN) (SINCE 1992)

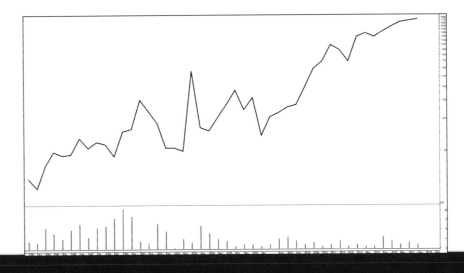

The Reynolds Winans Apollo Collection Index (RWACI) tracks the prices of Apollo 11 autographed crew photos and other crew-signed items. As can be seen, prices of Apollo 11 memorabilia have risen dramatically. A mint-condition 8½ x 10 photo signed by the Apollo 11 crew sold in 2017 for $12,400. This same photo has appreciated 2,155% since 1992. (US new homes increased 153% during this same time.)

It is also amazing that personal items the astronauts took on their lunar missions have recently sold for well over $1 million!

Armstrong, Collins, and Aldrin are said to have taken 214 postal covers along…All of the Apollo 11 flown covers were autographed by the three crewmen during post-flight quarantine…Apollo 11 crew signatures are probably the most commonly encountered forgeries on the market in the United States.

—Russell Still, *Relics of the Space Race*, 1995

COLLECTIBLES SUMMARY

Collectibles can be a profitable addition to an investment portfolio. Here are some important things to remember to be a successful collector.

Be an expert. Experienced collectors are experts in their specific fields of interest. They balance the emotional desire to add a unique item to their portfolio with its costs. Many have built their own database of historical prices and have developed an extensive network of other collectors and dealers to keep them posted on desirable items for sale at good prices.

Watch out for fades or collecting bubbles. Remember Cabbage Patch Kids or Beanie Babies? They were *hot* collectibles that rose in price to ridiculous levels and rapidly collapsed in value as interest waned. Stick with conventional items that your grandparents would have collected.

Be mindful of numerous costs. Collecting is expensive, with numerous expenses. Auction costs, storage and security expenses, and insurance premiums are just a few of the costs that serious collectors with extensive portfolios have to contend with. Also tax laws surrounding collectibles can be complicated.

Stick with rare items for at least a five-year holding period. Focus on expensive, marquee items with an appealing appearance for long-term investment. Scarcity is the key to profitable collecting, so it is better to have a smaller collection of expensive items that will command good prices in soft times.

Understand how the internet has changed collecting. The web has had an immense impact on collecting through low-cost auction websites in the twenty-first century, such as eBay. In fact, eBay is one of the few companies created during the internet boom of the 1990s to survive the dot-com bubble (see chart). Like all change, there are good and bad aspects to it. The good news is that auctions costs have fallen drastically, and ease of access has attracted many new collectors into niche areas such as historical memorabilia. The bad news is that because you can't personally inspect the items before bidding, there is an increased risk of buying fake or forged items.

If you are a buyer and you're looking for a real steal, you might be hard-pressed to find one on a desirable item at eBay. Although the sellers benefit from having six million sets of eyes seeing their items, this is often a curse for buyers… don't expect to find an autographed Babe Ruth baseball card without others seeing it as well.

—Dennis Prince, *Online Auctions @ eBay*, 1999

EBAY (1998–2017)

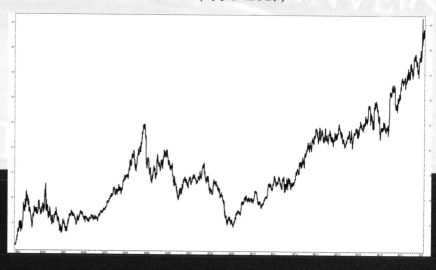

The Federal Reserve Board's Fine Arts Program was established in 1975 by former Chairman Arthur F. Burns. The Board's collection has grown to consists of more than 1,000 works of art, including drawings, paintings, photographs, prints, and sculptures.

—Federal Reserve website, 2016

CASH –
CAN BE KING

WASHINGTON, I

SERIES OF

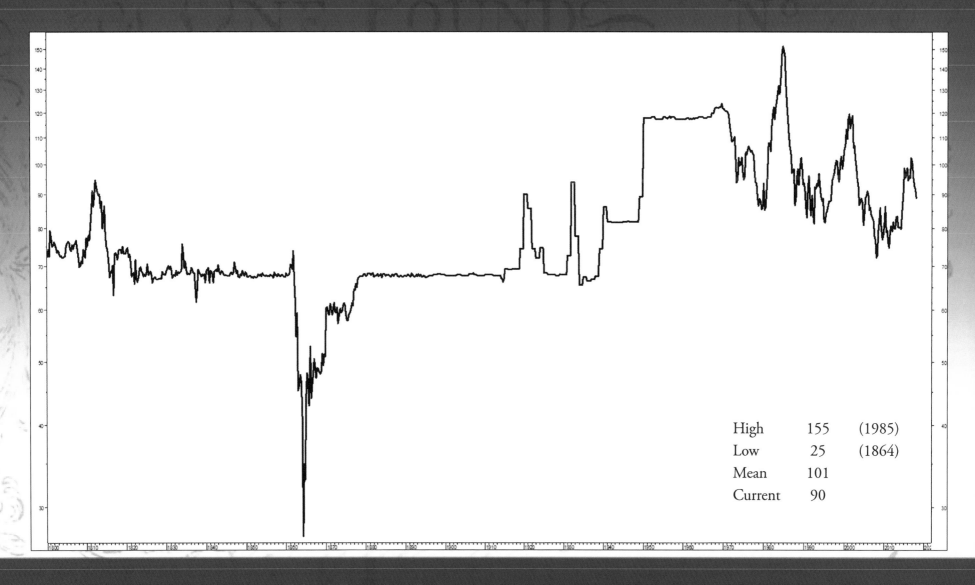

High	155	(1985)
Low	25	(1864)
Mean	101	
Current	90	

Every dollar bill issued by the Treasury or the Fed since 1863 is as good today
as it ever was. You can even use one today to pay your tax.

—Jason Goodwin, *GreenBack*, 2003

90-DAY T-BILLS AND COMMERCIAL PAPER

The long-term relationship between the value of the US dollar (versus foreign currencies) and the level and direction of short-term US interest rates (T-bills and commercial paper) isn't as strong as commonly believed.

The highs and lows of the US dollar and US short-term interest rates don't match up well. The dollar's value (versus the British pound, America's longtime trading partner) had sharply fallen to a low point in 1864, during the US Civil War, while interest rates increased modestly.

The US dollar index (a basket of major foreign currencies) hit an all-time high in 1985 while short-term interest rates were 47% below their highest levels of 17% in 1980.

While short-term interest rates were near 0% at their all-time low point during the Great Depression of the 1930s, the dollar's value versus the British pound was near the value it had been at since the late 1800s.

NINETY-DAY T-BILL YIELD (SINCE 1820)

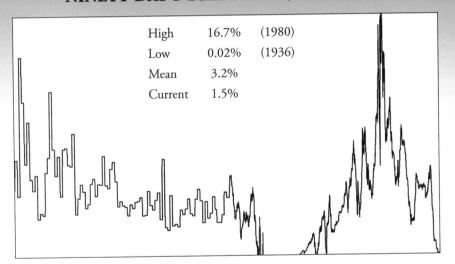

High	16.7%	(1980)
Low	0.02%	(1936)
Mean	3.2%	
Current	1.5%	

COMMERCIAL PAPER YIELD (SINCE 1830)

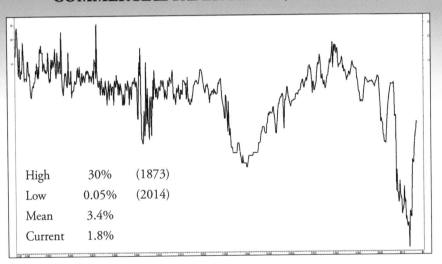

High	30%	(1873)
Low	0.05%	(2014)
Mean	3.4%	
Current	1.8%	

All cares, hopes, joys, affections, virtues, and associations seemed to be melted down into dollars.

—Charles Dickens, 1844

Treasury Maturity Yield Spread—Since 1820

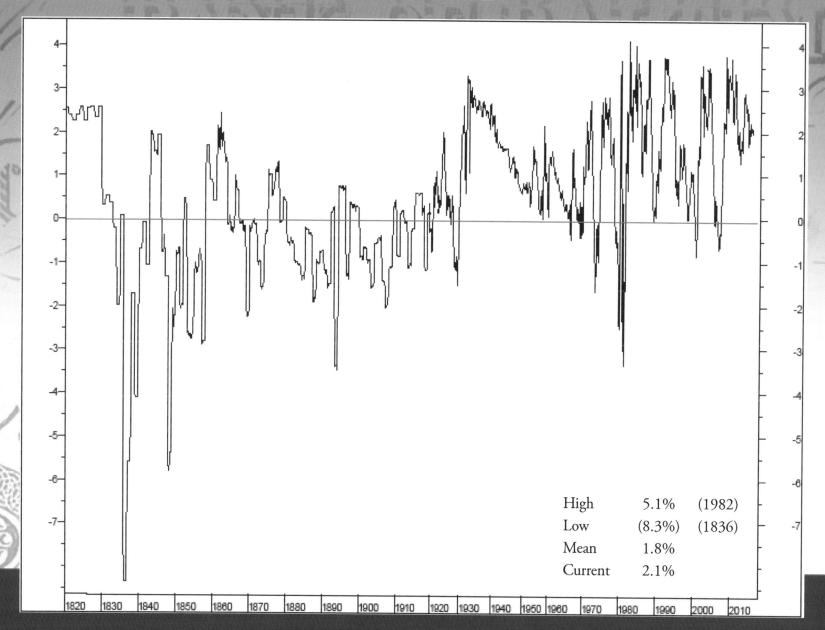

High	5.1%	(1982)
Low	(8.3%)	(1836)
Mean	1.8%	
Current	2.1%	

Inverted (yield) curves often come toward the end of Fed rate-increase cycle.

—*The Wall Street Journal*, January 8, 2007

"Go to cash" is an instinctive move for investors that is just a phone call or Enter keystroke away during scary, volatile times. It can be the defining judgment that allows investors to keep the easy profits made during an investment bubble that sets an investor up for life. Think of those lucky souls who cashed out at the top in August 1929, December 1972, or January 2008.

While consistently getting out at the top is pure luck, investors need to remember that stock and real estate investments have had significant annual declines, more than 29% of the time, since 1900. It is essential that investors decide whether they plan to ride through the bear markets or pay the taxes and commissions and cash out after making significant gains to come back to fight another day.

Fortunately, money market instruments (mutual funds that mostly hold short-term debt obligations of governments and corporations and one of Wall Street's greatest inventions) are universally used by all investors at some time and make it easy to "go to cash" regardless of the investor's time frame and not skip a beat in collecting interest.

Information Table		
90-Day T-Bill Yield (since 1900)		
High	16.7%	1980
Low	0.01%	2011
Average Return Since		
1900		3.6%
1960		4.7%
1990		2.9%
2000		1.8%
2010		0.32%

The really sophisticated investors liquidate to cash at each bear market rally.

—*Time*, July 1, 1962

A Few Key Facts to Remember

Not all money market accounts are the same. Thinking it's always insured by the government, many investors pick the highest-yielding money market account offered by a brokerage house and investigate no further than the fund's name. Caveat emptor—like all other types of investments, there are high-quality and low-rated products. This is not the place to take risk. Stick to quality versus yield!

Cash-equivalent investments hedge well against inflation. Because short-term rates have changed quickly, they have adjusted for inflationary pressures well since 1900 (average T-bill yield, 3.6%, versus CPI, 3.0%).

Inverted yield curves are common. As can be seen on the previous chart (Treasury yield spread), there have been long periods of time when short-term investments pay higher yields than longer-term bonds.

Money market returns have changed rapidly in both directions. Short-term interest rates are heavily influenced by government actions and can rapidly drop in favor of other types of investments. Remember the near-zero interest rates policies of the 1930s and today's "new normal."

The dollar's value is relative. It's tempting to tell yourself that a dollar earned is a dollar saved. However, in today's global investment environment, adverse currency swings can be long-lasting and result in significant devaluation of foreign investments. Bottom-line: keep an eye on the direction of the US dollar.

SAME ADVICE OVER TIME

AND THE WINNERS ARE ... STOCKS!

Performance Summary Table							A $1 Investment made in 1900 is worth today?	
Average Annual Returns	Line Color	1900	1960	1990	2000	2010	Nominal	Inflation Adjusted
US Common Stocks	Black	12.0%	11.0%	10.9%	6.8%	13.9%	71,039	2,075
US Preferred Stocks	Orange	7.7%	10.2%	10.3%	9.7%	10.5%	3,388	92.55
US Corporate Bonds	Brown	6.2%	7.9%	7.0%	6.1%	4.9%	935.91	26.19
US Homes (100% Owned)	Pink	5.2%	5.9%	3.5%	3.9%	5.2%	121.38	4.27
10-Year T-Bond Yields	Green	4.6%	6.1%	4.6%	3.6%	2.5%	189.63	5.62
Commodities	Blue	2.8%	2.2%	0.8%	1.7%	-2.5%	4.78	0.13

1900   1910   1920   1930   1940   1950   1960   1970   1980   1990   2000   2010

BEAR MARKETS
The Expressions Never Change!

MARKET CYCLES
FROM EASY MONEY TO CRASH LANDINGS

TIME
THE CRASH
After a wild week on Wall Street, the world is different

In the last section, we reviewed the overall performance of six different types of investments. Though this knowledge is important, when to buy or sell can be as important as what to buy or sell, especially when investment debt is used to try to enhance returns. History has repeatedly shown that investors blow up portfolios of sound investments in stocks and real estate by using lethal levels of high leverage during bear markets.

This section will focus on the most significant bull and bear markets for US common stocks and homes since 1850 and how time-tested tools can provide important early clues to possible changes in direction for stocks and real estate.

These old pros would think that the idea of most investors being 100% invested in stocks 100% of the time was laughable.

—Forbes.com, October 29, 2015

BULL MARKETS—THE BEST OF TIMES

US Common Stocks

Five stock bull markets have exceeded seven years in duration since 1850. Their average annual return was 67% higher than the markets average performance (18.4% vs. 11%). Although the Roaring Twenties posted the best annual average return of 25%, the twenty two-year run of the Decade of Greed coupled with the era of the dot-coms took first place as the longest-running stock bull market in spite of the 1987 market crash.

US COMMON STOCKS
Longest bull markets (since 1850)

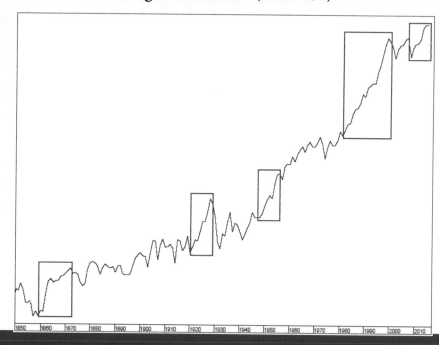

			Annual Total Returns				
Period	Number of Years	Cumulative Return	Average	Median	Best	Worst	Dividend Yield
1982-1999	22	3017%	17.5%	19.2%	36.6%	-3.0%	3.6%
1858-1872	15	691%	15.8%	12.5%	61.2%	-3.2%	6.1%
1947-1956	10	414%	18.7%	17.6%	51.1%	-1.1%	6.0%
2009-2017	9	247%	15.2%	13.5%	31.5%	1.5%	2.0%
1921-1928	8	474%	25.2%	30.6%	42.7%	2.8%	6.0%
Average	**13**	**969%**	**18.5%**	**18.7%**	**44.6%**	**-0.6%**	**4.7%**

US Common Stocks: Longest Bull Markets

Criteria:
Timeframe is at least 7 years
No negative year worse than 3.5%
Cumulative return to exceed 150%

A history of the Great Bull Market of 1982–99 is more than a financial story. Ultimately, that breakneck ride would mark an epoch in US cultural history. While share prices spiraled, investing replaced baseball as the national pastime. CNBC's stars began to edge the soaps off the screen. The New Economy spawned a New Society, and, as the baby boomers aged, even the symbols of success changed: SUVs trumped BMW. Trophy mansions replaced trophy wives.

—Maggie Mahar, *Bull!*, 2003

US Homes

Five real estate bull markets have exceeded five years in duration since 1850. Their average annual return was 125% higher than average performance (11.0% vs. 4.9%). The twenty-year run of the 1971–1990 housing market was the longest, but the second best bull market started two years later, the fifteen-year run of the 1992–2006.

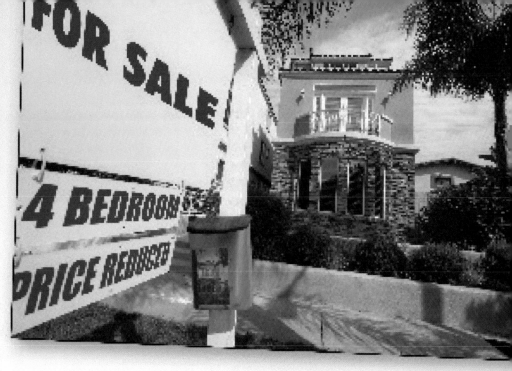

US HOMES
Longest bull markets (since 1850)

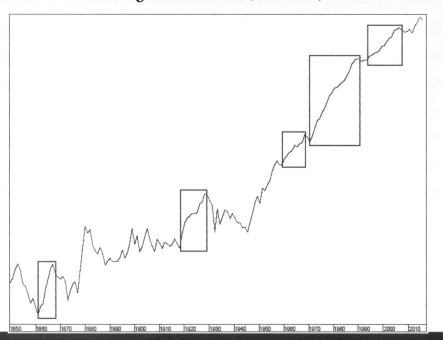

US Common Stocks: Longest Bull Markets						
Period	Number of Years	Cumulative Return	Annual Total Returns			
			Average	Median	Best	Worst
1971–1990	20	511%	9.6%	10.0%	20.3%	0.3%
1992–2006	15	478%	5.0%	3.4%	14.2%	-0.3%
1919–1928	10	222%	12.9%	8.2%	36.4%	-0.3%
1959–1968	10	94%	7.0%	6.3%	19.5%	-3.4%
1862–1867	6	196%	20.4%	21.9%	37.1%	5.5%
Average	12.2	300%	11.0%	10.0%	25.5%	-0.4%

Criteria:
Timeframe is at least 5 years
No negative year worse than 3.5%
Cumulative return to exceed 90%

You're seeing people now for whom investing in real estate is their life. It's a move taken straight from the old day traders of the stock market.

—Fortune, June 6, 2005

MARKET TOPS
Is it Time to Sell? How to Tell

There are several tools that stock investors can use to gauge the health of an old bull market similarly to how doctors use various tests during physical exams on their patients. Unfortunately, many investors fruitlessly search for a magic indicator to pick the top of a bull market. Experienced investors use a series of indicators to gain a consensus as to the market's overall strength. Although many tools are used in stock market analysis, the forty-week moving average of major stock market indices combined with the NYSE advance decline line are used to evaluate the market tops of 1929 and 2007.

US COMMON STOCKS (1928–1930)
with forty-week moving average

Moving averages are used to determine market direction. If the index is above the moving average, then the index is in an uptrend. If the index is below the moving average, then the index is in a downtrend.

NYSE ADVANCE/DECLINE LINE (1928–1930)
with forty-week moving average

This measures the number of individual stocks where prices are moving up versus down. It uses the forty-week moving average similar to price charts.

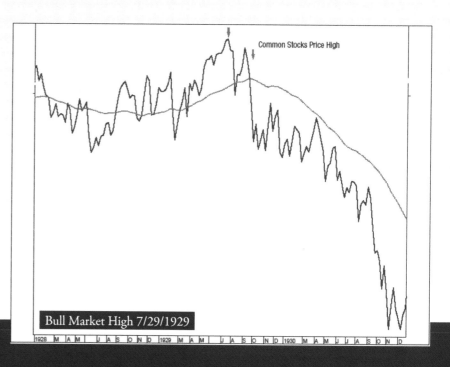

Bull market high:	9/7/1929	32.90
40 moving Average Crossing:	10/23/1929	26.60
Bear market low:	6/1/1932	4.40

1929 Crash

NYSE Volume

Common Stocks Price High

Bull Market High 7/29/1929

The statement is again being heard that we are in a new era of market valuation.

—*Barron's*, August 19, 1929

US common stocks in 1929 and 2007

As can be seen in both examples, the internal strength of the market had been eroding many months before a new high was made on the index itself. For example, the NYSE advance decline line had started to decline many months before the S&P 500 Index crossed below the forty-week moving average, thus beginning a new bear market in both cases.

Bull market—the name given to an advancing market in the 1700s because a bull fights by using its horns to throw its victims up.

US COMMON STOCKS (2007–2008)
with forty-week moving average

Moving averages are used to determine market direction. If the index is above the moving average, then the index is in an uptrend. If the index is below the moving average, then the index is in a downtrend.

NYSE ADVANCE/DECLINE LINE (2007–2008)
with forty-week moving average

This measures the number of individual stocks where prices are moving up versus down. It uses the forty-week moving average similar to price charts.

Bull market high:	1,576	(10/11/2007)
Forty-week moving average crossing:	1,474	(11/7/2007)
Bear market low:	667	(3/6/2009)

NYSE A/D Line High (6/4/2007)

Common Stocks Price High

Capital can move in and out of the market with mercurial speed…Little wonder that market prices often anticipate economic trends long in advance.

—Forbes, May 1, 1967

MARKET TOPS
U.S. Residential Real Estate

Many of the tools used for market analysis of real estate did not exist before the 1960s, so attention is focused on the bull markets of the 1960s and 2000s.

Although there are many tools used in market analysis, the fifteen-month moving average of the Winans Real Estate Index™ combined with the number of months a new house was on the market before it was sold are used to evaluate the market tops of 1968 and 2007.

US NEW HOME PRICES (1968–1970) with fifteen-month moving average	MONTHS THAT NEW HOMES WERE ON THE MARKET (1968–1970)
Moving averages are used to determine market direction. If the index is above the moving average, then the index is in an uptrend. If the index is below the moving average, then the index is in a downtrend.	This measures the number of months that new houses in the United States were for sale before they were sold.

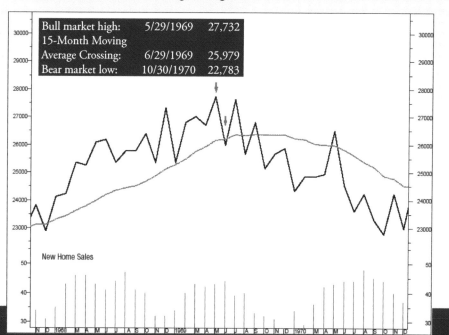

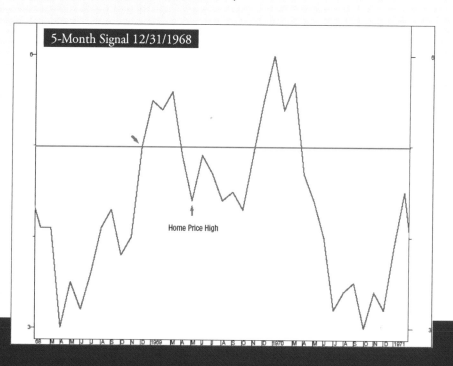

Skeletons of unfinished houses in Los Angeles testify to the suddenness with which scarcity of money and high mortgage rates can cut off demand.

—*Life* magazine, June 5, 1970

New Homes in 1968 and 2007

As can be seen in both examples, when the WIREI™ crossed below its fifteen-month moving average and the months on market climbed above five months, there was strong evidence that the bull markets were coming to an end.

US NEW HOME PRICES (2005–2007)
with fifteen-month moving average

Moving averages are used to determine market direction. If the index is above the moving average, then the index is in an uptrend. If the index is below the moving average, then the index is in a downtrend.

MONTHS THAT NEW HOMES WERE ON THE MARKET (2005–2007)

This measures the number of months that new houses in the United States were for sale before they were sold.

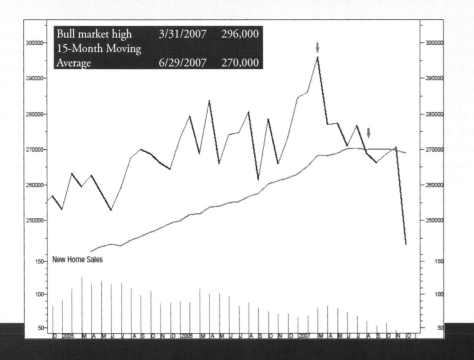

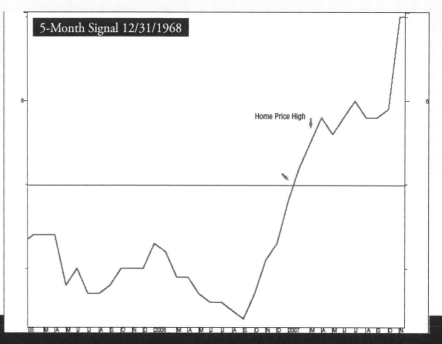

Today's residential real estate markets are booming, and I and many other prominent housing economists believe they will most likely climb into the next decade.

—David Lereah, *Are You Missing the Real Estate Boom*, 2005

BEAR MARKET—THE WORST OF TIMES

Volume of New York Stock Exchange Transactions

Absence of Tangible Business Improvement Results in Uncertain Trend

How Far Can This Market Go?

US Common Stocks

Five stock bear markets have exceeded two years in duration since 1850. Their average annual decline was -15%, and it took nearly ten years on average to return to the market's previous high. The four-year decline of the Great Depression was the worst in 165 years, with a cumulative decline of -63%.

US COMMON STOCKS LONGEST BEAR MARKETS (SINCE 1850)

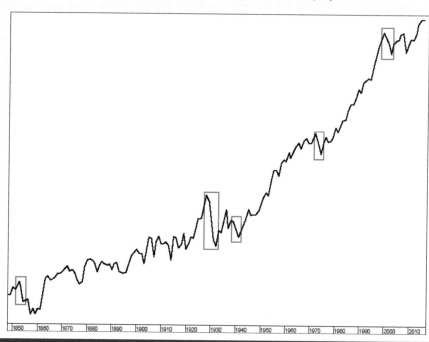

US Common Stocks: Longest Bear Markets							
	Number	Cumulative	Annual Total Returns				
Period	of Years	Return	Average	Median	Best	Worst	Yield
1929–1932	4	-63%	-20.8%	-16.6%	-8.0%	-42.0%	4.9%
2000–2002	3	-37%	-14.3%	-11.8%	-9.1%	-21.5%	1.2%
1939–1941	3	-20%	-7.1%	-9.8%	-0.5%	-11.2%	5.7%
1973–1974	2	-34%	-18.7%	-18.7%	-13.3%	-24.0%	4.9%
1853–1854	2	-21%	-13.1%	-13.1%	-5.8%	-20.5%	8.3%
Average	**2.8**	**-35%**	**-14.8%**	**-14.0%**	**-7.3%**	**-23.8%**	**5.0%**

Criteria:
Timeframe is at least 2 years
No positive years
Cumulative return worse than -19%

During the long continued rise in stocks which began in 1924 the slogan "common stocks for investment" became a popular watchword. People were obsessed with the notion that bear markets were a thing of the past and could never recur.

—Roger Babson, *Investment Fundamentals*, 1930

US Homes

Five housing bear markets have exceeded three years in duration since 1850. Their average annual decline was -14%, and it took nearly twelve years on average to return to the previous high. The six years of decline during World War II was the longest in 165 years, with a cumulative decline of -33%. But the five-year decline of 1854–1858 was far worse, with a cumulative decline of -58%.

US HOMES'
longest bear markets (since 1850)

US Homes: Longest Bear Markets						
Period	Number of Years	Cumulative Return	**Annual Total Returns**			
			Average	Median	Best	Worst
1929-1932	6	-33%	-6.4%	-9.1%	1.3%	-10.2%
1854–1858	5	-58%	-15.5%	-15.4%	-6.9%	-24.6%
1854–1858	4	-57%	-17.1%	-10.7%	-3.3%	-43.6%
1883–1885	3	-40%	-15.4%	-11.9%	-6.8%	-27.4%
1883–1885	3	-39%	-14.9%	-15.5%	-10.3%	-19.0%
Average	**4.2**	**-45%**	**-13.8%**	**-12.5%**	**-5.2%**	**-25.0%**

Criteria:
Timeframe is at least 3 years
No positive year to exceed 3.5%
Losses are at least -30%
No leverage

Brace yourself: Home prices could fall an additional 25%, on average, before bottoming out. Such a drop would be unprecedented in modern times.

—Businessweek, February 11, 2008

MARKET BOTTOMS
Is It Time to Buy? How to Tell

Stock investors can use several tools to determine whether a bear market is getting close to ending. Unfortunately, many investors fruitlessly search for a magic indicator to pick the bottom of a bear market. Experienced investors use a series of indicators to gain a consensus as to the market's overall strength or weakness and learn to ignore all the doom and gloom projections coming from media sources. Although many tools are used in market analysis, the forty-week moving average of a broad market index (such as the S&P 500 Index) combined with the NYSE advance decline line are used to evaluate the market bottoms of 1932 and 2009.

US COMMON STOCKS (1929–1932)
with forty-week moving average

Moving averages are used to determine market direction. If the index is above the moving average, then the index is in an uptrend. If the index is below the moving average, then the index is in a downtrend.

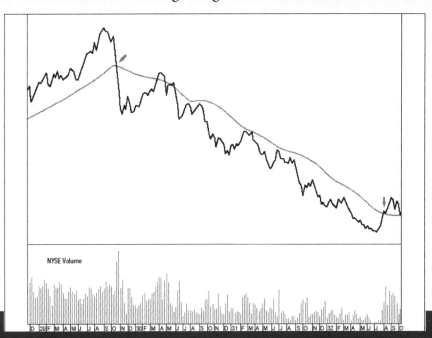

NYSE ADVANCE/DECLINE LINE (1929–1932)

This measures the number of individual stocks where prices are moving up versus down. It uses the forty-week moving average similar to price charts.

While the 1921–1932 period is the shortest gap between bear market bottoms it was still accompanied by significant structural change in the stock market. There were many more securities to choose from in 1932 compared to 1921.

—Russell Napier, *Anatomy of the Bear*, 2005

US Common Stocks in 1932 and 2009

As can be seen in both examples, waiting for both the indicators to cross above their individual forty-week moving averages gave a strong indication the bear market was coming to an end.

US COMMON STOCKS (2007–2009)
with forty-week moving average

Moving averages are used to determine market direction. If the index is above the moving average, then the index is in an uptrend. If the index is below the moving average, then the index is in a downtrend.

NYSE ADVANCE/DECLINE LINE (2007–2009)
with forty-week moving average

This measures the number of individual stocks where prices are moving up versus down. It uses the forty-week moving average similar to price charts.

Investors who followed the 200-day moving average buy and sell rules enjoyed larger returns than those who bought and held on between 1988 through 2008.

—USA Today, October 20, 2009

MARKET BOTTOMS
U.S. Residential Real Estate

Many of the tools for market analysis of real estate did not exist before the 1960s. Therefore, attention is focused on the bear markets of 1970–72 and 2007–12.

Although many tools are used in market analysis, the fifteen-month moving average of the Winans Real Estate Index™ combined with the number of months a new house was on the market before it was sold are used to evaluate the market bottoms of 1970 and 2011.

US HOMES (1968–1971)
with fifteen-month moving average

Moving averages are used to determine market direction. If the index is above the moving average, then the index is in an uptrend. If the index is below the moving average, then the index is in a downtrend.

US HOME SALES, MONTHS UNTIL SOLD (1968–1971)

This measures the number of months that new houses in the United States were for sale before they were sold.

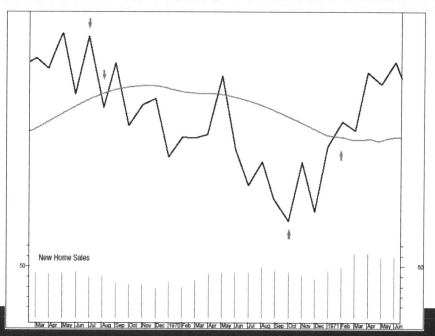

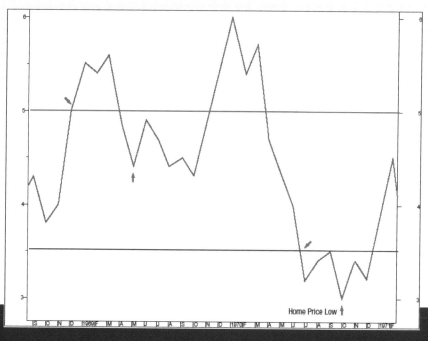

Over the last 60 years, housing bear markets ended when the BLS compiled "Months for Sale" dropped below 3.5 months.

—*Financial History Magazine*, spring 2011

New Homes in 1970 and 2012

As can be seen in both examples, when the WIREI crossed above its fifteen-month moving average, and the months on market reached 3.5 months, there was strong evidence that the bear markets were reaching a close.

US NEW HOME PRICES (2007–2012)
with fifteen-month moving average

Moving averages are used to determine market direction. If the index is above the moving average, then the index is in an uptrend. If the index is below the moving average, then the index is in a downtrend.

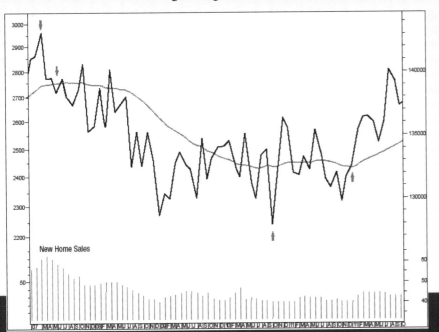

US NEW HOME SALES, MONTHS UNTIL SOLD (2007–2012)

This measures the number of months that new houses in the United States were for sale before they were sold.

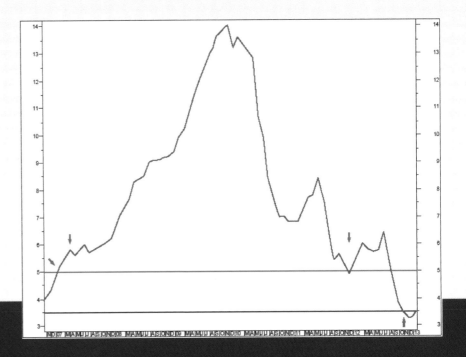

Buy land, they're not making it anymore.

—Mark Twain

FINANCIAL STORMS

Like major hurricanes that frequently strike our nation, these one-year cliff-dropping bear markets are unique but not uncommon. Since 1903, there have been thirteen times in which the Dow Jones Industrial Average declined more than 28% within a single year. Worse yet, there are no storm shelters to escape to as real estate, bonds, and commodities also suffered steep declines during most of these periods and cracked the foundations of even the best-diversified portfolios (see table below).

THE *HOWS* AND *WHYS* SEEM TO RHYME!

Let's look briefly at some of the factors that caused these disastrous bear markets.

1903: The Rich Man's Panic was caused by the sudden illiquidity of overpriced publicly traded trusts. Wall Street simply overestimated the demand and risks of these leveraged, illiquid inventions.

1907: A copper bubble burst, and a number of large financial trust companies failed. Global stock markets plunged due to overleverage.

1917: US entered World War I, and the federal government took over the nation's railroads.

1920: A commodities bubble burst, as the Federal Reserve raised interest rates by 47% and thus overtightened the money supply. A bomb exploded on Wall Street, which injured four hundred people. GOP candidate Warren G. Harding was elected president, ending eight years of democratic administrations.

1929: A stock market bubble ended with the worst one-day crash in US history and a two-month drop of 48%. Professionally managed, highly leveraged pools and investment trusts were quickly liquidated at low prices.

1930: Hawley-Smoot Tariff bill was enacted and started one of the largest trade wars in modern history.

1931: The Great Depression's high unemployment rate threatened the world's social and political stability. Some two hundred banks closed each month, and public anger at Wall Street drove federal investigations on short selling. England abandoned the gold standard for its currency.

1932: Bank failures set record levels, and the government enacted housing price supports and a foreclosure moratorium for homeowners. A perceived anti–Wall Street president was elected (i.e., FDR).

1937: The Japanese sank a US gunboat as it invaded China and thus started a US trade embargo with Japan. Reduced margin rates and SEC oversight failed to stem the stock market's volatility. The

Worst Financial Panics				
	Stocks Interyear	Home Prices	Corp. Bonds	Commodities
1903	-34%	13%	-11%	-6%
1907	-44%	-15%	-15%	-2%
1917	-31%	-10%	-14%	1%
1920	-38%	25%	-10%	-30%
1929	-34%	-3%	4%	-15%
1930	-37%	-11%	-1%	-31%
1931	-55%	-10%	-23%	-31%
1932	-47%	-44%	-15%	-27%
1937	-37%	-4%	-13%	-26%
1962	-28%	7%	0%	-4%
1974	-33%	5%	-12%	-7%
2002	-28%	6%	-7%	-2%
2008	-44%	-11%	-16%	-42%
Average	-38%	-4%	-11%	-17%
w/o 29–32	-35%	2%	-11%	-13%

Federal Reserve overtightened, and New Deal programs were perceived as not working.

1962: The Cuban missile crisis nearly started a new world war. The SEC investigated American Stock Exchange floor trading abuses and large-scale insider trading cases.

1974: The continuing Arab oil embargo was a result of the Yom Kippur War. The Federal Reserve raised interest rates to record levels. Most real estate investment trusts (REITs) collapsed in value. The Watergate scandal brought about President Nixon's resignation.

2002: Thirty-three large publicly traded corporations and the Big Four accounting firms were guilty of wide-scale accounting scandals. This led to several large bankruptcies and the criminal convictions of well-known CEOs. The Sarbanes-Oxley Law was enacted to significantly enforce corporate financial conduct. Congress authorized the president to use force against Iraq for noncompliance of UN sanctions.

2008: Commodity and real estate bubbles collapsed with housing having its worst decline since World War II. Highly leveraged mortgage-backed investments collapsed in price, leading to a global credit freeze as several major international investment firms failed. The collapse of Lehman Brothers and Washington Mutual were the largest financial failures in US history.

The federal government authorized a $700 billion bailout package to purchase failing bank assets. Democrats took control of both the White House and Congress for the first time since the early 1990s.

There are common themes in each of these market panics:

1. The combination of over leverage and illiquidity burst bubbles in all financial instruments.
2. Many of Wall Street's investment innovations went awry.
3. Investments responded negatively to failed government actions and overregulation.
4. The military conflicts or the threat of conflicts caused widespread investor panic.

Simply put, the names and dates might have changed, but the causes were similar.

Fortunately, these financial panics were usually followed by powerful stock market rallies and long before the media's headlines became bullish.

As can be seen in the table, these tough years have been followed with strong performances ten out of thirteen years, averaging 20%. Even more impressive, these market rallies typically extend for two years, 85% of the time, in fact, with an average total return (including dividends) of 44%. If the Great Depression years of 1929–32 are removed from the calculations, the two-year cumulative total increases to an impressive 62%!

Postpanic Rallies				
	DJIA Year-end	Year 2	Year 3	Cumulative Total Return
1903	-24%	42%	38%	104%
1907	-38%	47%	15%	79%
1917	-22%	11%	31%	59%
1920	-33%	13%	22%	51%
1929	-17%	-34%	-53%	-59%
1930	-34%	-53%	-23%	-52%
1931	-53%	-23%	67%	40%
1932	-23%	67%	4%	84%
1937	-33%	28%	-3%	34%
1962	-11%	17%	15%	41%
1974	-28%	38%	18%	72%
2002	-17%	25%	3%	33%
2008	-34%	19%	11%	34%
Average	-28%	20%	10%	44%
w/o 29–32	-26%	34%	15%	62%

Bubbles lie at the intersection between finance, economics, and psychology.

—Peter Garber, *Famous First Bubbles*, 2000

BUBBLES, FADS and SCANDALS

SOUTH SEAS COMPANY BUBBLE (1711–1750)

South Seas Company transaction receipt, 1720

The dot-com stock of the 1700s! The stock
price declined by 84% in six months.

When Sir Isaac Newton was asked about the continuance
of the rising South Sea Stock? He answered that he
could not calculate the madness of people.

—Joseph Spence, 1720

Equity Funding Corporation, 1973

Wall Street's Watergate! This insurance company committed
a $1 billion fraud, and its stock price went from a high of
$80 to $0.50 within nine months. Twenty-two company
executives were indicted for fraud and conspiracy.

Federal District Judge condemned his crimes as
"extraordinarily evil" and imposed a 150-year sentence…
Mr. Madoff blamed his pride, which would not allow
him to admit his failures as a money manager.

—*The New York Times*, June 30, 2009

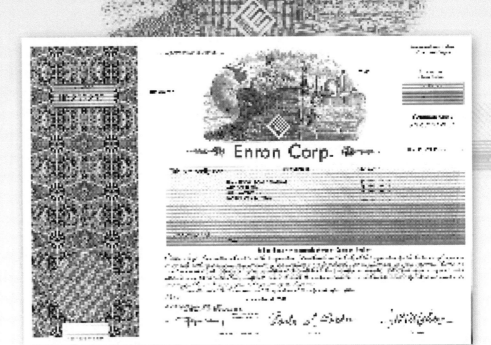

Planet Hollywood, 1996

This company was backed by many of Hollywood's biggest stars. It went public at $32 a share during April 1996 and was trading at only $0.90 by early 1999.

Enron Corporation, 2001

The largest bankruptcy in history due to a massive accounting fraud. The stock declined from $90 to $0.37 within fifteen months. Its top executives received prison sentences between twenty-four and forty-five years.

Planet Hollywood has stood as a cautionary tale about the perils of celebrity and hype, as the company filed bankruptcy protection not once but twice shortly after the Las Vegas groundbreaking.

—*The New York Times*, September 24, 2007

Something is rotten with the state of Enron.

—*The New York Times*, September 9, 2001

ACCOUNTING SCAMS
Watch Shareholder Dilution!

During the accounting scandals of 2002, what did companies like Enron, WorldCom, and Tyco have in common (besides stocks that "blew up" due to fraudulent accounting practices)? Excessive shareholder dilution—reckless growth in the number of split-adjusted shares outstanding.

The table below shows shares outstanding between 1991 and 2001. The dilution levels of these three tainted companies were significantly higher than the Dow Jones Industrial Average.

Many companies resort to aggressive accounting methods and high levels of shareholder dilution to hide reckless expansion, ridiculous employee compensation, and illegal business practices.

This statistic can be a good indicator of companies with potential accounting problems. History has shown that if investors want to avoid owning companies that could be using fraudulent accounting practices, then they should avoid companies that have levels of shareholder dilution exceeding 70% over the past ten years.

Company	Cumulative Outstanding (Millions of Shares)		Dilution (Postsplits)
	1991	2001	
Enron	405	752	86%
WorldCom	299	2,965	893%
Tyco International	377	1936	414%
DJIA 30 Stocks Average Cumulative Dilution			17%

Many commodity pool operators advertise and solicit investors based on false claims of high profits and low risk…The funds are often misused and spent on improper expenses.

—Commodity Futures Trading Commission brochure, 2015

HISTORICAL EVENTS
DOES WALL STREET CARE?

Throughout our lives, we have been shaped by the events we have experienced. Baby boomers have a different take on life than their Greatest Generation parents, their Generation X kids, or their millennial grandchildren. This is clearly defined by their investment choices.

To this day, many senior citizens still fear (and avoid) the stock market because of painful childhood memories of the 1930s Great Depression. To the other extreme, many of their children enjoy today's conveniences and wide-ranging choices of equity investments offered by the investment community and hold little or no cash for a rainy day.

But are our financial reactions to major events really any different from those of past generations? Can we learn from their investment mistakes and successes during difficult and ecstatic times in the past?

In this section, we review how investors in stocks, homes, and treasury bonds reacted to the major government policies, wars, natural disasters, man-made tragedies, and great national achievements since 1812 in hopes of finding useful investment guidance for future events.

Though it might be difficult to view dark times for all of mankind as investment opportunities, it is important to consider these events from many different perspectives and learn from the past actions of uninformed individuals who sold solid investments because of scary headlines rather than learning from the lessons of history.

If there is ever a time to be a logical, disciplined investor, it is during major historical events!

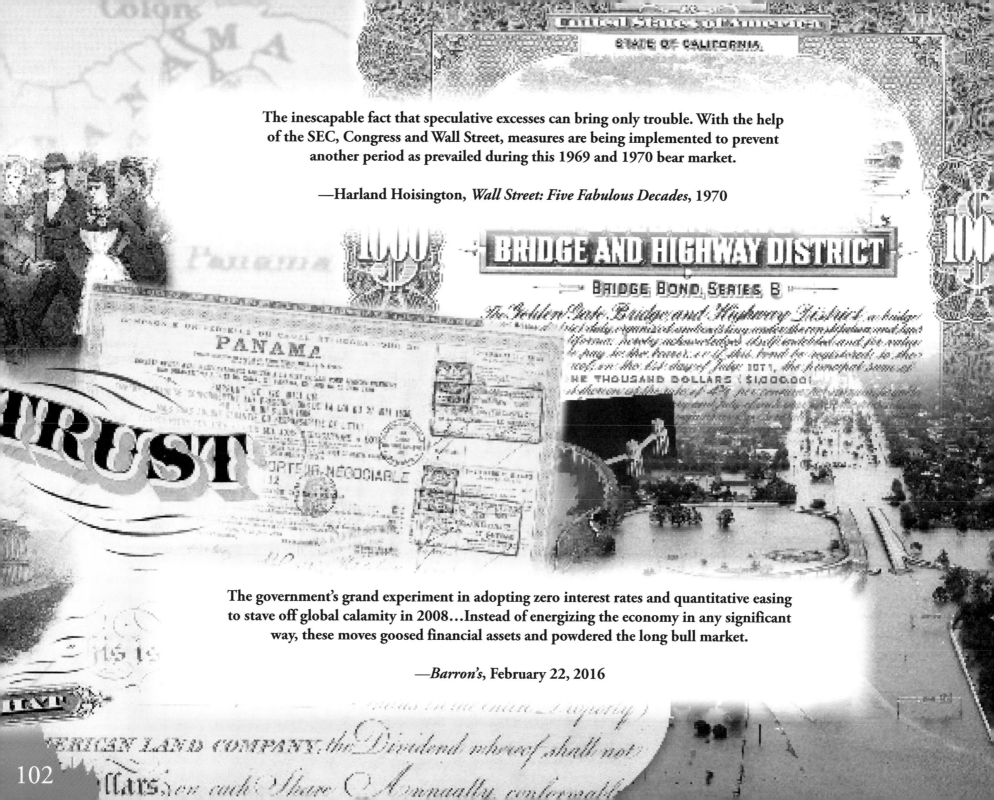

The inescapable fact that speculative excesses can bring only trouble. With the help of the SEC, Congress and Wall Street, measures are being implemented to prevent another period as prevailed during this 1969 and 1970 bear market.

—Harland Hoisington, *Wall Street: Five Fabulous Decades*, 1970

The government's grand experiment in adopting zero interest rates and quantitative easing to stave off global calamity in 2008…Instead of energizing the economy in any significant way, these moves goosed financial assets and powdered the long bull market.

—*Barron's*, February 22, 2016

UNCLE SAM:
ECONOMIC PARTY ANIMAL OR PARTY CRASHER?

POLITICS and INVESTING

Since the beginning of our nation's history, many politicians (from opposing parties) have been wealthy, successful investors. In fact, many congressional, senatorial, and presidential campaigns have been financed by the fruits of the candidates' (or their families') investment success.

Do winds of political change really have an effect on investing in America? Ultimately, investors (regardless of their political views) want to see their stocks and real estate holdings appreciate in value within a low-interest-rate environment.

Presidents and Investments	Percentage Change				
	Beg. Term Year	Investments	Common Stocks	Homes	Corporate Bonds
Best Single Terms					
Hayes	1877	369%	97%	233%	39%
Coolidge	1925	258%	176%	55%	28%
Roosevelt, F.	1933	226%	95%	62%	69%
Best Multiple Terms					
Reagan	1981–1988	371%	138%	72%	162%
Clinton	1993–2000	263%	171%	33%	59%
Eisenhower	1953–1960	252%	148%	85%	19%
Worst Single Terms					
Hoover	1929	-118%	-63%	-57%	-2%
Pierce	1853	-49%	-11%	-39%	na
Roosevelt, F.	1937	-33%	-23%	-16%	6%
Worst Multiple Terms					
Roosevelt, F.	1937–1944	23%	10%	-34%	48%
Bush (G. W.)	2001–2008	58%	-20%	30%	48%

You might not be surprised to know that President Ronald Reagan's two terms showed a 138% increase in stocks, a 72% increase in home prices, and 162% in corporate bonds (371% combined return), but the best one term was that of the obscure Rutherford B. Hayes when investments increased to an amazing 369% in four years!

Not all bull markets are generated on the Republican side. The best return for a Democrat was Bill Clinton's post–Cold War tenure of 263%, the second best on record.

Clearly, the well-followed scandals of the Reagan and Clinton administrations didn't matter to Wall Street!

On the flip side, both parties have had bear markets on their watch. The Republican Herbert Hoover and Democrat Franklin Pierce posted disastrous investment losses. Finally, no president had the highs and lows of Franklin D. Roosevelt. His administration made the lists for best and worst single terms.

The prospect of big losses for business-friendly Republicans in tomorrow's mid-term elections is eliciting more shrugs than fears on Wall Street…The first and most frequently cited rationale for Wall Street's nonchalance at the specter of a Democratic triumph is the old "gridlock is good" maxim.

—*The Wall Street Journal*, November 5, 2006

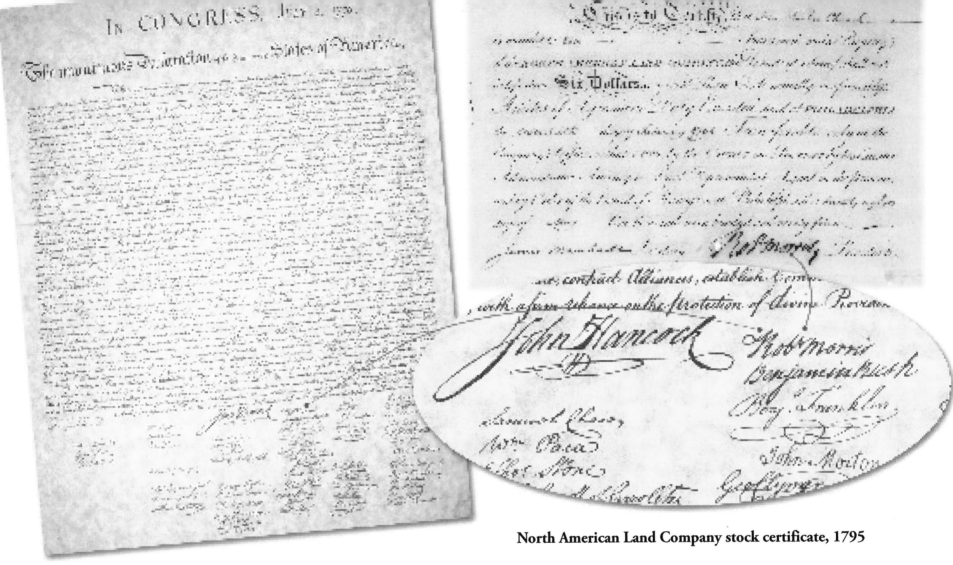

North American Land Company stock certificate, 1795

Founder of this company was Robert Morris, one of America's earliest millionaires, who helped finance the American Revolution. He also signed the Declaration of Independence.

Since 1833, presidential elections every four years have a profound impact on the economy and the stock market. Wars, recessions, and bear markets tend to start or occur in the first half of the term; prosperous times and bull markets, in the latter half.

—Jeffrey Hirsch and J. Taylor Brown, *The Almanac Investor*, 2006

Beg. Term Year	Administrations	Rank	Investments % Chg	Multiple Terms	Common Stocks % Chg	Homes % Chg	Corporate Bonds % Chg	T-Bill Yields Term-end
	Republicans and Whigs							
1849	Taylor / Filmore	15	77%		66%	11%		4.66%
1861	Lincoln	4	215%		169%	45%		5.42%
1864	Lincoln / Johnson	12	109%		37%	42%	31%	5.36%
1869	Grant	17	64%		38%	-7%	34%	5.14%
1874	Grant	20	56%	120%	6%	-11%	61%	4.31%
1877	Hayes	1	369%		97%	233%	39%	4.13%
1881	Garfield / Arthur	22	-24%		-6%	-41%	22%	4.57%
1889	Harrison	19	60%		26%	9%	24%	3.18%
1897	McKinley	5	198%		80%	90%	28%	3.76%
1901	McKinley / Roosevelt, T.	22	-24%		-11%	-32%	18%	4.45%
1905	Roosevelt, T.	9	144%		117%	-10%	38%	4.31%
1909	Taft	18	62%		24%	22%	16%	3.52%
1921	Harding / Coolidge	6	179%		109%	22%	48%	2.61%
1925	Coolidge	2	258%		176%	55%	28%	4.26%
1929	Hoover	23	-118%		-63%	-57%	2%	0.08%
1953	Eisenhower	7	157%		96%	52%	10%	2.56%
1957	Eisenhower	13	94%	252%	52%	33%	9%	2.27%
1969	Nixon	14	78%		29%	12%	37%	5.06%
1973	Nixon / Ford	11	117%		11%	58%	48%	4.35%
1981	Reagan	8	150%		50%	18%	83%	7.86%
1985	Reagan	3	221%	371%	88%	54%	79%	8.10%
1989	Bush, G. H. W.	10	141%		74%	1%	65%	3.09%
2001	Bush, G. W.	16	76%		-2%	39%	40%	2.22%
2004	Bush, G. W.	21	-18%	58%	-18%	-9%	8%	0.01%
Average			110%		52%	26%	35%	3.97%
High	Best Performance		369%		176%	233%	83%	8.10%
Low	Worst Performance		-118%		-63%	-57%	2%	0.01%

Just consider Thursday's strong rally in the stock market, which came in the wake of the report, Wednesday night, that President Bush's approval rating had sunk to its lowest level ever…There are lots of things that investors can legitimately worry about these days. But President Bush's low approval rating does not appear to be one of them.

—Marketwatch.com, June 15, 2007

Since 1849, the average Republican presidential term has posted a 52% return in stocks, a 26% increase in home prices, and a 35% return in corporate bonds. Of the twenty-four Republican administrations, only five had declines in the stock market, and seven saw declines in home prices.

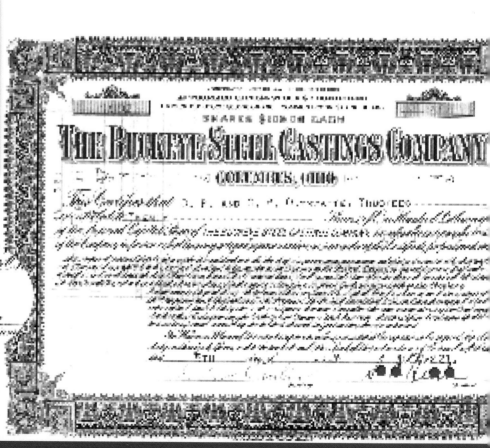

Signed by Samuel Bush,
President George W. Bush's great-grandfather

The eyes of the US last week turned anxiously toward Wall Street, where drama and despair marked the stock market's worst plunge since 1950. The sad news on the Big Board did not mean that the US economy was in bad trouble. But, it did highlight a dilemma for the Kennedy Administration.

—*Time*, June 1, 1962

	Democrats							
Beg. Term Year	Administrations	Rank	Investments % Chg	Multiple Terms	Common Stocks % Chg	Homes % Chg	Corporate Bonds % Chg	T-Bill Yields Term-end
1853	Pierce	17	-49%		-11%	-39%		6.50%
1857	Buchanan	15	-25%		10%	-35%		1.93%
1885	Cleveland	13	50%		41%	-27%	37%	4.06%
1893	Cleveland	12	52%	102%	21%	7%	23%	4.66%
1913	Wilson	8	101%		75%	8%	18%	2.95%
1917	Wilson	14	40%	140%	1%	40%	-1%	5.67%
1933	F. Roosevelt	1	226%		95%	62%	69%	0.00%
1937	F. Roosevelt	16	-33%	192%	-23%	-16%	6%	0.00%
1940	F. Roosevelt	11	57%	23%	33%	-18%	42%	0.38%
1945	F. Roosevelt / Truman	3	142%		66%	69%	8%	1.15%
1949	Truman	2	166%		121%	30%	15%	2.13%
1961	Kennedy / Johnson	9	98%		65%	31%	1%	3.86%
1965	Johnson	10	95%		38%	26%	30%	5.92%
1977	Carter	7	111%		57%	54%	0%	14.99%
1993	Clinton	4	134%		86%	16%	32%	5.06%
1997	Clinton	5	129%	263%	85%	17%	27%	5.87%
2009	Obama	6	124%		69%	7%	48%	0.05%
2013	Obama	9	98%	222%	70%	28%	1%	0.54%
Average			84%		50%	14%	22%	3.65%
High	Best Performance		226%		121%	69%	69%	14.99%
Low	Worst Performance		-49%		-23%	-39%	-1%	0.00%

Since 1849, the average Democrat presidential term has posted a 50% return in stocks, a 14% increase in home prices, and a 22% return in corporate bonds. Of the seventeen Democratic administrations, only two had declines in the stock market and five saw declines in home prices.

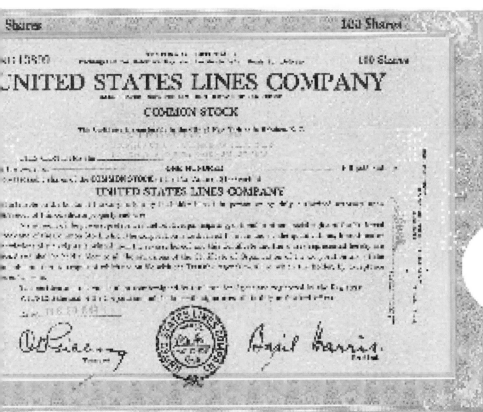

Stock certificate issued to a Kennedy family trust, 1944

That has been the suspicion from the late 1980s onwards, when the Federal Reserve began cutting rates when equity markets wobbled… Investors may thus have learned that if they throw a toddler's tantrum, central banks will eventually come to their rescue.

—*The Economist*, February 16, 2016

Whom should investors pay the most attention to: the president, Congress, or the Federal Reserve? Historically, the president has been praised and blamed for the economy. For instance, Hoover is the popular choice to blame for the Great Depression while House Speaker Nicholas Longworth or Federal Reserve Chairman Roy A. Young are not even mentioned for their roles in the disaster.

Up until Chairman Paul Volcker, the public didn't pay much attention to the Federal Reserve, and yet an argument can easily be made that the actions of this body have the most direct effect on the investment world.

Today, Capitol Hill, the White House, Wall Street, and the media have a love-hate relationship with the Fed, and there have been times all of them have wanted to tar and feather the Fed chairman.

Has America economically performed better with the Federal Reserve at the helm in trying to control inflation and enhance economic growth?

In looking at charts of inflation and economic growth since 1800, it can be seen that economic growth is more stable under the Fed's watch. Deflation is less prevalent, yet inflation still seems to have been a persistent problem since the Federal Reserve's establishment in 1913.

US GROSS DOMESTIC PRODUCT
% CHANGE (SINCE 1800)

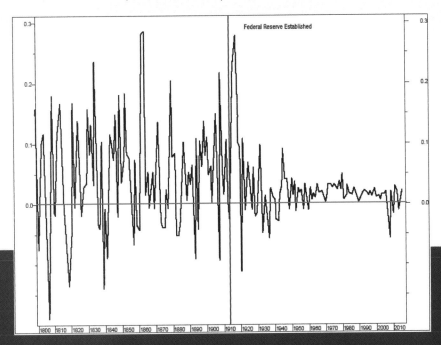

US INFLATION RATE (SINCE 1800)

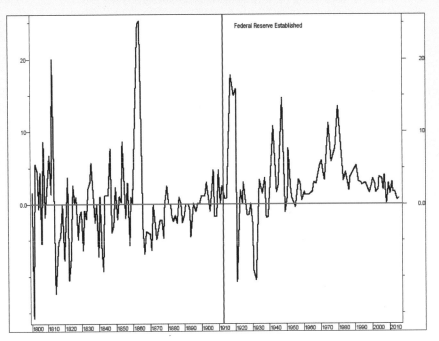

None of the post-war expansions died of old age. They were all murdered by the Fed.

—The Economist, August 25, 2007

There's an awful lot of power there held by unelected people.
I'm not sure it's good for a President to be held responsible
for monetary policy when he has no control over it.

—Donald Regan, treasury secretary, 1984

Federal Reserve Chairman											
Administrations	Tenure (Years)	Inflation Rate (CPI)			Fed Funds Rate			Common Stocks % Chg	T-Bond Yields % Chg	New Homes % Chg	Stocks% +Homes% -Inflation%	Rank
		High	Low	Average	High	Low	Average					
Hamlin	2.0	7.4%	0.8%	4.1%	5.0%	3.0%	4.0%	44%	0%	9%	49%	1
Harding	6.0	17.7%	-10.8%	3.4%	7.0%	3.0%	5.0%	0%	3%	11%	7%	8
Crissinger	4.4	2.9%	-6.5%	-1.8%	4.5%	3.0%	3.8%	24%	-6%	8%	34%	2
Young	2.9	0.1%	-1.4%	-0.7%	6.0%	2.0%	4.0%	8%	0%	1%	9%	8 (tie)
Meyer	2.6	-2.4%	-4.9%	-3.7%	4.5%	1.5%	3.0%	-22%	1%	-6%	-24%	12
Black	1.2	3.2%	-4.9%	-0.8%	3.5%	1.5%	2.5%	2%	-6%	-23%	-20%	11
Eccles	13.2	14.6%	-1.7%	6.4%	2.0%	0.5%	1.3%	4%	-2%	4%	2%	10
McCabe	3.0	7.9%	-1.0%	3.4%	1.8%	1.0%	1.4%	13%	3%	12%	22%	4 (tie)
Martin	18.8	7.6%	-0.3%	3.7%	9.0%	0.6%	4.8%	16%	12%	10%	22%	4 (tie)
Burns	8.0	11.1%	3.3%	7.2%	14.0%	3.3%	8.6%	1%	0%	15%	9%	8 (tie)
Miller	1.4	11.3%	6.6%	9.0%	10.9%	5.0%	7.9%	13%	8%	16%	20%	5
Volcker	8.0	13.5%	1.9%	7.7%	24.0%	5.4%	14.7%	27%	0%	9%	29%	3
Greenspan	18.5	5.4%	1.5%	3.5%	9.9%	0.9%	5.4%	15%	-3%	7%	19%	6
Bernanke	8	4.0%	-0.2%	1.9%	5.3%	0.1%	2.7%	5%	-6%	1%	4%	9
Yellen	4	2.1%	0.6%	1.4%	1.5%	0.3%	0.9%	12%	10%	6%	16%	7
Average	6.8			3.0%			4.7%	10.7%	0.3%	5.3%	13.0%	
High (Top Performance)	18.8			9.0%			14.7%	43.8%	12.3%	15.6%	48.5%	
Low (Worst Performance)	1.2			-3.7%			0.9%	-22.2%	-6.2%	-23.0%	-24.5%	

The verdict upon the Federal Reserve System is thus necessarily mixed. Foreign observers regard it with favor, as witness the extensive copying of the System in various countries. Many home critics have blamed it for acts, which constitute its principal claim for merit. It has suffered very greatly from the lack of an informed and effective public opinion which understood the meaning of the different policies that were being applied.

—*The Magazine of Wall Street,* September 29, 1923

THE FED

Chairman Paul Volcker, seated at rear, presiding at a meeting in Washington of the governors of the Federal Reserve Board, 1980

There have been fifteen chairmen of the Federal Reserve, with tenures ranging from 1.2 to 18.8 years. Stocks and homes posted their best inflation-adjusted gains during the tenures of Charles Sumner Hamlin, Daniel Richard Crissinger, and Volcker. The long tenures of William McChesney Martin and Alan Greenspan were marked with strong investment performance even though inflation was nearly twice as high during Miller's terms. The only Fed chairman to have declines in both stocks and housing during his term was Eugene Meyer during the 1930s.

Short-term interest rates were more stable in the early days of the Federal Reserve. From 1914–1951, there were eight Federal Reserve chairmen, and the federal funds rate range was 2.4% (the highest inflation rate averaged 6.7%). Since 1951, there have been seven different Federal Reserve chairmen, and the federal funds rate range increased to 9.6% (the highest inflation rate averaged 8.8%). The long tenure of Greenspan had a profound effect on modern-day Fed policy where inflation was benign, yet short-term interest rates ranged widely from 9.9% to 0.9%.

The President (Reagan) and the Federal Reserve chairman (Volcker) shared in the warming glow of public opinion. Ronald Reagan took personal credit for halting high inflation, though the task was actually done by the Federal Reserve.

—William Greider, *Secrets of the Temple*, 1987

TAXATION

The old saying "It's not what you make, but what you get to keep" really holds true with investing and taxes. Taxes strongly influence which investments are used, when profits and losses are realized, and which types of accounts are used (taxable versus tax-deferred). Over time, taxes ebb and flow, and the government has developed a complicated maze of investment-related taxes such as income tax (with dividends taxed twice due to taxes paid by the corporate entity), capital gains, estate taxes, and penalties for early and late IRA withdrawals, just to name a few.

Much has been written about taxes on investment, and though these articles and books have been written at different times about different situations, they all deal with the need for an individual's investment strategy to strike a balance between realizing maximum profits and minimizing the impact of taxes. Simply put, selling an investment at the top is always an investor's goal, and yet in the world of taxes, it might not be the most profitable solution.

The complexity of some opportunities now being offered in the investment markets and elsewhere make the task of predicting tax results even more daunting.

—Arlene Hibschweiler and Marion Kopin, *Investment Taxation*, 2004

Stock transaction tax stamps, 1903

The art of taxation consists in so plucking the goose as to obtain the largest possible amount of feathers with the smallest amount of hissing.

—Jean-Baptiste Colbert, 1672

US INVESTMENT TAXES (SINCE 1913)
Income and capital gain % rates

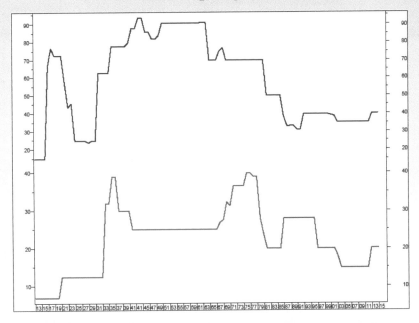

US COMMON STOCKS VERSUS INVESTMENT TAXES (SINCE 1913)

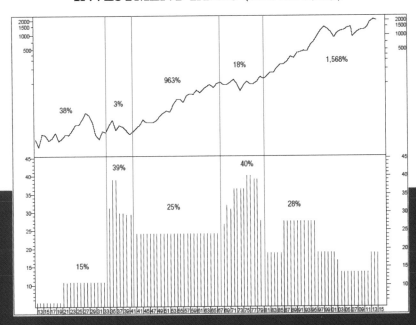

Investment Taxes 1913–2017						
	Corporate Tax	Largest Annual % Chg	Individual Tax %	Largest Annual % Chg	Capital Gains Tax %	Largest Annual % Chg
Current	21.0		32.0		20.0	
Average	33.9		58.6		22.5	
Highest	52.8	200%	94.0	347%	39.9	156%
Lowest	1.0	-17%	15.0	-46%	7.0	-29%

As can be seen in the charts and table on this page, income taxes were permanently imposed on US citizens in 1913 and have been increased and reduced on twenty-two separate occasions. Top income tax rates have ranged from 15% in 1916 to 94% in 1944. Capital gains tax has ranged from 7% in 1913 to 39.9% in 1975. Big jumps in tax rates (such as in 1917, 1932, and 1934) were not well received on Wall Street.

There is also a strong inverse relationship between the level of the capital gains tax rate and the stock market. As can be seen in the preceding chart, during the two periods ranging from eight to ten years in which this tax exceeded 30%, the stock market performed miserably.

It is also important to note that though the level of tax rates has been in a general decline since the late 1940s, investment tax law has become very complicated and can easily make a good investment into a tax nightmare (like most tax-free municipal bonds subjected to AMT penalties).

Treasury estimates the biggest boost to economic growth comes from the cuts in capital gains and dividend taxes.

—The Wall Street Journal, January 27, 2006

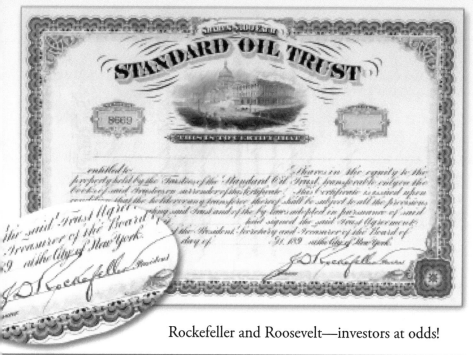

Rockefeller and Roosevelt—investors at odds!

Standard Oil shown as a monopoly, 1903 cartoon

Roosevelt distrusted wealthy businessmen and dissolved forty monopolistic corporations as a 'trust buster' (including Standard Oil trusts). He was clear, however, to show he did not disagree with trusts and capitalism in principle but was only against corrupt, illegal practices.

—Wikipedia.com, 2007

The sensational newspapers, which are always attacking John D. Rockefeller and his associates for their wealth, have put millions into the treasury of the Standard Oil Company.

—Henry Rodgers, legendary stock trader, 1920

HUMPTY DUMPTY BACK TOGETHER—AGAIN

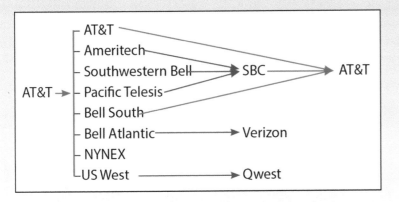

There is such a thing as too much success! Throughout history, governments have always felt compelled to attack monopolistic threats and change the investment landscape.

In the past one hundred years, there were two well-publicized government-imposed corporate breakups, Standard Oil (1911) and AT&T (1984), and the near breakup of Microsoft (2001). But political agendas do change, and the election of George W. Bush in 2000 spared Microsoft a breakup. Changes in government policy have also allowed many pieces of the former Standard Oil and AT&T to come back together again.

AT&T

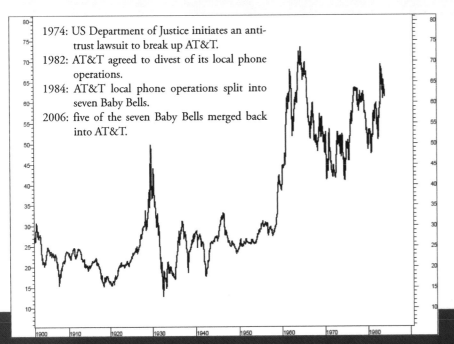

1974: US Department of Justice initiates an antitrust lawsuit to break up AT&T.
1982: AT&T agreed to divest of its local phone operations.
1984: AT&T local phone operations split into seven Baby Bells.
2006: five of the seven Baby Bells merged back into AT&T.

MICROSOFT

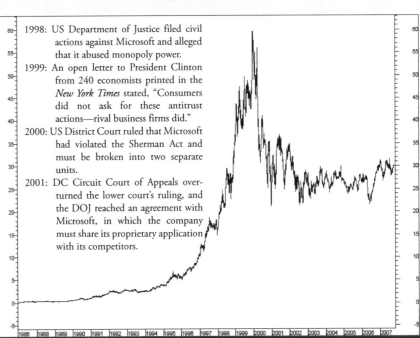

1998: US Department of Justice filed civil actions against Microsoft and alleged that it abused monopoly power.
1999: An open letter to President Clinton from 240 economists printed in the *New York Times* stated, "Consumers did not ask for these antitrust actions—rival business firms did."
2000: US District Court ruled that Microsoft had violated the Sherman Act and must be broken into two separate units.
2001: DC Circuit Court of Appeals overturned the lower court's ruling, and the DOJ reached an agreement with Microsoft, in which the company must share its proprietary application with its competitors.

History will probably judge the misguided post-2008 crisis regulations like Dodd-Frank and retribution against Wall Street to have sown the seeds of the next financial crisis.

—*The Wall Street Journal,* February 20, 2016

WHO REALLY CAUSED THE GREAT DEPRESSION?

One of the public's mistaken beliefs about Wall Street is that the 1929 stock market crash caused the Great Depression.

Though the stock market reacted to the deteriorating economic conditions of the 1930s, the US government's disastrous policies of large increases in interest rates, imposing high barriers to foreign trade, increasing income taxes 152%, and a massive increase of the government regulation of business were the real culprits in the economic meltdown and the slow recovery. In fact, it took more than twenty-two years for both stocks and real estate to get back to their highs of 1929.

One of the great defects of our kind of monetary system is that its performance depends so much on the quality of the people who are put in charge. We have seen that in the history of our own Federal Reserve System. Surely a computer would have produced far better results during the 1930s and during both world wars.

—Milton Friedman, 2006

US COMMON STOCKS WITH NYSE VOLUME

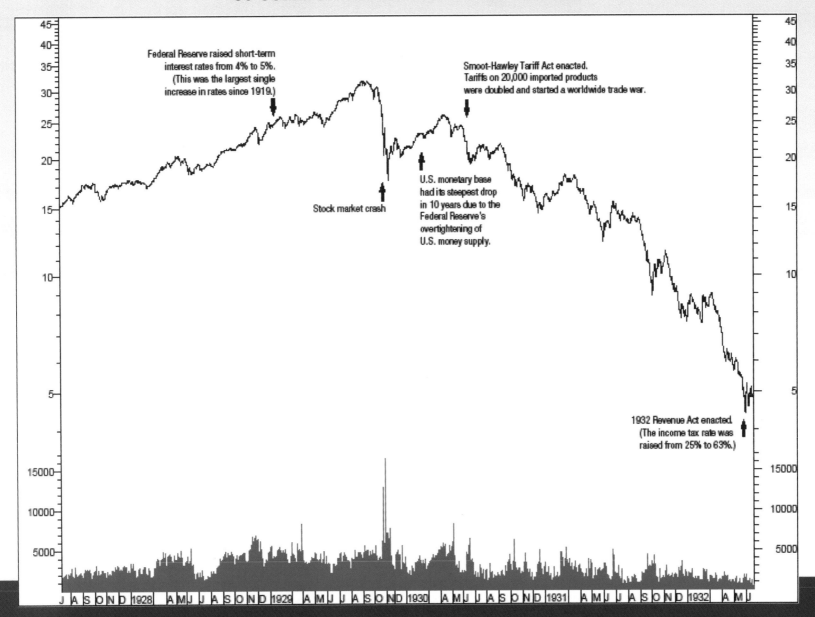

Federal Reserve raised short-term interest rates from 4% to 5%. (This was the largest single increase in rates since 1919.)

Smoot-Hawley Tariff Act enacted. Tariffs on 20,000 imported products were doubled and started a worldwide trade war.

Stock market crash

U.S. monetary base had its steepest drop in 10 years due to the Federal Reserve's overtightening of U.S. money supply.

1932 Revenue Act enacted. (The income tax rate was raised from 25% to 63%.)

Stock market reform long denied has a way of going to excess, often producing results more distasteful than the abuses aimed at. It appears to be so with proposed Federal regulation of security exchanges.

—*The Magazine of Wall Street*, March 31, 1934

UNCLE SAM SUMMARY

We come now to the prospects of business recovering soon enough and fast enough both to curb extraordinary government outlays and to provide abundant taxes and public loans. If it does we shall avoid dangerous inflation of either the currency or credit through government instrumentality.

—The Magazine of Wall Street, February 17, 1934

The table lists taxes (set by the president and Congress), Fed funds rate (set by the Federal Reserve), and stocks and real estate prices. Several key facts materialize when reviewing the investment carnage after 1915, the 1930s, the early 1970s, and the early 2000s:

1. The Federal Reserve significantly increased interest rates prior to and during each of these periods.
2. Investment-related taxes were significantly increased in three of these four periods.
3. The combination of increases in both taxes and interest rates were present during severe, multiyear bear markets in both stocks and real estate.

When it comes to government economic miscues, there is plenty of blame to go around. Whom should investors pay the most attention to: the president, Congress, or the Federal Reserve? Answer: all of them!

Government Actions and Investments									
			Investment Taxes				Short-Term Interest Rates		
Beginning of Year	President	House Speaker	Individual Income Tax	% Chg	Capital Gains Tax	% Chg	Fed Chairman	Fed Funds Rate	% Chg
1916	Wilson (D)	Clark (D)	15	0%	7	0%	Harding	3.00	0%
1917	Wilson (D)	Clark (D)	67	347%	7	0%	Harding	3.00	0%
1918	Harding (R)	Clark (D)	77	15%	7	0%	Harding	4.00	33%
1929	Hoover (R)	Longworth (R)	24	-4%	12.5	0%	Young	4.50	-10%
1930	Hoover (R)	Longworth (R)	25	4%	12.5	0%	Young	2.00	-56%
1931	Hoover (R)	Longworth (R)	25	0%	12.5	0%	Meyer	3.50	75%
1932	Hoover (R)	Garner (D)	63	152%	12.5	0%	Meyer	2.50	-29%
1933	F. Roosevelt (D)	Garner (D)	63	0%	12.5	0%	Meyer	2.00	-20%
1934	F. Roosevelt (D)	Rainey (D)	63	0%	32	156%	Eccles	1.50	-25%
1935	F. Roosevelt (D)	Byrns (D)	63	0%	32	0%	Eccles	1.50	0%
1936	F. Roosevelt (D)	Byrns (D)	78	24%	39	22%	Eccles	1.50	0%
1937	F. Roosevelt (D)	Bankhead (D)	78	0%	39	0%	Eccles	1.00	-33%
1938	F. Roosevelt (D)	Bankhead (D)	78	0%	30	-23%	Eccles	1.00	0%
1939	F. Roosevelt (D)	Bankhead (D)	78	0%	30	0%	Eccles	1.00	0%
1940	F. Roosevelt (D)	Bankhead (D)	78	0%	30	0%	Eccles	1.00	0%
1941	F. Roosevelt (D)	Rayburn (D)	80	3%	30	0%	Eccles	1.00	0%
1942	F. Roosevelt (D)	Rayburn (D)	88	10%	25	-17%	Eccles	0.50	-50%
1943	F. Roosevelt (D)	Rayburn (D)	88	0%	25	0%	Eccles	0.50	0%
1969	Nixon (R)	McCormack (D)	77	3%	27.5	2%	Martin	8.97	49%
1970	Nixon (R)	McCormack (D)	70	-9%	32.3	17%	Martin	4.90	-45%
1971	Nixon (R)	Albery (D)	70	0%	31.3	-3%	Burns	4.14	-16%
1972	Nixon (R)	Albery (D)	70	0%	36.5	17%	Burns	5.33	29%
1973	Nixon (R)	Albery (D)	70	0%	36.5	0%	Burns	9.95	87%
1974	Ford (R)	Albery (D)	70	0%	36.5	0%	Burns	8.86	-11%
2000	Clinton (D)	Hastert (R)	39.6	0%	20	0%	Greenspan	6.25	9%
2001	GW Bush (R)	Hastert (R)	39.1	-1%	20	0%	Greenspan	1.63	-74%
2002	GW Bush (R)	Hastert (R)	38.6	-1%	20	0%	Greenspan	1.19	-27%
Median			70.0	0%	25.0	0%		3.7	0%
Average			60.6	4%	23.0	2%		4.3	6%
High			94.0	347%	39.9	156%		20.0	141%
Low			15.0	-46%	7.0	-29%		0.5	-74%

Large Tax Rate Decreases
Large Tax Rate Increases

WAR

FROM INDIANS TO IRAQ, HOW WARS INFLUENCE INVESTING

VICTORY DAY ON WALL STREET
NOVEMBER 11, 1918

Since 1812, the United States has been involved in ten major military conflicts. Though war has always been a dark spot on humanity, it has been financially good for American investors. Stocks and real estate generally appreciated in the range of 40%–50% on average during these large military conflicts as huge increases in government spending drove the wartime economy. (In fact, the only conflict in which American shareholders didn't prosper was the War of 1812.) Amazingly, this appreciation occurred during times when US interest rates fluctuated wildly as large amounts of government war debt hit the market.

Even though the conflicts are very different in why, how, and where they have been fought, wartime investments display common, predictable characteristics. In comparing the charts of stock and home prices during the War of 1812, Mexican-American War, Civil War, Indian Wars of the late 1800s, Spanish-American War, World War I, World War II, and the Cold War battlefields of Korea and Vietnam, investments usually declined in value during the initial phases of the war, reversed direction while the outcome was uncertain, and were significantly higher at the end of the conflict—win, lose, or draw.

Our wartime adversaries often used their financial markets to finance their military needs, and their financial assets typically moved in the opposite direction of US investments as the winds of war shifted direction. Ironically, US corporations often revived these foreign investment markets after the conflict through peacetime rebuilding efforts and increased worldwide trade at about the same time many of America's business titans were accused of war profiteering.

As you review the following charts, you will notice that the two-hundred-day moving average (shown as a red dotted line) has proven to be a useful indicator in determining the stock market's trend during these turbulent times.

The War on Terror is following its predecessors; it seems that history once again repeats itself!

"Hey, Dad, what war was this?"

The Wall Street Journal, 1979

WAR of 1812

Land certificate for 120 acres of public
land for military service in 1812

Stock certificate for the private armed ship Yorktown

The War of 1812 gave the first genuine impulse to stock speculation. There were endless fluctuations
and the lazy-going capitalists of the time managed to gain or lose handsome fortunes.

—Samuel Nelson, *The ABC of Stock Speculation*, 1903

WAR OF 1812 US COMMON STOCKS WITH 200-DAY MOVING AVERAGE

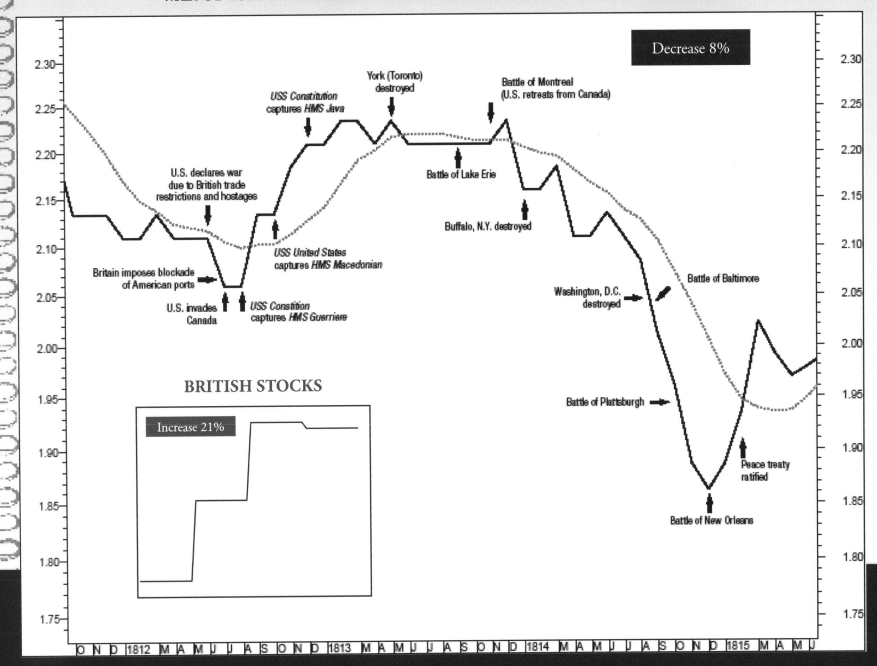

Decrease 8%

York (Toronto) destroyed

Battle of Montreal (U.S. retreats from Canada)

USS Constitution captures HMS Java

U.S. declares war due to British trade restrictions and hostages

Battle of Lake Erie

Britain imposes blockade of American ports

USS United States captures HMS Macedonian

U.S. invades Canada

USS Constitution captures HMS Guerriere

Buffalo, N.Y. destroyed

Washington, D.C. destroyed

Battle of Baltimore

BRITISH STOCKS

Increase 21%

Battle of Plattsburgh

Peace treaty ratified

Battle of New Orleans

O N D 1812 M A M J J A S O N D 1813 M A M J J A S O N D 1814 M A M J J A S O N D 1815 M A M J

123

| US Stocks | down 8% |
| US Interest Rates | up 15% |

Chart Notes

Early victories were greeted by a strong rally in US stocks. As American forces retreated out of Canada and British forces destroyed American towns and cities, US financial assets suffered huge losses while British stocks and bonds posted equally impressive gains.

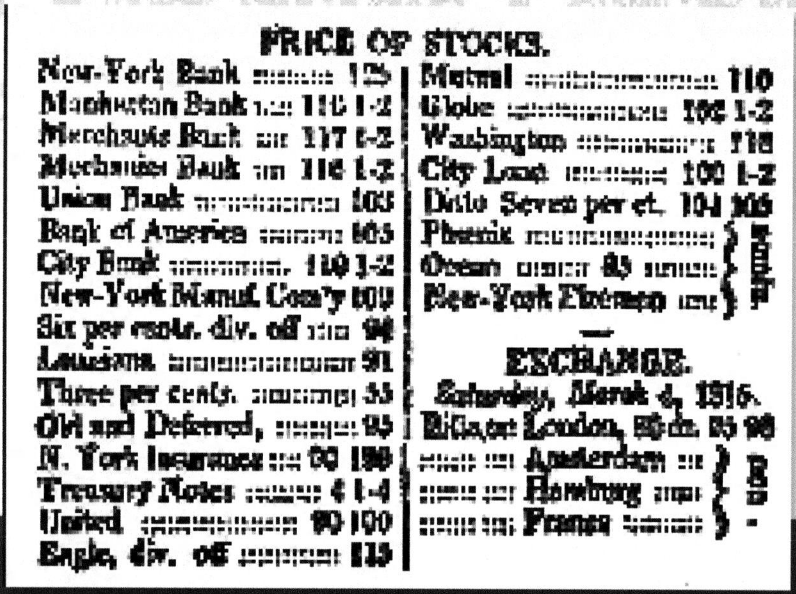

The first complete price list of stocks ever published in a newspaper, March 10, 1815

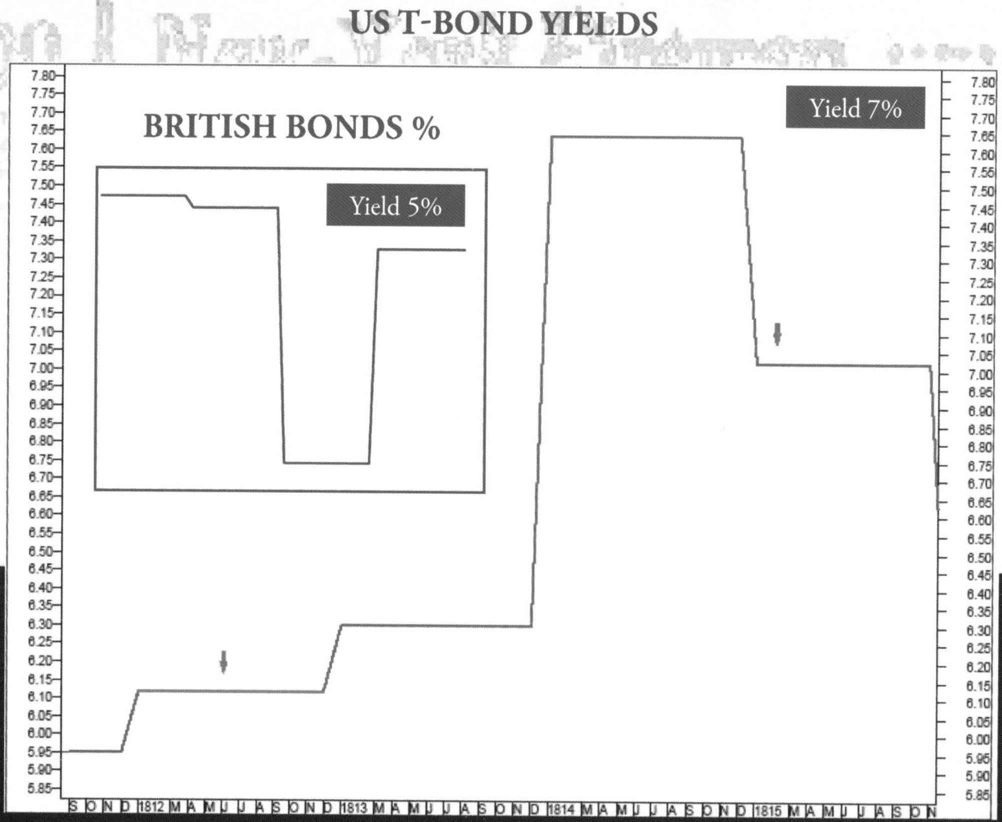

US T-BOND YIELDS

BRITISH BONDS %

Yield 7%

Yield 5%

New York and Erie Railroad letter to New York state comptroller Millard Fillmore (soon to be thirteenth US president) regarding bond investments, November 30, 1848

The panic in Europe in 1847 exerted but little influence in this country, although there was a serious loss in specie, and the Mexican war had some effect in checking enterprises. These effects, were neutralized somewhat by large exports of breadstuffs and the later discovery of gold in 1848–49.

—Charles Dow's editorial on past financial crisis, July 2, 1902

MEXICAN-AMERICAN WAR US COMMON STOCKS WITH 200-DAY MOVING AVERAGE

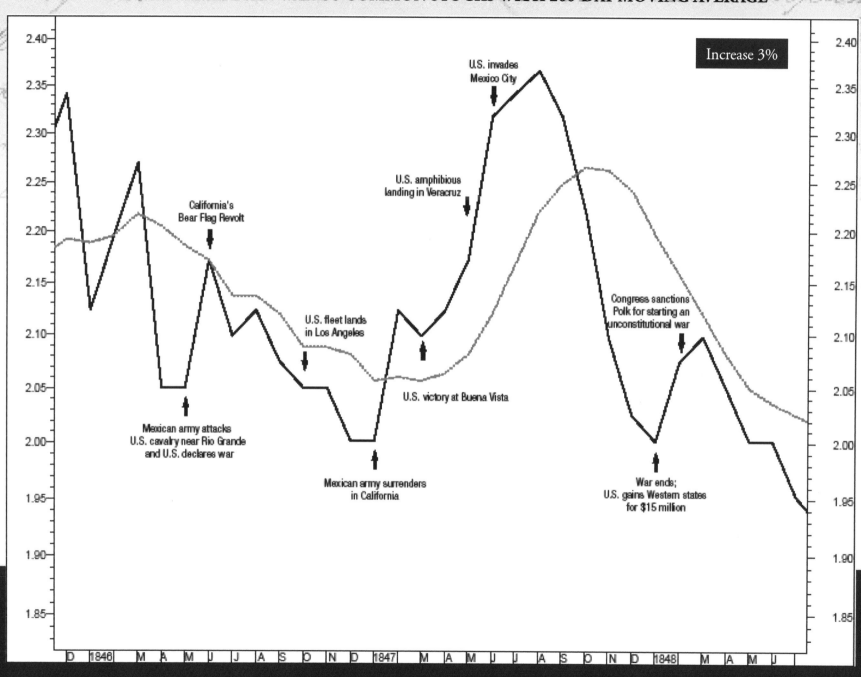

Increase 3%

California's
Bear Flag Revolt

U.S. amphibious
landing in Veracruz

U.S. invades
Mexico City

U.S. fleet lands
in Los Angeles

Congress sanctions
Polk for starting an
unconstitutional war

Mexican army attacks
U.S. cavalry near Rio Grande
and U.S. declares war

U.S. victory at Buena Vista

Mexican army surrenders
in California

War ends;
U.S. gains Western states
for $15 million

US NEW HOMES

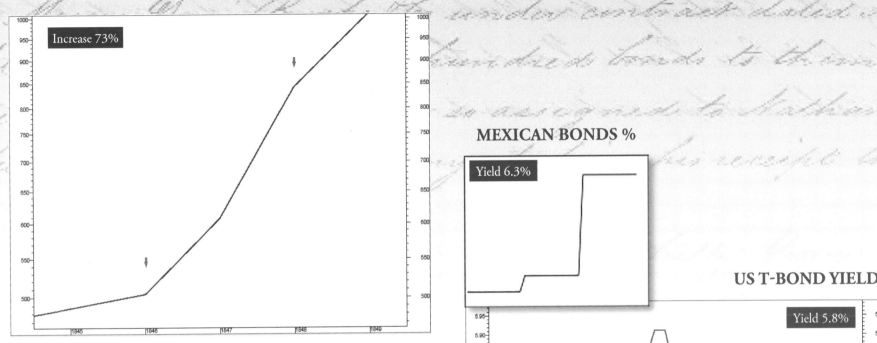

Increase 73%

MEXICAN BONDS %

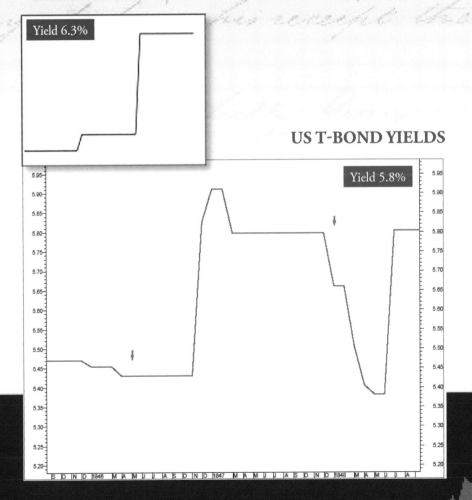

Yield 6.3%

US T-BOND YIELDS

Yield 5.8%

US Stocks	up 3%
US Home Prices	up 73%
US Interest Rates	up 7%

Chart Notes

Wall Street initially greeted this unpopular war with a whimper. The war rally started after victories in California and hit a climax with the invasion of Mexico City. Although equity gains were meager, real estate values gained 73% in light of America obtaining valuable new territories. Interest rates in Mexico rose dramatically as the US invaded Mexico City.

U.S. CIVIL WAR—1861 to 1865

CIVIL WAR US COMMON STOCKS WITH 200-DAY MOVING AVERAGE

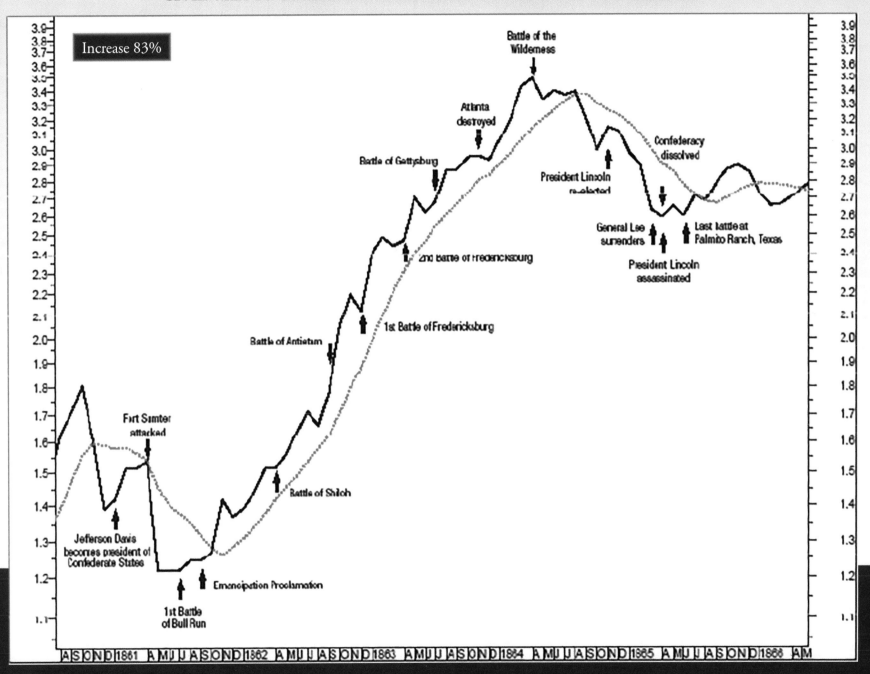

Increase 83%

Battle of the Wilderness

Atlanta destroyed

Confederacy dissolved

Battle of Gettysburg

President Lincoln re-elected

2nd Battle of Fredericksburg

General Lee surrenders

Last battle at Palmito Ranch, Texas

President Lincoln assassinated

1st Battle of Fredericksburg

Battle of Antietam

Fort Sumter attacked

Battle of Shiloh

Jefferson Davis becomes president of Confederate States

Emancipation Proclamation

1st Battle of Bull Run

A S O N D 1861 A M J J A S O N D 1862 A M J J A S O N D 1863 A M J J A S O N D 1864 A M J J A S O N D 1865 A M J J A S O N D 1866 A M

129

US Stocks	up 83%
US Home Prices	up 115%
US Interest Rates	down 16%

Chart Notes

After the initial decline from the Battle of Fort Sumter, the market hit bottom before the First Battle of Bull Run. The stock market's high was made just after the little-known Battle of the Wilderness. The returns in stocks and real estate were the highest posted of any wartime period in American history while bonds were relatively stable in light of high inflation and a devalued currency. One of the worst investments of the US Civil War was debts issued by the government of the Confederate States of America. After appreciating through most of 1864, Confederate cotton bonds (7%, due 1868) stopped trading in London at 8 cents on $1 shortly after the Confederacy dissolved in early 1865.

US NEW HOMES

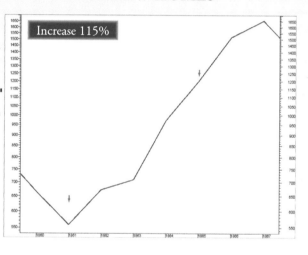

Increase 115%

US T-BOND YIELDS

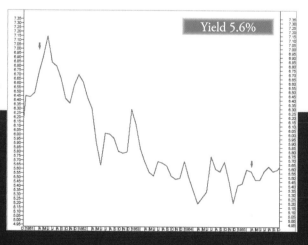

Yield 5.6%

The Winans Steam Gun, created by Ross Winans, was captured by General Benjamin Butler's command near the Relay House, Maryland.

It should be that early in the [civil] war, Union successes were used as arguments in favor of a rise in stocks, but as the war went on, Union defeats were used as arguments in favor of a rise.

—William Fowler, *Ten Years in Wall Street*, 1870

CONFEDERATE 7% COTTON BOND DUE 1868, TRADED IN LONDON

Decrease 91%

INDIAN WARS – 1866 to 1890

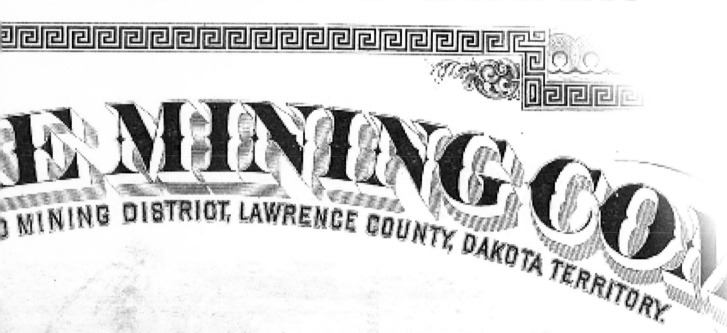

E MINING CO.

MINING DISTRICT, LAWRENCE COUNTY, DAKOTA TERRITORY.

Custer's campaign against the wild Sioux was undertaken with disadvantageous circumstances owing to the refusal of Congress to appropriate money for the establishment of military post (to protect settlers and miners).

—*The New York Times*, July 7, 1887

Homestake Mining stock certificate, 1883

INDIAN WARS US COMMON STOCKS WITH 200-DAY MOVING AVERAGE AND NYSE VOLUME

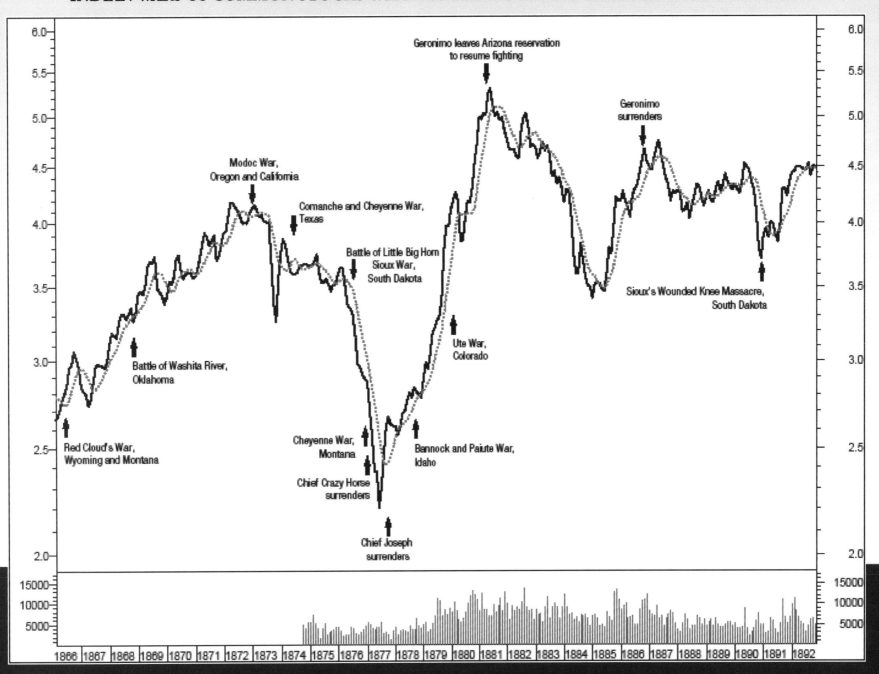

133

US Stocks	up 60%
US Home Prices	up 58%
US Interest Rates	down 30%

Chart Notes

The Indian Wars of the late 1800s were a series of guerilla-style conflicts by various tribes caused by the great population migration into the Western territories and a series of gold and silver rushes on Indian ancestral lands. The most pronounced decline was tied to the shock of Custer's Last Stand near the Little Big Horn and the panic of future large-scale Indian attacks on Western settlers. Stock and real estate investments staged impressive gains as Indian leaders such as Joseph and Crazy Horse surrendered.

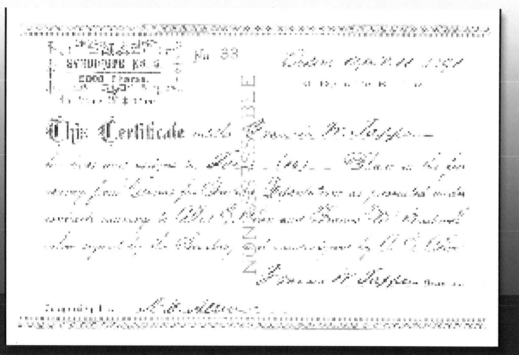

Claims for Indian depredations, 1891. Used to reimburse victims of crimes committed by Indians on the frontier.

US T-BOND YIELDS

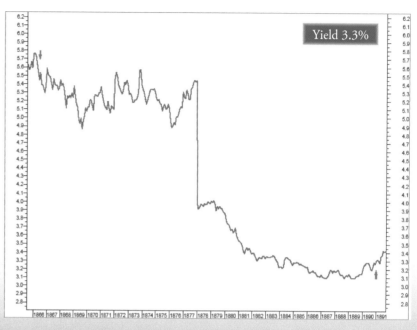

Yield 3.3%

US NEW HOMES

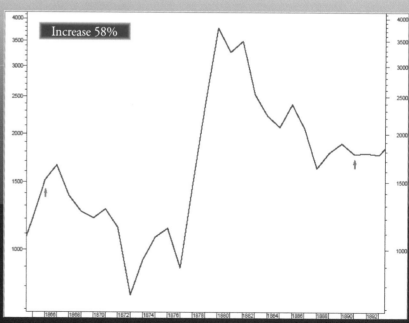

Increase 58%

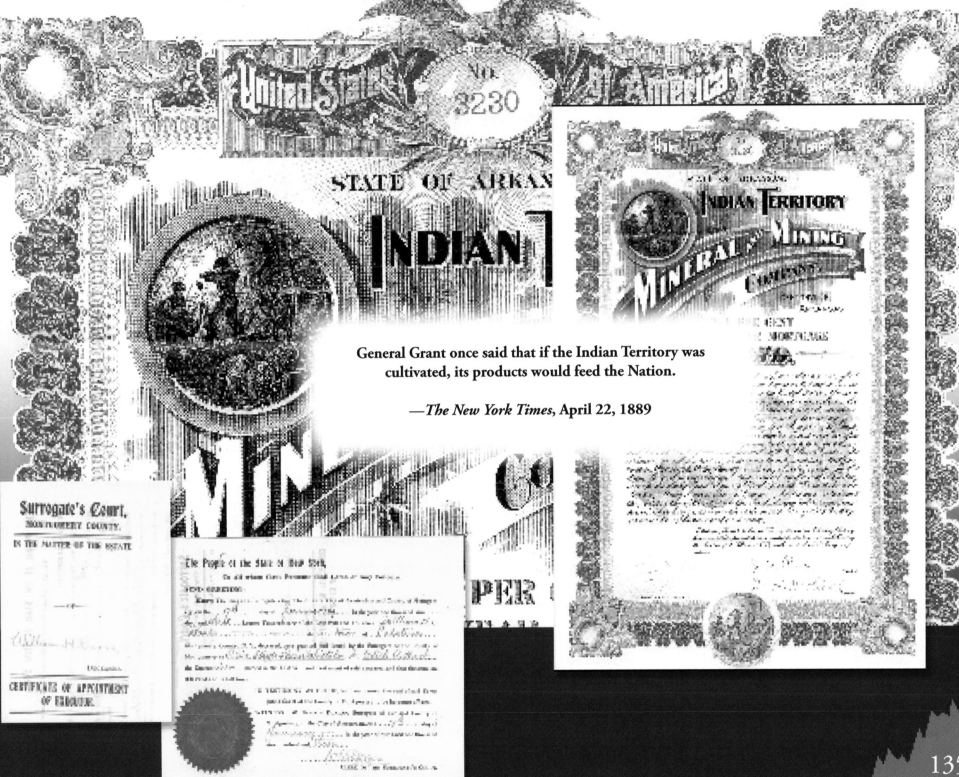

General Grant once said that if the Indian Territory was cultivated, its products would feed the Nation.

—*The New York Times*, April 22, 1889

135

Wreckage of USS *Maine* in Havana Harbor.
Photo taken by an ancestor of Ken Winans.

SPANISH-AMERICAN WAR US COMMON STOCKS WITH 200-DAY MOVING AVERAGE AND NYSE VOLUME

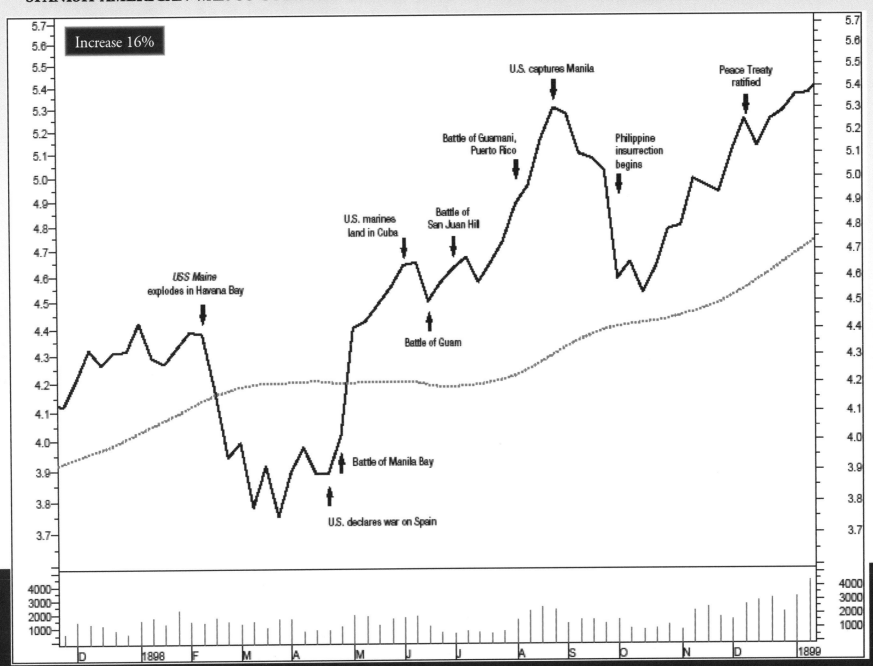

Increase 16%

USS Maine explodes in Havana Bay

U.S. declares war on Spain

Battle of Manila Bay

U.S. marines land in Cuba

Battle of Guam

Battle of San Juan Hill

Battle of Guamani, Puerto Rico

U.S. captures Manila

Philippine insurrection begins

Peace Treaty ratified

US Stocks	up 16.0%
US Home Prices	up 10.0%
US Interest Rates	down 0.6%

Chart Notes

As can be seen in the *Leslie's* magazine sketch on the following page, there was an initial panic on Wall Street after the battleship USS *Maine* exploded in Havana Harbor. Investments quickly rebounded after war was declared and Admiral Dewey's won the Battle of Manila Bay. Interest rates in Spain declined throughout this short war.

SPANISH INTEREST RATES

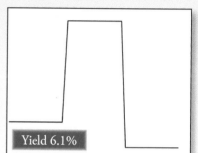

Yield 6.1%

US NEW HOMES

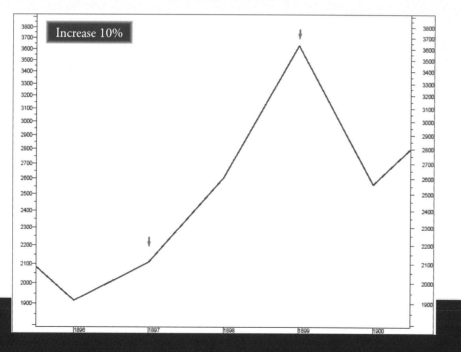

Increase 10%

US T-BOND YIELDS

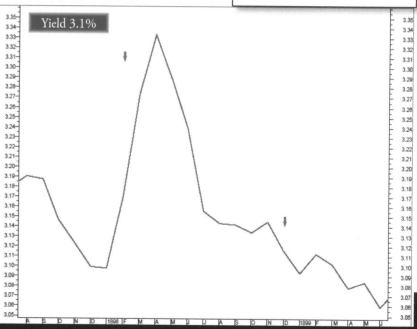

Yield 3.1%

UNLISTED SECURITIES

WAR RUMORS IN WALL STREET.

Leslie's magazine, February 1898

San Francisco Dry Docks, 1916

The Great War threatened the US with financial disaster. Europeans began to liquidate their Wall Street investments and transfer gold to Europe to pay for the war.

—William Silber, *When Washington Shut Down Wall Street*, 2007

WORLD WAR I US COMMON STOCKS
with 200-day moving average and NYSE volume

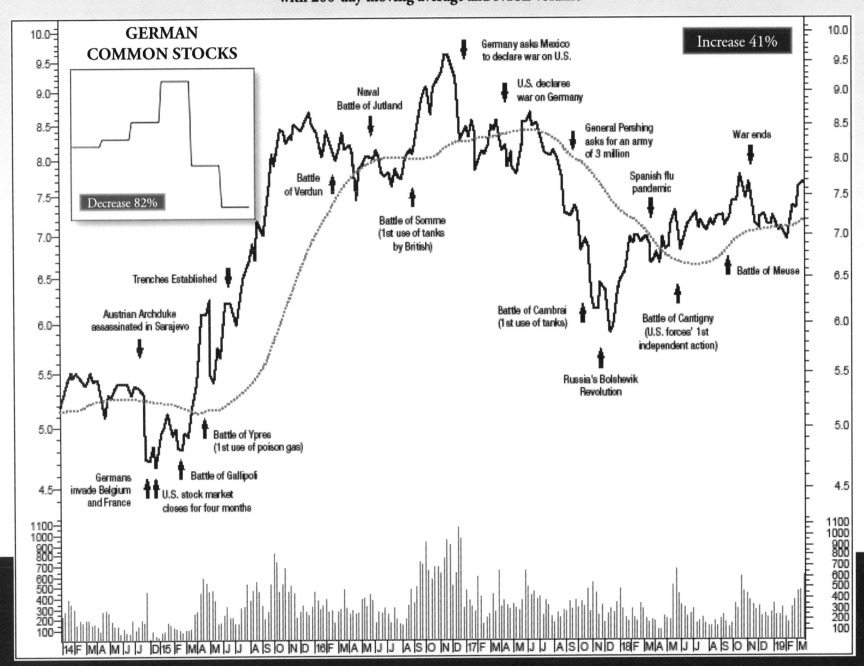

GERMAN COMMON STOCKS

Decrease 82%

Increase 41%

Germany asks Mexico to declare war on U.S.

U.S. declares war on Germany

Naval Battle of Jutland

General Pershing asks for an army of 3 million

War ends

Battle of Verdun

Battle of Somme (1st use of tanks by British)

Spanish flu pandemic

Trenches Established

Battle of Meuse

Austrian Archduke assassinated in Sarajevo

Battle of Cambrai (1st use of tanks)

Battle of Cantigny (U.S. forces' 1st independent action)

Russia's Bolshevik Revolution

Battle of Ypres (1st use of poison gas)

Germans invade Belgium and France

Battle of Gallipoli

U.S. stock market closes for four months

US NEW HOMES

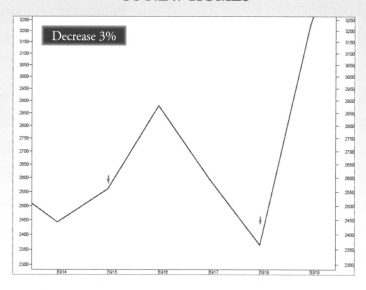

Decrease 3%

US Stocks	up 41%
US Home Prices	down 3%
US Interest Rates	up 3%

Chart Notes

The beginning of World War I led to the longest disruption in world financial markets of the past one hundred years. The NYSE closed for four months after Germany invaded France. When trading resumed, the market quickly rallied until the US entered the war, and General Pershing requested a three-million-man US army for Europe's bloody trenches. Ironically, the beginning of Soviet Communism was met with a significant rally. Real estate was in the midst of a severe bear market through most of the war. German financial markets suffered enormous losses due to their defeat and the financial penalties imposed by the Allies for starting the war.

US T-BOND YIELDS

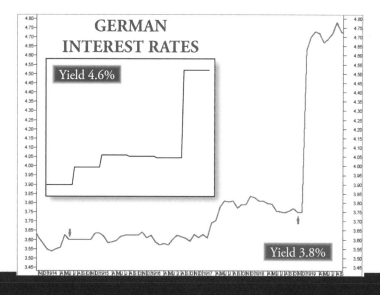

GERMAN INTEREST RATES

Yield 4.6%

Yield 3.8%

French defense bond, 1915

These German reconstruction loans (financed by Wall Street) became a vehicle that did more to promote World War II than to establish peace after World War I.

—Anthony Sutton, *Wall Street and the Rise of Hitler*, 2002

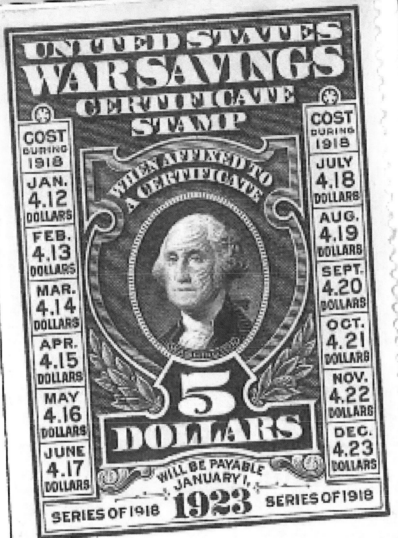

US government war bond with stamps, 1918

Disney war bond, state of Wisconsin, 1944

Since April 1942 stocks listed on the New York Stock Exchange have risen in value from $31 billion to $73 billion, with almost half the rise taking place in 1945.

—*Life* magazine, January 1, 1946

WORLD WAR II US COMMON STOCKS
with 200-day moving average and NYSE volume

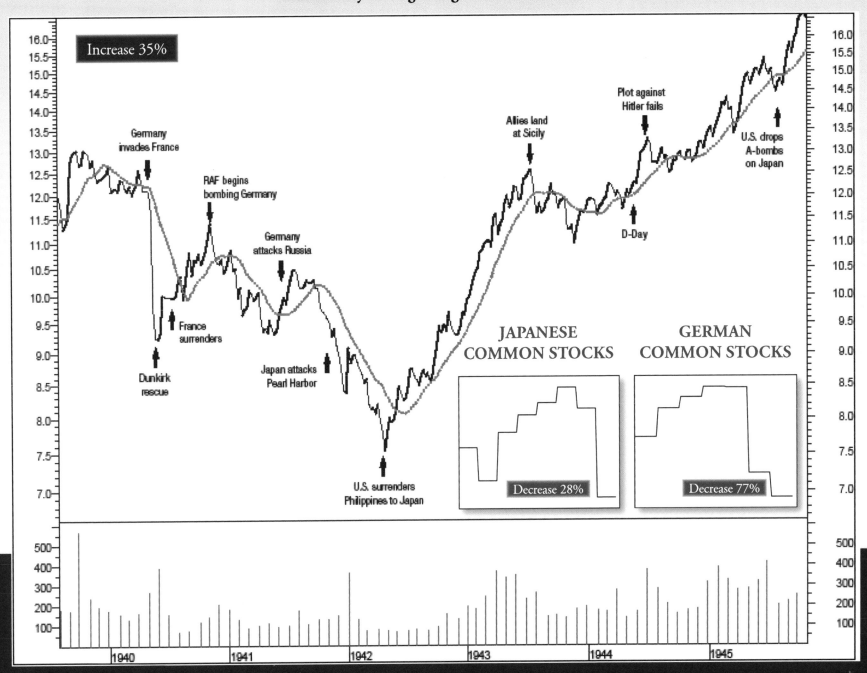

Increase 35%

Germany invades France

RAF begins bombing Germany

Germany attacks Russia

France surrenders

Dunkirk rescue

Japan attacks Pearl Harbor

U.S. surrenders Philippines to Japan

Allies land at Sicily

Plot against Hitler fails

D-Day

U.S. drops A-bombs on Japan

JAPANESE COMMON STOCKS

Decrease 28%

GERMAN COMMON STOCKS

Decrease 77%

US NEW HOMES

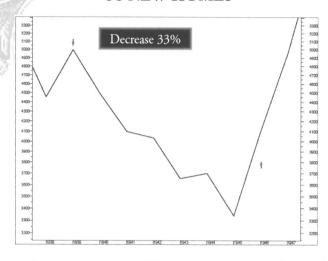

Decrease 33%

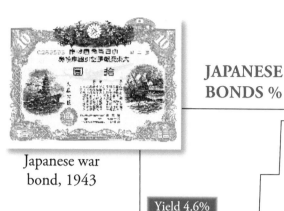

Japanese war
bond, 1943

JAPANESE BONDS %

Yield 4.6%

Nazi war
bond, 1937

GERMAN BONDS %

Yield 5.5%

US Stocks	up 35%
US Home Prices	down 33%
US Interest Rates	down 39%

Chart Notes

The stock market started this war in a prolonged downtrend as Allied losses mounted. A powerful rally in stocks started right after America's worst military defeat in history (the surrender of the Philippine Islands to Japan) and continued through the end of the war. US Treasury bonds posted their best wartime performance. German and Japanese equities and bonds followed an inverse course to US financial investments while US real estate suffered its worst wartime performance due to a shortage of mortgages as investors poured savings into the war bonds of the most expensive war in American history.

US T-BOND YIELDS

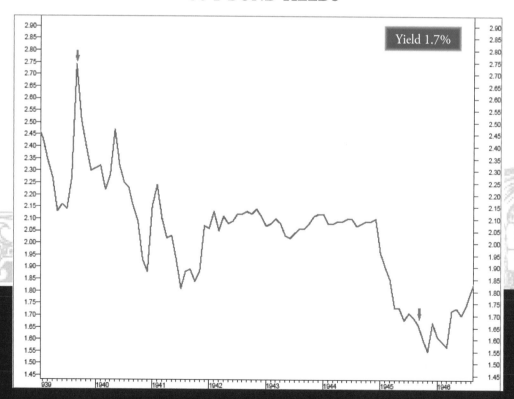

Yield 1.7%

Price control, financing, rationing, controls of consumption, investment and international trade have all undergone significant changes in the past twelve months.

In the past two years, the falling off in demand for stocks has resulted from the fear of higher taxes, the effects of war priorities, and the general uncertainty concerning the future.

—The Economics of America at War, 1943

Scandinavia is one of our chief sources of supply for wood pulp, and when Germany invaded Norway it looked as if our imports of pulp would be cut off for the duration of the war, and, therefore, that pulp stocks might be a good buy. They enjoyed an agreeable rise and about a month later Germany attacked the Netherlands.
In view of Germany's all-out method of Blitzkrieg war, it was reasonable to expect that Germany would either defeat France or be defeated herself within a fairly short time period. What should one do, therefore, about the pulp stocks? It did not take much thought to produce the following conclusions: a) If Germany were defeated, the supplies of pulp from Norway would start coming in again which would be bad for pulp stocks, b) If France were defeated, the threat of our being involved in the war would have such a serious effect on our economic system that all stocks would be affected.

—Making Money in Stock Trading, 1943

US savings bond, Series E, 1944

Although our maximum military effort still lies ahead, we have already gone over the top in industrial production for war to such an extent that large, although selective, cutbacks in war output are both familiar and increasing.

—*The Magazine of Wall Street*, February 5, 1944

Actually Germany cannot take much comfort out of the widely publicized difference among the Big Three (i.e., contract scandals)…On the contrary the Allies are united as ever on the paramount objective—which is to defeat the Nazis, although they may see certain related factors with different eyes. No Breaks for the Axis.

—*The Magazine of Wall Street*, February 5, 1944

The recovery of the market following Pearl Harbor was very gradual and painful…All during 1942, stocks were on the bargain counter.

—*The Magazine of Wall Street*, February 5, 1944

From 1949 to 1989, the top defense firms outperformed the stocks market by a huge margin. An investor who held a portfolio of top defense stocks during those four decades would have earned 2.4 times more than one who invested an equal amount in a diversified portfolio.

—Robert Higgs, *Depression, War, and Cold War*, 2006

The problem in defense spending is to figure how far you should go without destroying from within what you are trying to defend from without.

—President Eisenhower, 1955

You say we want war, but you have now got yourselves into a position I would call idiotic, but we don't want to profit by it. If you withdraw your troops from Germany, France, and Britain—I'm speaking of American troops—we will not stay one day in Poland, Hungary, and Romania. But we, Mister Capitalists, we are beginning to understand your methods…It doesn't depend on you whether or not we exist. If you don't like us, don't accept our invitations, and don't invite us to come to see you. Whether you like it or not, history is on our side. We will bury you!

—Nikita Khrushchev, premier of USSR, November 26, 1956

In 1958 the US just missed the moon (i.e., response to Russia's lunar satellite). But Wall Street's Bull made it—and over, with ease.

—Business in 1958, *Time*, December 29, 1958

UNDER THE LAWS OF THE STATE OF DELAWARE

Y CORPORA

Sperry Corporation, a
major defense company

The wrong war, at the wrong place, at the
wrong time, and with the wrong enemy.
—General Omar Bradley, one of six
five-star generals, 1951

149

KOREAN WAR US COMMON STOCKS
with 200-day moving average and NYSE volume

Increase 40%

President-elect Eisenhower visits Korea

Cease-fire truce signed

Battle of Heartbreak Ridge

President Truman fires General MacArthur

General MacArthur requests use of atomic weapons

U.N. Air Force stops all bombing in "Mig Alley"

Battle of the Hook

U.N. enters N. Korea

A fortified line established—truce talks begin

U.N. lands at Inchon
N. Korean army leaves S. Korea

U.N. forces recapture Seoul

U.N. retreats from N. Korea
China captures Seoul

Communist China enters the war

U.N. forces pushed to edge of Korean Peninsula at Pusan

Communist N. Korea captures Seoul

Korea's economy had been integrated with the Empire of Japan, and with that relationship now broken, so too was its economy. Japanese forces in Korea surrendered to the Americans in 1945, marking the end of three and a half decades of Japanese rule in Korea. The Russians made matters worse by sealing their zone of occupation from the southern zone, halting coal deliveries to southern Korea, halting also railway traffic, mail deliveries, and the transfer of electrical power southward across the 38th parallel.

—MacroHistory.com, 2007

US Stocks	up 40%
US Home Prices	up 49%
US Interest Rates	up 51%

Chart Notes
The first confrontation of the Cold War was met with the shock of Communist North Korea's invasion. But US investments staged a long, linear bull market as UN forces pushed Communist troops out of South Korea through to the end of hostilities. At the end of the war, South Korean government bond interest rates exceeded 25%.

US NEW HOMES

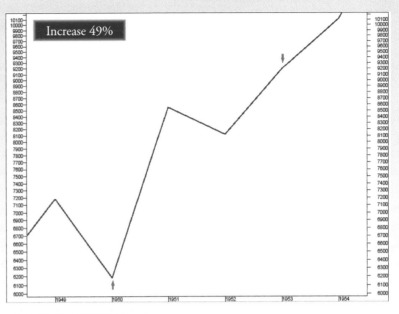

Increase 49%

SOUTH KOREAN INTEREST RATES

US T-BOND YIELDS

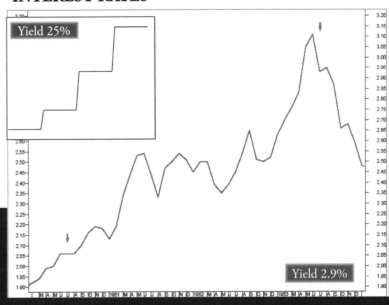

Yield 25%

Yield 2.9%

VIETNAM WAR—1964 to 1973

North American Aviation, major supplier of military aircraft and spacecraft. Dated on the twenty-fourth anniversary of Pearl Harbor attack.

Stein, president of Dreyfus Funds, was an outspoken critic of the Vietnam War long before dovishness became fashionable in the Wall Street community.

—*Change and Turmoil on Wall Street*, *Time*, August 24, 1970

VIETNAM WAR US COMMON STOCKS
with 200-day moving average and NYSE volume

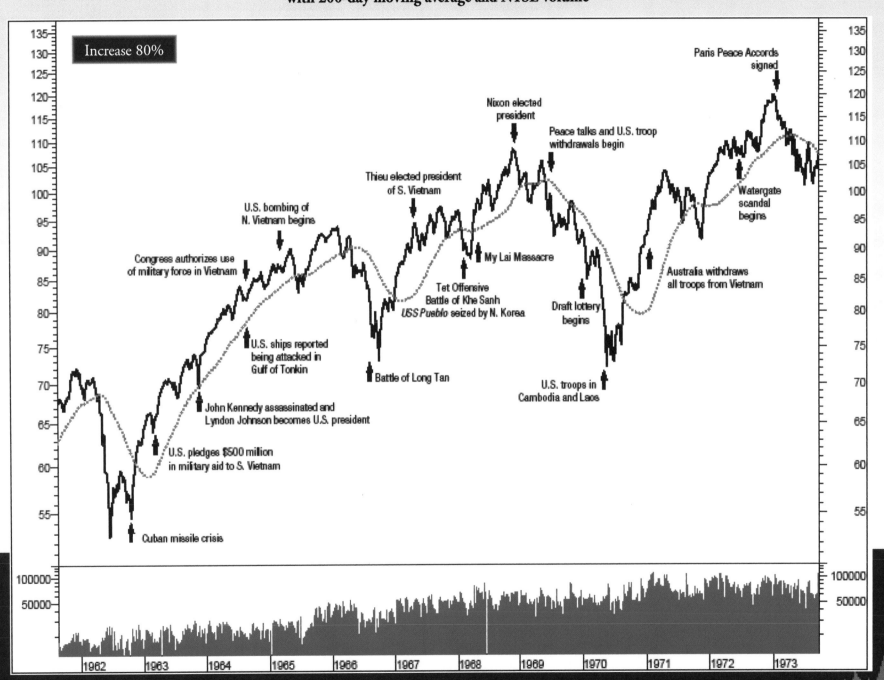

Increase 80%

Paris Peace Accords signed

Nixon elected president

Peace talks and U.S. troop withdrawals begin

Thieu elected president of S. Vietnam

Watergate scandal begins

U.S. bombing of N. Vietnam begins

Congress authorizes use of military force in Vietnam

My Lai Massacre

Tet Offensive
Battle of Khe Sanh
USS Pueblo seized by N. Korea

Australia withdraws all troops from Vietnam

U.S. ships reported being attacked in Gulf of Tonkin

Draft lottery begins

John Kennedy assassinated and Lyndon Johnson becomes U.S. president

Battle of Long Tan

U.S. troops in Cambodia and Laos

U.S. pledges $500 million in military aid to S. Vietnam

Cuban missile crisis

1962   1963   1964   1965   1966   1967   1968   1969   1970   1971   1972   1973

Carrier-based pocket bomber packs a nuclear punch

Aerospace advertising, 1962

The Vietnam War cost the United States more than 58,000 lives and claimed hundreds of thousands of Vietnamese. It cost more than $500 billion in today's dollars.

—US News & World Report, November 12, 2006

Draft protest at the Pentagon, 1970

American priorities

The Minneapolis Tribune, December 13, 1972

By means of their influence on the operation of the Pentagon, military-industry firms seem to get away with large profits.

—Seymour Melman, *Pentagon Capitalism*, 1970

Even with large gold reserves the dollar can be shaken by a drop in confidence. Devaluation of the dollar and a concomitant increase in the price of gold would lead to a run on gold.

—Walt Rostow, President Johnson's National Security advisor, January 13, 1968

SOUTH VIETNAM INTEREST RATES

US T-BOND YIELDS

Yield 33%

Yield 6.6%

US Stocks	up 80%
US Home Prices	up 86%
US Interest Rates	up 55%

Chart Notes

After the Cuban missile crisis, the stock market started a long bull run with only a couple of hiccups such as the initial bombing of North Vietnam that was feared would bring Communist China into the conflict and the beginning of the peace treaty process followed by initial US troop withdrawals. Next to the Civil War, equities and real estate posted their best wartime performance in spite of the highest interest rates since the War of 1812. At the time of the signing of the peace treaty, South Vietnam's government bond yields exceeded 33%.

US NEW HOMES WITH NEW HOME SALES

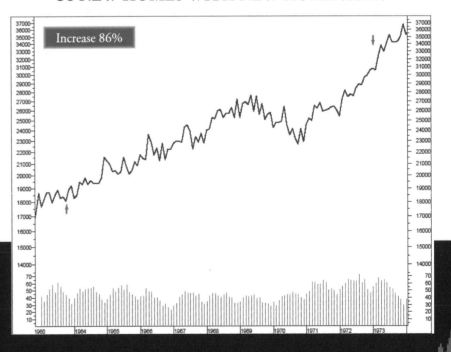

Increase 86%

Vietnam made clear 'even the mighty United States' lacks the means to fight anywhere, anytime and prevail and a call for de-escalation and fiscal restraint are needed now.

—*Businessweek*, March 14, 1968

WAR ON TERRORISM— 2001 to ...

HAVE YOU SEEN ME?

I'm about to get my ass nuked off the face of the planet!
—Osama Bin Laden
1-HEI-SSO-DEAD

Taped to the outside of the
New York Stock Exchange

Calling Iraq a serious threat, Bush vows that he'll disarm it, and also rebuild the US economy.

—*The New York Times*, January 29, 2003

WAR ON TERRORISM US COMMON STOCKS
with 200-day moving average and NYSE volume

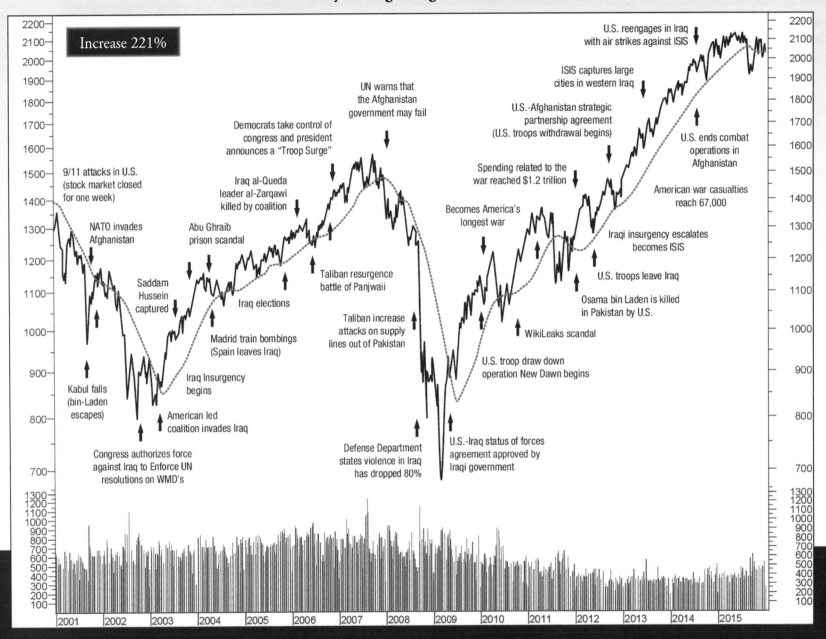

Increase 221%

U.S. reengages in Iraq with air strikes against ISIS

ISIS captures large cities in western Iraq

U.S.-Afghanistan strategic partnership agreement (U.S. troops withdrawal begins)

UN warns that the Afghanistan government may fail

U.S. ends combat operations in Afghanistan

American war casualties reach 67,000

Democrats take control of congress and president announces a "Troop Surge"

Spending related to the war reached $1.2 trillion

9/11 attacks in U.S. (stock market closed for one week)

Iraq al-Queda leader al-Zarqawi killed by coalition

Becomes America's longest war

Iraqi insurgency escalates becomes ISIS

NATO invades Afghanistan

Abu Ghraib prison scandal

U.S. troops leave Iraq

Saddam Hussein captured

Taliban resurgence battle of Panjwaii

Osama bin Laden is killed in Pakistan by U.S.

Iraq elections

Iraq Insurgency begins

WikiLeaks scandal

Madrid train bombings (Spain leaves Iraq)

Taliban increase attacks on supply lines out of Pakistan

Kabul falls (bin-Laden escapes)

U.S. troop draw down operation New Dawn begins

American led coalition invades Iraq

Congress authorizes force against Iraq to Enforce UN resolutions on WMD's

Defense Department states violence in Iraq has dropped 80%

U.S.-Iraq status of forces agreement approved by Iraqi government

2001 2002 2003 2004 2005 2006 2007 2008 2009 2010 2011 2012 2013 2014 2015

157

Wall Streeters now fall mainly into two camps: Those who think the war in Iraq was itself a horrible mistake and those who think it could have been a good choice but was bungled in the execution. It is not the $800 billion the Iraq War is projected to cost that drives us nuts. A $13 trillion economy can make adjustments. But it is the troop draw down, and the failure to finish the job in Afghanistan.

—TomPaine.com, June 26, 2006

Investor's Business Daily, June 2, 2006

Investor's Business Daily, December 22, 2006

It is a budget fight that highlights the deep stresses on a military force tussling for more money and manpower while it struggles to protect expensive combat systems in a time when war worn equipment remains in need of critical repairs and posts across the country are struggling to pay their electric bills.

—US News & World Report, October 30, 2006

But wonder is almost overwhelmed by relief. Mr. Obama's election offers a sense that the imperial power capable of doing such good and harm—a country that preached justice but tortured its captives, launched a disastrous war in Iraq…and greedily dragged the world into economic chaos.

—*The New York Times*, November 5, 2008

US Stocks	up 217%
US Home Prices	up 70%
US Interest Rates	down 53%

Chart Notes

After the 9/11 attacks, the US stock and bond markets were closed for five days. After an initial panic, the stock market "bounced," following the prompt invasion of Afghanistan by NATO forces. The stock market hit a low point on the day of Congress' controversial decision to authorize US military forces against Iraq as the second front of this war. To date, both stocks and real estate have posted gains comparable to those seen during the Vietnam War with the lowest interest rates since the Great Depression. Iraqi and Afghan bank rates are at 9%.

Certificate of Martyrdom · Iraqi government bond

IRAQI INTEREST RATES

Yield 9%

Yield 2.27%

U.S. NEW HOMES WITH SALES

Increase 70%

U.S. T-BOND YIELDS

PAYING FOR A WAR

1878 Civil War bond redemption notice. US Treasury started to pay off war debts ten years after the Civil War.

Confederate States of America deposit form, 1883. This was used by foreign investors to collect principal payments from the defunct Confederacy. The US would not honor the obligation.

Gas ration book with stamps, 1944

WARTIME INVESTMENTS SUMMARY

Conflicts	Number of Years	Percentage Change				
		Stocks Prices	Negative Years	Homes	Negative Years	T-Bond Yields
Average (w/o Cold War)	7.4	57%	28%	47%	41%	-1%
Total (w/o Cold War)	74	567%	21	425%	30	-8%
War of 1812	3	-8%	2			15%
Mexican-American War	2	3%	1	73%		7%
Civil War	4	83%	1	115%	1	-16%
Indian Wars	24	60%	7	58%	13	-30%
Spanish-American War	1	16%	0	10%	0	-1%
World War I	4	41%	2	-3%	2	3%
World War II	6	35%	2	-33%	4	-39%
Cold War	45	2054%	6	3131%		330%
Korean War	3	40%	1	49%	2	51%
Vietnam War	11	80%	2	86%	3	55%
War on Terror	16	217%	3	70%	5	-53%

The following phrase best sums up how to be a wartime investor:

This is as good a place as any to emphasize the necessity of not letting your mind be paralyzed by the events… Never forget to think and take action!

—Making Money in Stock Trading, 1943

WELCOMING THE TROOPS HOME!

Victory Parade, 1991

VJ Day, New York City, 1945

War is the trade of Kings.

—John Dryden, poet, 1680

What a country calls its vital economic interests are
not the things which enable its citizens to live, but the
things which enable it to make war. Petrol is more likely
than wheat to be a use of international conflict.

—Simone Weil, philosopher, 1937

Wars are made to make debt.

—Ezra Pound, poet, 1963

DISASTERS

FROM KENNEDY'S DEATH TO KATRINA:
BUY OR SELL?

163

San Francisco fires, 1906

San Francisco Fire Protection bond, 1920

Hurricanes, tsunamis, tornadoes, volcanic eruptions, earthquakes, fires, pandemics, and environmental catastrophes—there is no place and no one in the world that hasn't been affected by at least one of these natural disasters. Acts of Mother Nature have shaped civilizations past and present. In fact, pandemics have been called a key factor in the decline of the Roman Empire.

How have investors reacted to sudden events and prolonged tragedies? In this section, eleven major natural disasters in US history (which led to the destruction of four major cities and the deaths of hundreds of thousands of people) are examined in light of their short- and long-term effects on various types of investments to see if they really matter to Wall Street.

Hurricane
Katrina, 2005

When a vast destruction of life and property takes place in a few hours, through an earthquake, the big commercial nations seem to realize that humanitarianism and economic interest alike demand both temporary measures of emergency relief, and more fundamental measures for the reconstruction of the economic life of the affected area at the earliest date possible.

—*The Magazine of Wall Street*, September 29, 1923

An ancestor of the author took these photographs.

SAN FRANCISCO EARTHQUAKE—1906

US NEW HOME PRICES

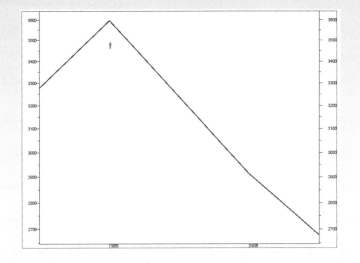

US COMMON STOCKS WITH NYSE VOLUME

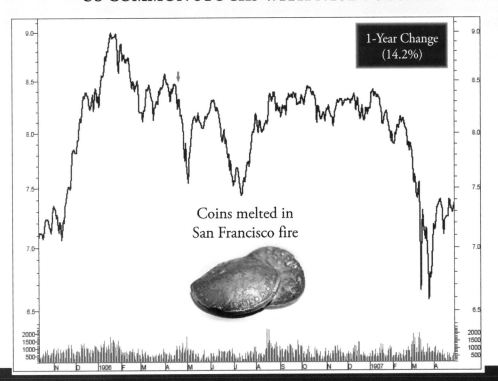

1-Year Change
(14.2%)

Coins melted in
San Francisco fire

US T-BOND YIELDS

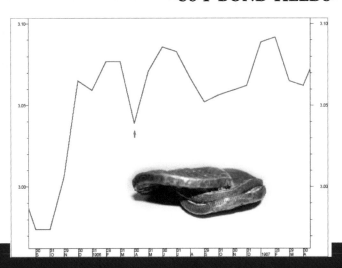

Right in the path of the largest, hottest blaze, a few dozen men at the San Francisco Mint stood fast. Led by a political appointee with no experience in crisis management, they fought back against an inferno that melted the glass in the mint's windows and burned the clothes off their backs. Although their story is largely forgotten, by safeguarding gold and silver worth $300 million in 1906, they may have saved the US economy from collapse.

—*Smithsonian* magazine, April 2006

FIRES

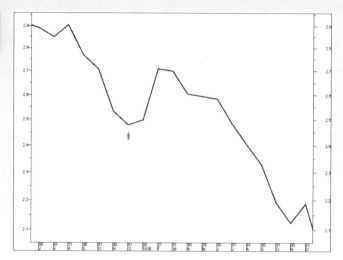

1-Year Change (13.5%)

Great Fire of New York, 1835

Great Chicago Fire, 1871

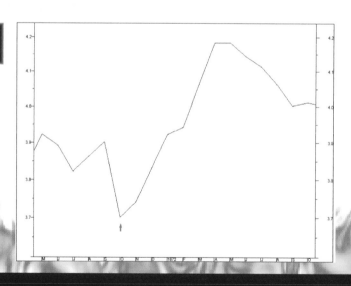

1-Year Change (13.3%)

Within a year of these disasters, the financial district (Wall Street) was restored, its lightning-like reconstruction driven by an appetite for commercial speculation that nothing seemed able to dampen.

—Steve Fraser, *Every Man a Speculator*, 2005

US T-BOND YIELDS

US NEW HOMES

When the Chicago fire occurred it immediately created a panic. When a calamity occurs
at any part of the country the shock is first felt in Wall Street.

—Henry Clews, *Twenty-Eight Years in Wall Street*, 1887

HURRICANE ANDREW—1992

US NEW HOME PRICES   U.S. T-BOND YIELDS   US COMMON STOCKS WITH NYSE VOLUME

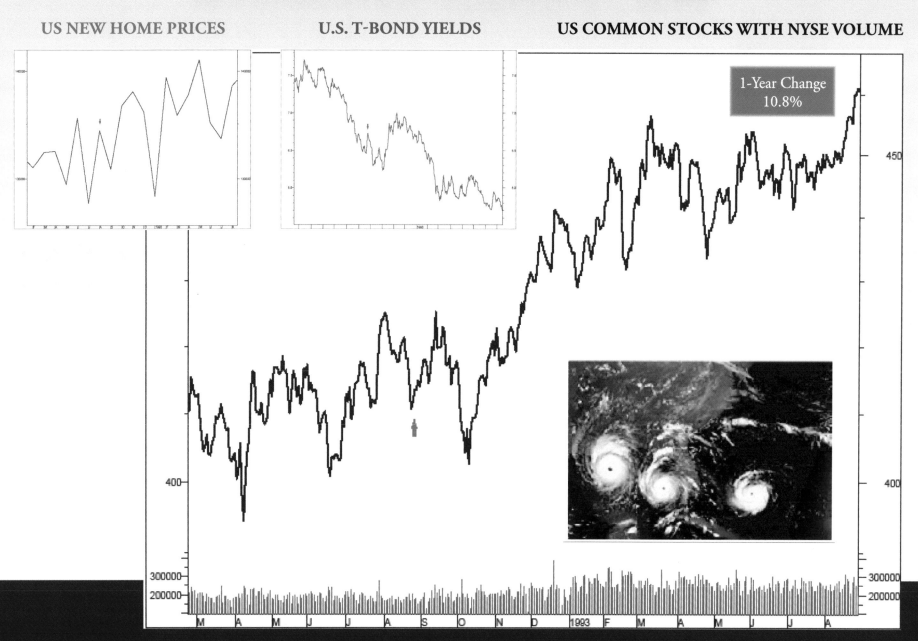

1-Year Change
10.8%

Unlike most hurricanes, the vast majority of the damage in Florida was caused by winds. The agricultural loss in Florida was $1.04 billion alone.

—Wikipedia.com, 2007

TSUNAMI and KATRINA—2005

US COMMON STOCKS WITH NYSE VOLUME

1-Year Change
5.8%

Sumatra-Andaman
earthquake and tsunamis

Hurricane Katrina
and flooding
of New Orleans

US NEW HOME PRICES

US T-BOND YIELDS

In the aftermath of Hurricane Katrina, Congress passed the Katrina Emergency Tax Relief Act
of 2005, which was signed by the President into law on September 23, 2005.

—J. K. Lasser, *Your Income Tax*, 2006

169

MOUNT ST. HELENS—1980

US COMMON STOCKS WITH NYSE VOLUME

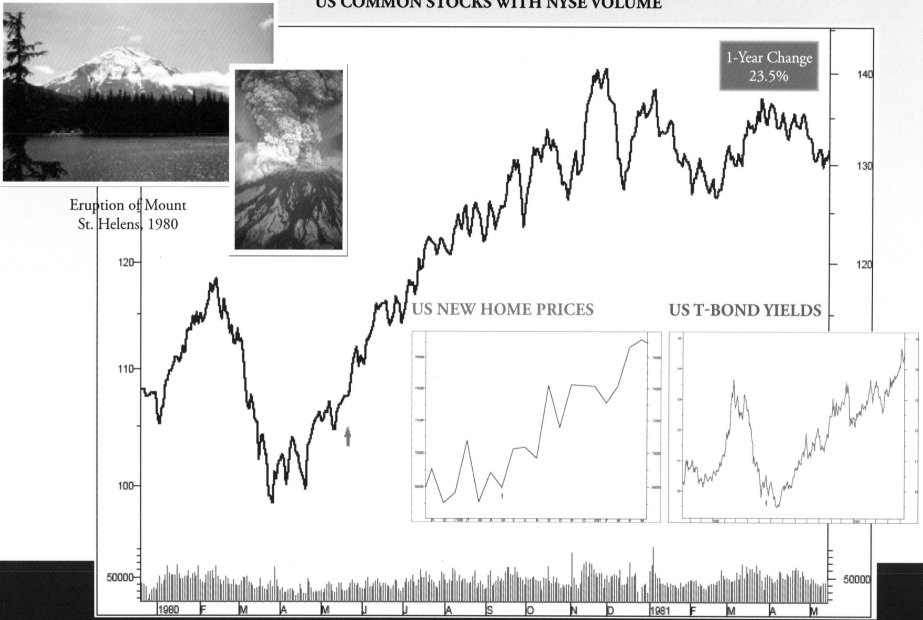

Eruption of Mount
St. Helens, 1980

1-Year Change
23.5%

US NEW HOME PRICES

US T-BOND YIELDS

Heavy volcanic activity is known to cause global cooling. They also start major forest fires.

—Richard Firestone, *The Cycle of Cosmic Catastrophes*, 2006

TORNADO STORMS—1974

US COMMON STOCKS WITH NYSE VOLUME

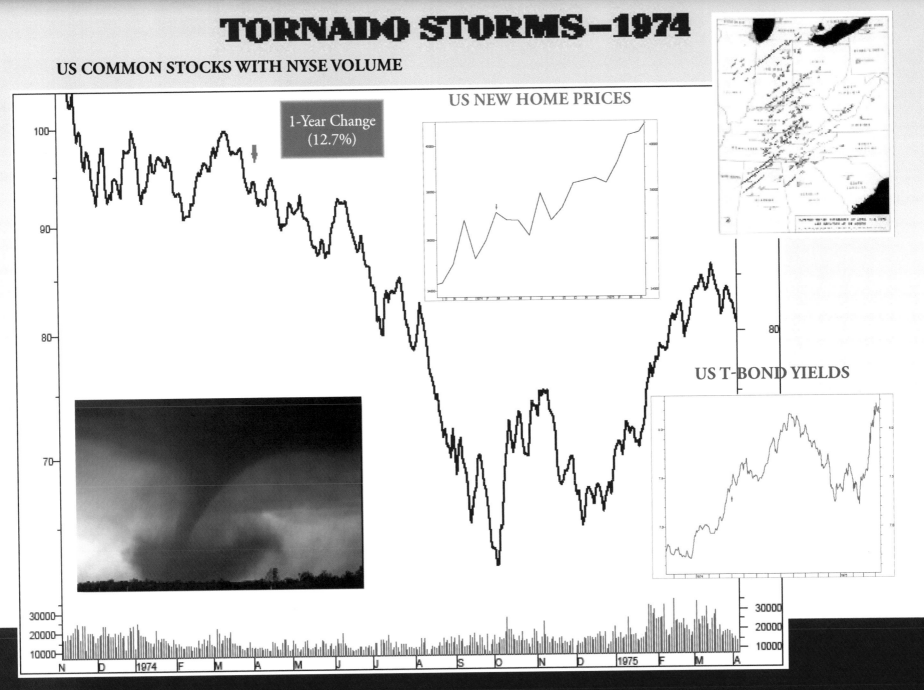

1-Year Change
(12.7%)

US NEW HOME PRICES

US T-BOND YIELDS

Although [the] number of fatalities [has] decreased, the number of people affected by tornados and costs incurred continues to increase.

—FEMA report, 2003

PANDEMICS

Forbes cover,
June 2006

Treatment ward
during the Spanish
flu pandemic

US COMMON STOCKS WITH NYSE VOLUME

SPANISH FLU, 1918

Total Change
39%

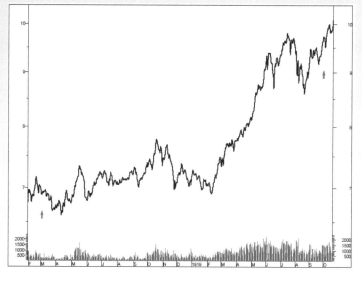

ASIAN FLU, 1957

Total Change
0.7%

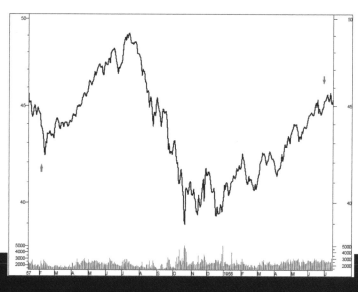

**More and more bugs are becoming untreatable. But, Big Pharma,
rather than riding to the rescue, has largely abandoned antibiotic
research, a low-ticket business, for more lucrative pursuits.**

—Forbes, June 2006

US T-BOND YIELDS

Spanish Flu

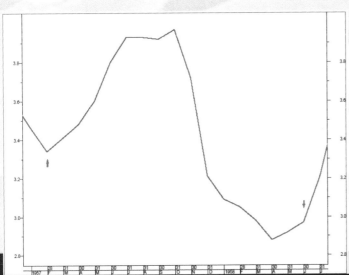

US NEW HOME PRICES

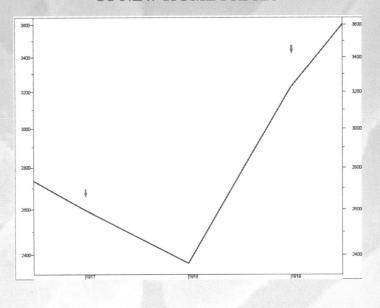

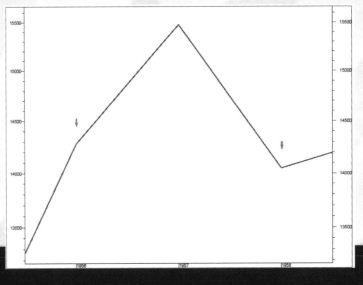

Background photo by Rocky Mountain Laboratories, NIAID, NIH

With people streaming in from all over the world to join the California gold rush, at a time when public health and sanitary conditions were frequently substandard, it now seems amazing that only one major plague ravaged the Golden State during those tumultuous days.

—William Secrest, *California Disasters*, 2005

US COMMON STOCKS WITH NYSE VOLUME

In the early 1930s, many farmers were trying to recover from economic losses suffered during the Great Depression. To compensate for these losses, they began to increase their crop yields. High production drove prices down, forcing farmers to keep increasing their production to pay for both their equipment and their land. When the Dust Bowl drought hit, farmers could no longer produce enough crops to pay off loans or even pay for essential needs. Even with Federal emergency aid, many Great Plains farmers could not withstand the economic crisis of the drought. Many farmers were forced off of their land, with one in ten farms changing possession at the peak of the farm transfers.

—NOAA.gov, 2001

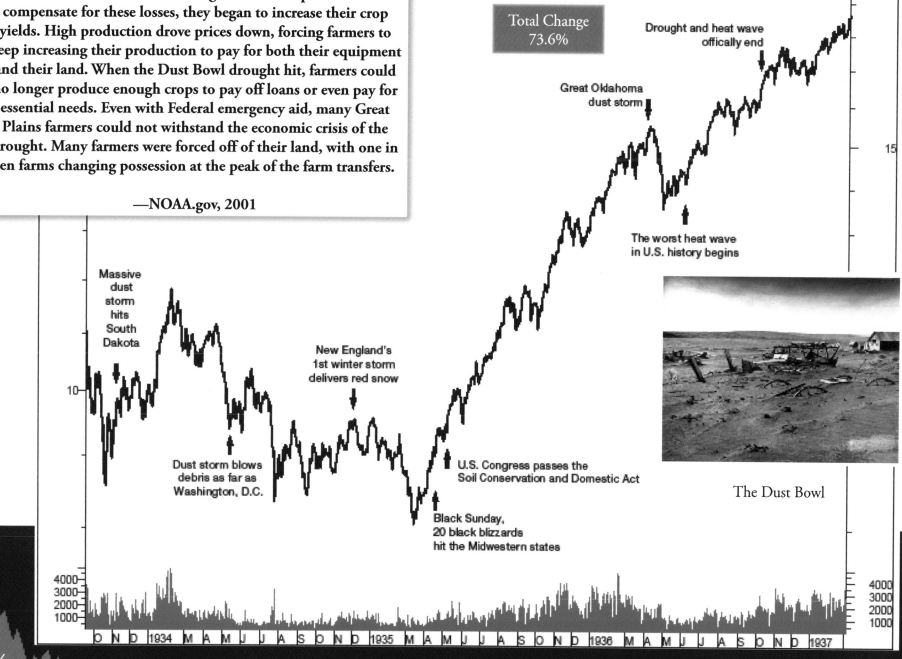

Total Change
73.6%

Drought and heat wave officially end

Great Oklahoma dust storm

The worst heat wave in U.S. history begins

Massive dust storm hits South Dakota

New England's 1st winter storm delivers red snow

Dust storm blows debris as far as Washington, D.C.

U.S. Congress passes the Soil Conservation and Domestic Act

Black Sunday, 20 black blizzards hit the Midwestern states

The Dust Bowl

US T-BOND YIELDS

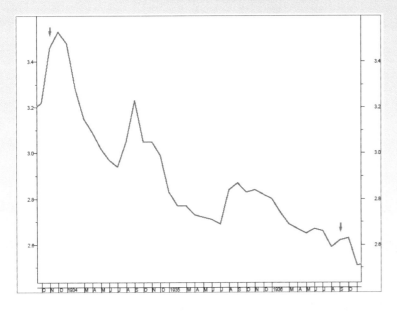

US NEW HOME PRICES

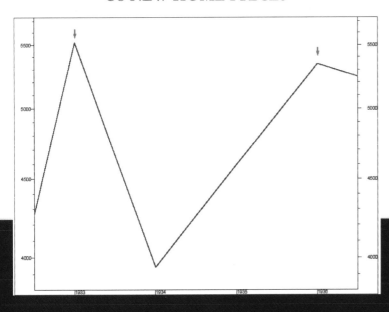

As the table on the next page shows, there have been various market reactions to these destructive disasters. The common pattern is a knee-jerk correction not exceeding (3.4%) in the stock market over a week, followed by annual advances in both equities and real estate. In fact, stocks and home prices combined have advanced 3.7% within one year (investment gains exceeded 6.8% for 63% of the time) of these acts of Mother Nature. Bond yields posted moderate increases.

The great fires in the financial centers of New York (1835), Chicago (1871), and San Francisco (1906) caused large one-year corrections in stocks while Hurricanes Andrew and Katrina had little effect on stock and real estate values nationwide, short- or long-term, while interest rate changes ranged from 14% to (14%) over a year.

Deadly pandemics and the environmental nightmare of the three-year Dust Bowl didn't faze investors, with investment prices advancing 44% on average throughout these events amid single-digit increases in interest rates.

The direct and indirect economic effects of this disaster will be enormous and will affect the entire nation. The loss of wealth will be huge, measured physically, but measured in money and trade the consequences are problematical.

—*The Magazine of Wall Street*, August 18, 1934

NATURAL DISASTERS SUMMARY

SINGLE EVENTS	Date	Description (What is it? What did it do?)	Common Stocks							T-Bond (10-year) Yield					Homes			Combined
			Price	1 Week After	% Chg	6 Months After	% Chg	1 Year After	% Chg	Yields	6 Months After	% Chg	1 Year After	% Chg	Prices	1 Year After	% Chg	% Chg
Great New York Fire (1, 2)	December 16–17, 1835	Destroyed 700 buildings (including NYSE) in lower Manhattan, $20 million in damages.	2.5	na	na	2.6	1.9%	2.2	-13.5%	4.83	4.96	2.7%	4.96	2.7%	1,673	2,189	30.8%	17.3%
Great Chicago Fire (1, 2)	October 8–10, 1871	The largest US natural disaster of the 19th century, $222 million in damage (four square miles of downtown Chicago destroyed—important commodities exchanges).	3.9	na	na	4.2	7.2%	3.4	-13.3%	5.06	5.39	6.5%	5.14	1.6%	1,274	1,142	-10.4%	-23.7%
Great San Francisco Earthquake and Fire (2)	April 18–20, 1906	500 city blocks destroyed; $400 million in damage; 3,000 people killed (15% of population), West Coast's major financial institutions destroyed.	8.5	8.2	-3.4%	8.3	-2.2%	7.3	-14.2%	3.08	3.05	-1.0%	3.07	-0.3%	3,596	2,913	-19.0%	-33.2%
The Super Tornado Outbreak	April 3–4, 1974	148 tornadoes struck 13 Midwestern states; $3.5 billion damage over 2,600 miles. Other Factor: Watergate scandal	93.3	92.0	-1.4%	62.3	-33.3%	81.5	-12.7%	7.43	8.04	8.2%	8.15	9.7%	37,112	40,600	9.4%	-3.3%
Mount St. Helens Eruption	May 18, 1980	Most destructive volcanic event in US history, $3 billion in damages (185 miles of major Northwest highways destroyed). Other Factor: record interest rates	107.3	110.6	3.0%	139.7	30.1%	132.5	23.5%	10.37	12.95	24.9%	13.80	33.1%	68,850	77,200	12.1%	35.6%
Hurricane Andrew	August 24, 1992	Second-most destructive hurricane in US history, $27 billion in damages outside Miami	414.9	414.0	-0.2%	440.9	6.3%	459.8	10.8%	6.53	6.01	-8.0%	5.60	-14.2%	127,850	138,600	8.4%	19.2%
Sumatra-Andaman Earthquake and Tsunamis	December 26, 2004	Second-largest earthquake in recorded history; 285,000 people killed in six countries with strong US financial interest. Other Factors: Hurricane Katrina; Al-Qaeda war	1210.2	1202.1	-0.7%	1190.7	-1.6%	1257.0	3.9%	4.23	3.90	-7.8%	4.34	2.6%	256,950	264,400	2.9%	6.8%
Hurricane Katrina New Orleans Floods	August 23–30, 2005	Costliest disaster in US history exceeded $82 billion throughout four states, 80% of New Orleans destroyed; 1,836 people killed	1221.8	1220.3	-0.1%	1287.8	5.4%	1293.0	5.8%	4.22	4.56	8.1%	4.81	14.0%	267,550	280,600	4.9%	10.7%
		Average			-0.5%		1.7%		-1.2%			4.2%		6.1%			4.9%	3.7%
		Median			-0.2%		3.6%		-4.4%			4.6%		2.6%			6.6%	8.7%
		High			3.0%		30.1%		23.5%			24.9%		33.1%			30.8%	35.6%
		Low			-3.4%		-33.3%		-14.2%			-8.0%		-14.2%			-19.0%	-33.2%

EXTENDED EVENTS	Date	Description (What is it? What did it do?)	Beginning			End	% Chg	1 Year After	% Chg	Beginning			End	% Chg	Beginning	1 Year After	End	% Chg
Spanish Flu Pandemic (2)	March 1918 to September 1919	17 million people died worldwide; 500,000 in US (of 100 million total population). Other Factor: World War I	7.0			9.7	39.0%			3.81			4.71	23.6%	2,597		3,226	24.2%	63.2%
The Dust Bowl (2)	November 1933 to September 1936	The largest environmental disaster in US history caused permanent migration of 500,000 people from the Midwest. Other Factor: Great Depression	9.2			16.0	73.6%			3.22			2.62	-18.6%	5,519		5,346	-3.1%	70.5%
Asian Flu Pandemic (2)	February 1957 to June 1958	70,000 deaths in US. Other Factors: USSR launched Sputnik, President Eisenhower suffered a stroke	44.9			45.2	0.7%			3.46			2.97	-14.2%	14,279		14,047	-1.6%	-0.9%

(1) Monthly Prices on Stocks	Best Performance		Average											-3.1%			6.5%	44.3%
(2) Year-End Prices on Real Estate	Worst Performance		Median				39.0%							-14.2%			-1.6%	63.2%
			High				73.6%							23.6%			24.2%	70.5%
			Low				0.7%							-18.6%			-3.1%	-0.9%

Veteran investors have found that major disasters tend to take place after the stock market has already given its clues that the rally is over.

—Investor's Business Daily, July 2005

MAN-MADE TRAGEDIES

Trade embargoes, terrorism, shipwrecks, spaceship explosions, presidential assassinations, and political controversies. Except for war, these man-made situations have been the indelible "time stoppers" for people who lived through them.

How have such events affected investors' actions?

In this section, sixteen of the most significant man-made tragedies (eleven sudden events and five protracted situations) that have occurred in America since the 1850s are examined in light of their short- and long-term effects on various types of investments.

Gas shortage lines of the 1970s

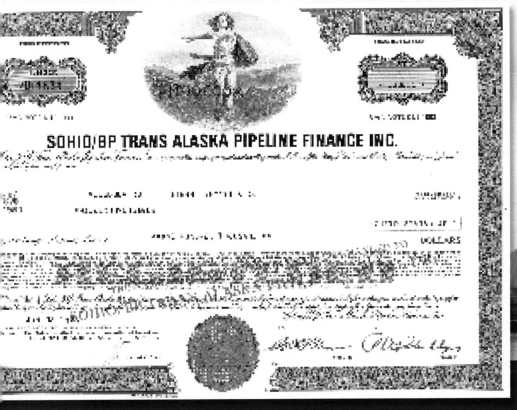

Alaska Pipeline, 1976

The first panic of any importance was that of 1837. This panic had its origin in a misunderstanding between the United States Bank and President Jackson, whose election the officials of the bank opposed.

—Henry Clews, *Twenty-Eight Years in Wall Street*, 1888

177

OIL EMBARGOES – 1967 and 1973

1944 and 1970
embargo cartoons

Franklin D. Roosevelt
with Saudi king

US COMMON STOCKS WITH NYSE VOLUME

1967

4% Increase

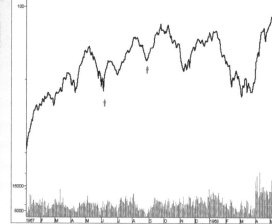

PRICE OF OIL

322% Increase

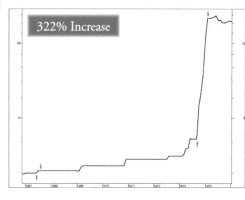

1973

25% Decrease

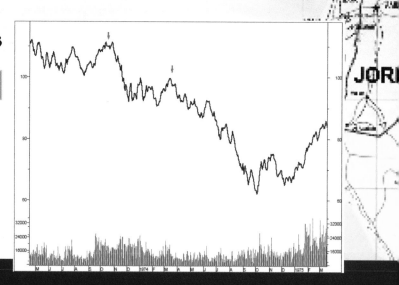

JOR

A $2 per barrel tariff imposed by President Ford on foreign crude oil is an attempt
to push prices high enough to force motorists to conserve fuel.

—*Time*, July 21, 1975

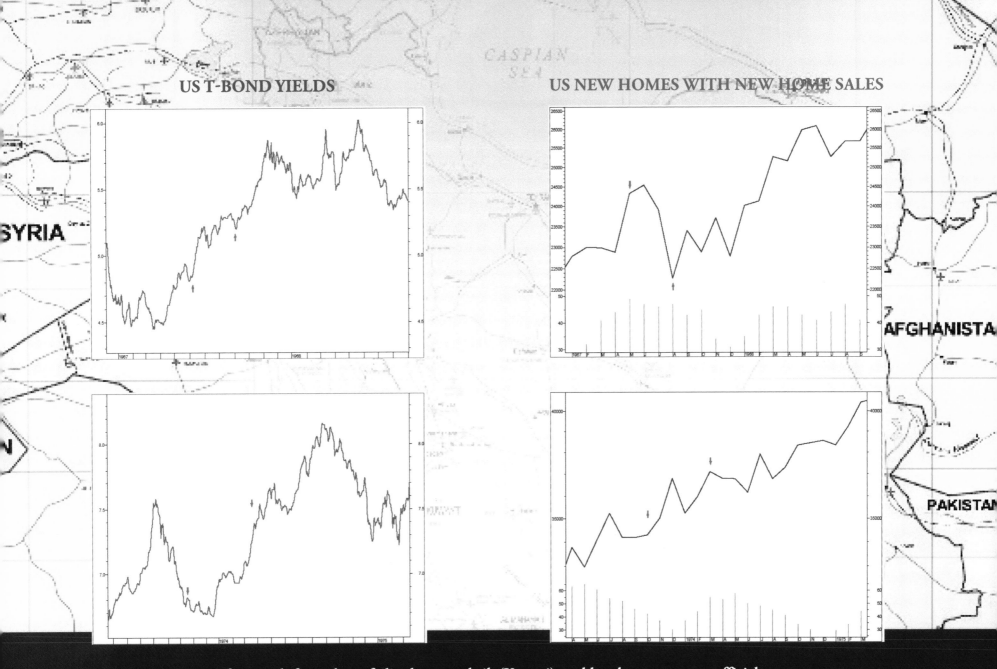

US T-BOND YIELDS

US NEW HOMES WITH NEW HOME SALES

A few words from the unfailingly suave sheik (Yamani) could make government officials
shudder and cause stock markets from New York to New Delhi to fall.

—*Time*, November 10, 1986

TERRORISM ON WALL STREET

Bomb Explosion in Wall Street District, New York

SCENE in front of United States Sub-Treasury a few minutes after the explosion took place on Sept. 16, 1920. Thirty people were killed and more than 100 injured, while the property damage done was es-

US COMMON STOCKS WITH NYSE VOLUME

WALL STREET, 1920

1-Year Change (19%)

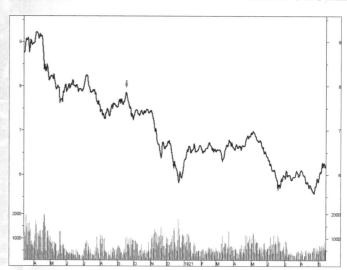

WORLD TRADE CENTER, 2001

1-Year Change (17%)

Wall Street has repeatedly been a target for violence by the disaffected, but heretofore its response has been to grieve, shrug and move on, ultimately reaching new heights.

—*The Wall Street Journal,* September 23, 2002

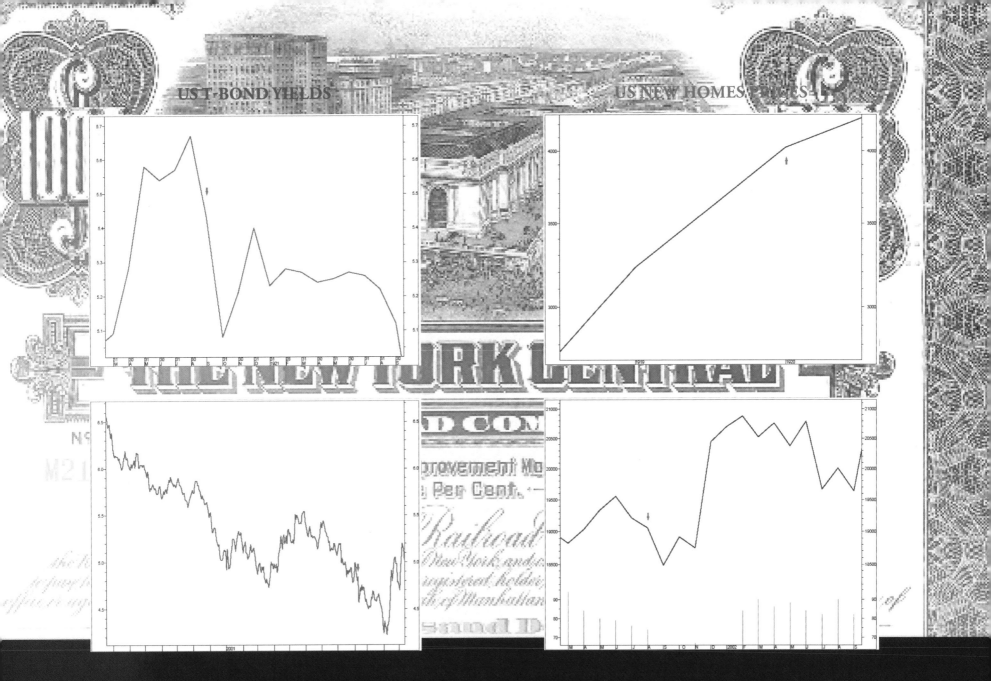

The New York Stock Exchange, a block away from the explosion, was a scene of chaos. Brokers traders, specialist, clerks all crowded to the center of the room, hoping to avoid flying glass, and the Exchange was closed immediately.

—*The Wall Street Journal*, September 17, 1920

181

SHIPWRECKS

SS *CENTRAL AMERICA* SINKS, 1857

1-Year Change
(10%)

TITANIC SINKS, 1912

1-Year Change
(9%)

International
Mercantile
Marine,
owner of
the *Titanic*

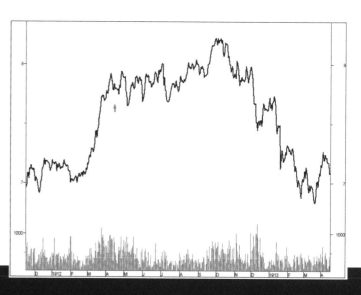

The first-class passengers for Titanic's maiden voyage included some of the richest and most prominent people in the world.

—Wikipedia.com, 2008

US T-BOND YIELDS

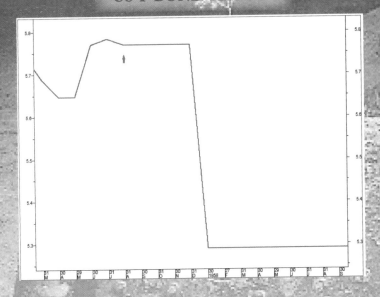

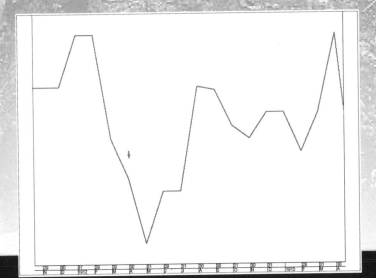

US NEW HOMES PRICES

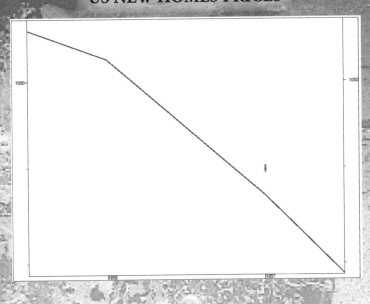

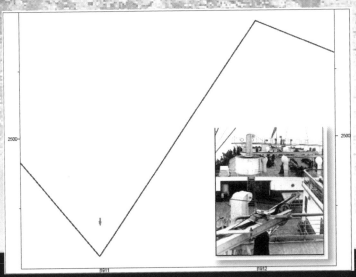

But overspeculation, following the enormous production of gold, and the abuses of credit in the promotion of new railroad and other companies, together with tariff disturbances, brought on the panic of 1857.

—Sereno Pratt, *Work of Wall Street*, 1916

SPACE TRAVEL CALAMITIES

US COMMON STOCKS WITH NYSE VOLUME

US T-BOND YIELDS

CHALLENGER,
1986

1-Year Change
33%

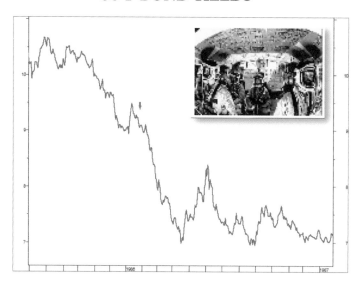

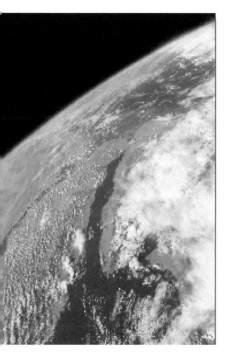

From a roll of unprocessed
film recovered from wreckage
of space shuttle *Columbia*

COLUMBIA,
2003

1-Year Change
33%

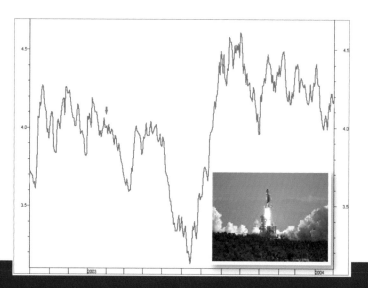

The space program has in fact returned the nation untold dividends in technological advancement and jobs.

—*Time* magazine, January 3, 1968

US NEW HOMES WITH NEW HOME SALES

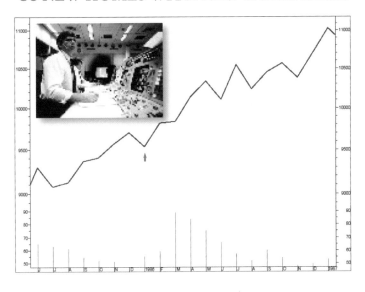

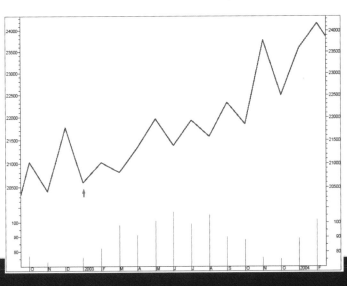

The second guessing will start soon enough. By Saturday
night the whistle-blowers were already beginning to
toot on the Internet and on the talking head shows,
claiming they had predicted disaster for years.

—*Newsweek*, February 10, 2003

POLITICAL ASSASSINATIONS

US COMMON STOCKS

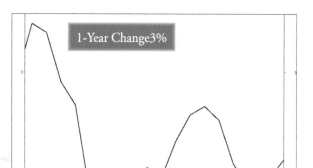

1-Year Change3%

US T-BOND YIELDS

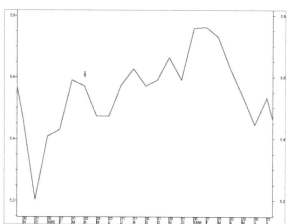

US NEW HOME PRICES

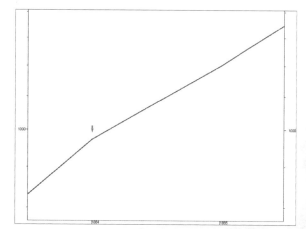

President Lincoln, 1865

The assassination of
President Lincoln at
Ford's Theatre, Washington, DC,
April 14, 1865

Stock market closed for over one week.

—NYSE.com, 2007

US COMMON STOCKS

US T-BOND YIELDS

US NEW HOME PRICES

President Garfield, 1881

The assassination of President Garfield, Washington, DC, July 2, 1881

President Garfield was shot on July 2. A railroad rate war broke out almost the next week; following which, the hot winds ruined the corn crop. All these occurrences were described, as usual, as thunderclaps from a clear sky—then the markets collapsed.

—Samuel Nelson, *The ABC of Stock Speculation*, 1903

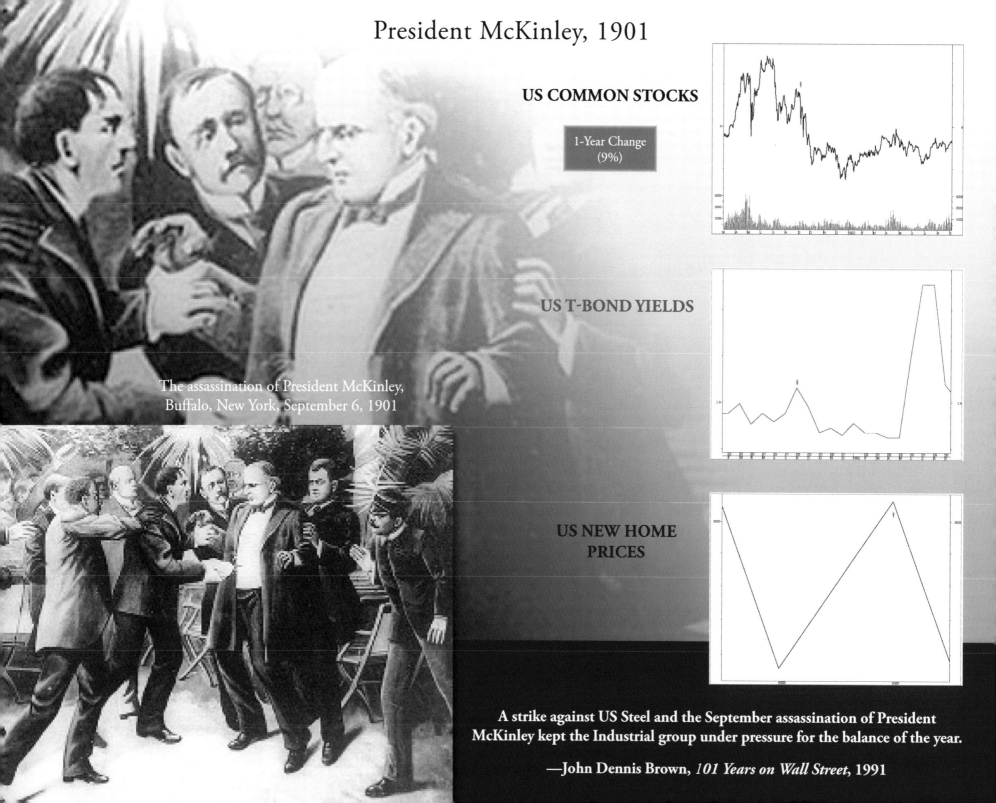

President McKinley, 1901

US COMMON STOCKS

1-Year Change
(9%)

US T-BOND YIELDS

The assassination of President McKinley,
Buffalo, New York, September 6, 1901

**US NEW HOME
PRICES**

A strike against US Steel and the September assassination of President
McKinley kept the Industrial group under pressure for the balance of the year.

—John Dennis Brown, *101 Years on Wall Street*, 1991

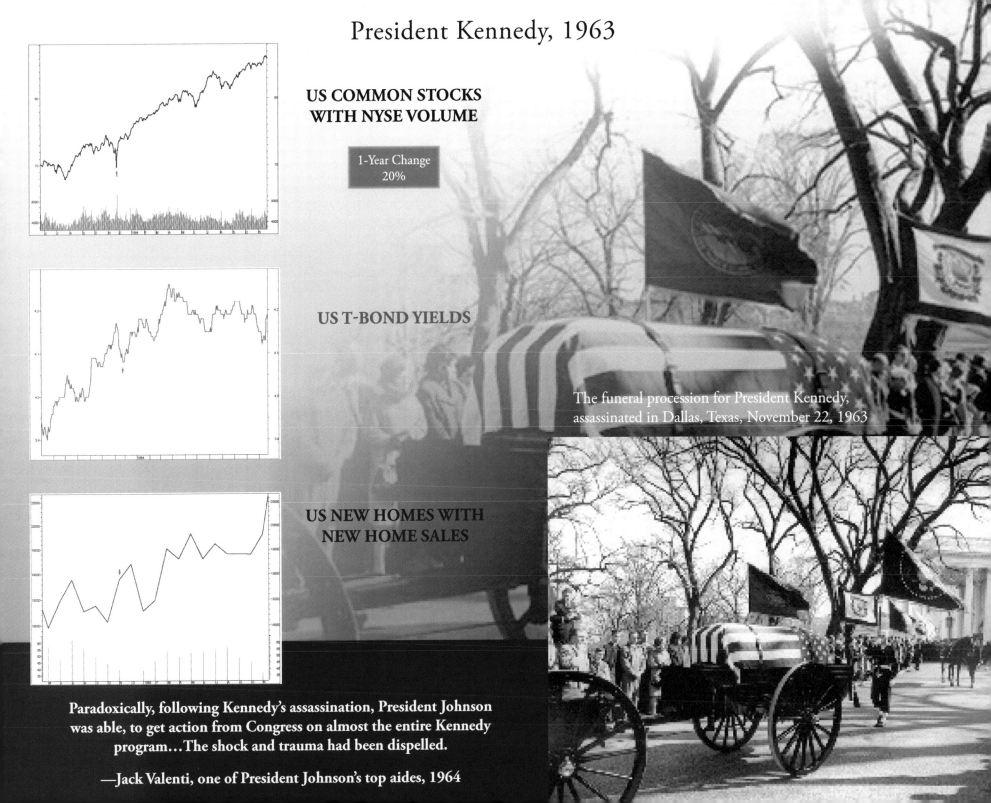

President Kennedy, 1963

**US COMMON STOCKS
WITH NYSE VOLUME**

1-Year Change
20%

US T-BOND YIELDS

**US NEW HOMES WITH
NEW HOME SALES**

The funeral procession for President Kennedy,
assassinated in Dallas, Texas, November 22, 1963

Paradoxically, following Kennedy's assassination, President Johnson
was able, to get action from Congress on almost the entire Kennedy
program…The shock and trauma had been dispelled.

—Jack Valenti, one of President Johnson's top aides, 1964

WATERGATE/NIXON RESIGNATION—1973

US COMMON STOCKS WITH NYSE VOLUME

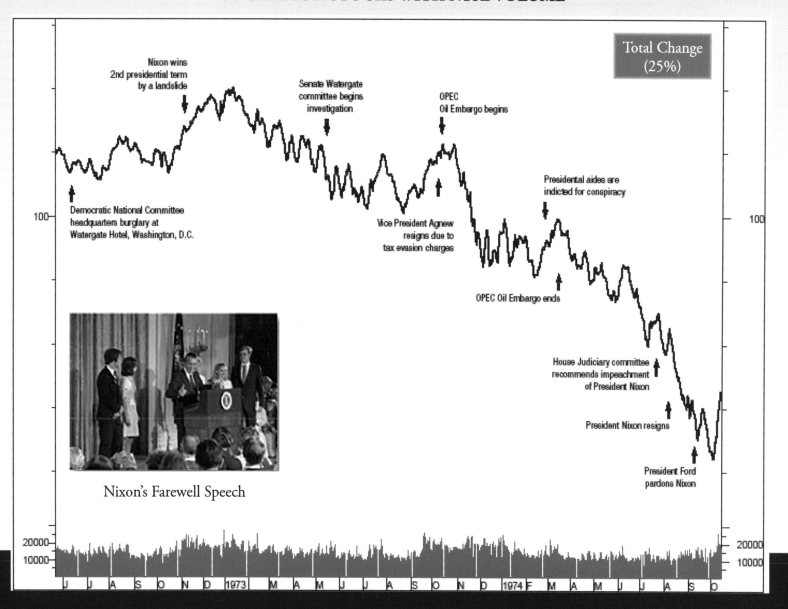

Total Change (25%)

Nixon wins 2nd presidential term by a landslide

Senate Watergate committee begins investigation

OPEC Oil Embargo begins

Democratic National Committee headquarters burglary at Watergate Hotel, Washington, D.C.

Presidental aides are indicted for conspiracy

Vice President Agnew resigns due to tax evasion charges

OPEC Oil Embargo ends

House Judiciary committee recommends impeachment of President Nixon

President Nixon resigns

President Ford pardons Nixon

Nixon's Farewell Speech

100

100

20000
10000

20000
10000

J J A S O N D 1973 M A M J J A S O N D 1974 F M A M J J A S O

Through acts that made no sense, discord would descend once again on a society already weakened by ten years of upheaval over Vietnam.

—Time, March 8, 1982

NF16618

COMMON STOCK
PAR VALUE $1.00

COMMON STOCK
PAR VALUE $1.00

PLAYBOY ENTERPRISES, INC.

Playboy Enterprises certificate issued during Watergate Scandal

US T-BOND YIELDS

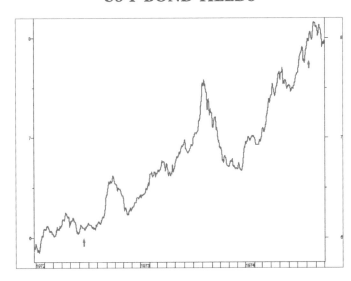

Political scandals: a timeless tradition

US NEW HOMES WITH NEW HOME SALES

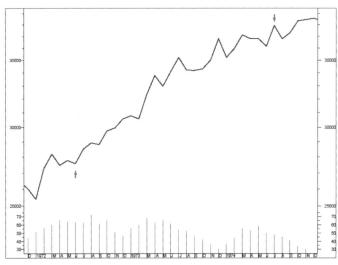

It was very succinctly described by Mr. Gould in his testimony before the Garfield Investigating Committee (into the president's role in the Gold Panic of 1869). He said, "The President (Grant) was an eager listener. The other gentlemen were discussing. Some were in favor of Treasurer Boutwell's selling gold, and some were opposed to it."

—Henry Clews, *Twenty-Eight Years in Wall Street*, 1887

PRESIDENT REAGAN SHOT–1981

US COMMON STOCKS WITH NYSE VOLUME

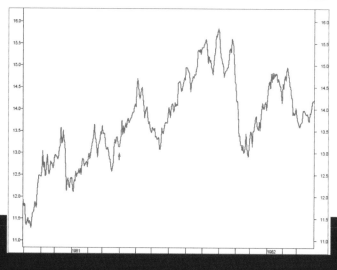

1-Year Change
(17%)

US NEW HOMES WITH NEW HOME SALES

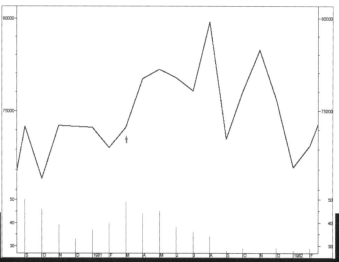

US T-BOND YIELDS

The first patient is healing, but his economic programs are ailing.

—*Time*, April 27, 1981

US COMMON STOCKS WITH NYSE VOLUME

US NEW HOMES WITH NEW HOME SALES

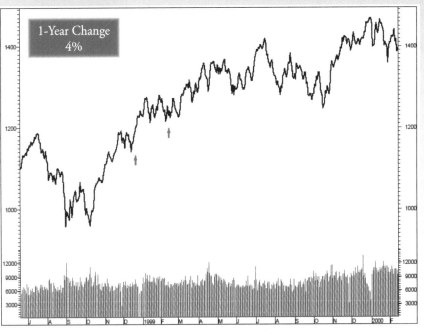

1-Year Change
4%

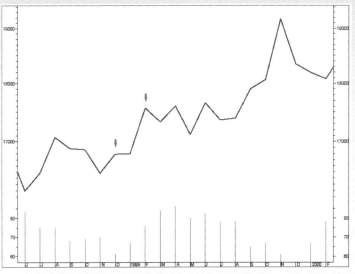

US T-BOND YIELDS

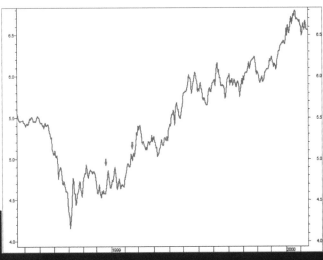

Elected men of the highest honor come out stained.

—Matthew Smith, *Bulls and Bears of New York*, 1875

BUSH/GORE ELECTION—2000

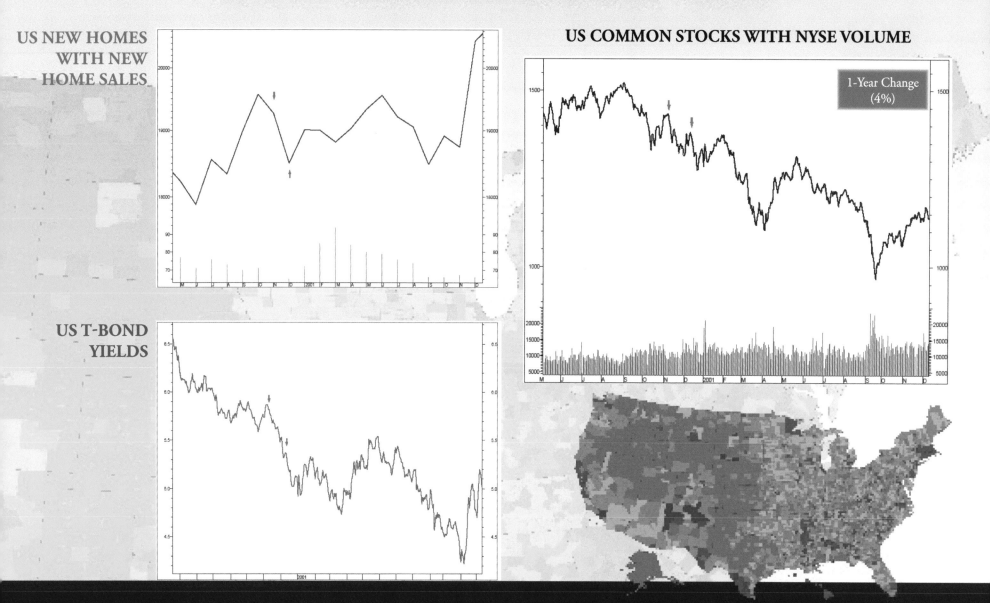

US NEW HOMES WITH NEW HOME SALES

US COMMON STOCKS WITH NYSE VOLUME

1-Year Change (4%)

US T-BOND YIELDS

A 1998 Report for the National Bureau of Standards recommends that punch card machines be eliminated due to frequent undervotes and recounting errors. Despite these warnings, states and localities did little or nothing; facing difficult budgetary choices, ensuring fair and accurate elections [were] viewed as less important than other priorities. At the same time, Congress took no action.

—Conyers Congressional Report, August 20, 2001

MAN-MADE DISASTERS SUMMARY

SINGLE EVENTS	Date	Description (What is it? What did it do?)	Common Stocks							T-Bond (10-year)					Homes			Combined
			Price	1 Week After	% Chg	6 Months After	% Chg	1 Year After	% Chg	Yields	6 Months After	% Chg	1 Year After	% Chg	Prices	1 Year After	% Chg	% Chg
Sinking of SS *Central America* (1, 2)	September 11, 1857	Sank in hurricane off South Carolina en route to Wall Street with 15 tons of gold. Other Factor: Financial panic of 1857	1.5	na	na	1.5	0.0%	1.3	-10.1%	5.77	5.29	-8.3%	5.29	-8.3%	717	803	12.0%	1.9%
Lincoln Assassination (1, 2)	April 14, 1865	Shot in Washington, DC, theater and died next day, several members of Cabinet wounded, stock market closed more than a week. Other Factor: Civil War	2.6	na	na	2.9	9.1%	2.7	3.0%	5.59	5.59	0.0%	5.63	0.7%	972	1,200	23.5%	26.5%
Garfield Assassination (1, 2)	July 2, 1881	Shot in Washington, DC, railway station four months after taking office; died two months later.	5.3	na	na	4.9	-8.4%	4.6	-13.7%	3.39	3.39	0.0%	3.32	-2.1%	3,776	3,270	-13.4%	-27.1%
McKinley Assassination (2)	September 6, 1901	Shot in Buffalo, NY, at Pan-American Exposition, died 8 days later.	6.4	6.2	-2.8%	5.7	-10.2%	5.8	-8.9%	2.92	2.87	-1.7%	3.03	3.8%	2,174	2,453	12.8%	3.9%
Titanic Sinking (2)	April 15, 1912	Luxury ocean liner sank after hitting iceberg in North Atlantic; 1,517 people died (including many prominent business people).	7.8	7.8	-0.4%	8.1	4.1%	7.1	-9.0%	3.51	3.52	0.3%	3.52	0.3%	2,332	2,676	14.8%	5.7%
Wall Street Bombing (2)	September 16, 1920	Foreign anarchists plant bomb in horse-drawn wagon at lunchtime in New York financial district; 38 killed, 400 injured.	7.7	7.6	-0.4%	6.6	-14.1%	6.2	-19.2%	5.67	5.27	-7.1%	5.12	-9.7%	4,027	4,489	11.5%	-7.7%
Kennedy Assassination (2)	November 22, 1963	Shot and killed in Dallas, Texas; NYSE closed immediately.	71.6	72.3	0.9%	80.7	12.7%	86.0	20.1%	4.10	4.20	2.4%	4.18	2.0%	18,065	19,816	9.7%	29.8%
Reagan Assassination Attempt	March 30, 1981	Shot and critically wounded in Washington, DC	134.6	135.5	0.6%	116.7	-13.3%	112.3	-16.6%	13.22	15.84	19.8%	14.19	7.3%	74,150	75,450	1.8%	-14.9%
Space Shuttle Challenger Explosion	January 28, 1986	Spacecraft exploded shortly after launch, first astronauts killed since 1967.	206.4	211.8	2.6%	249.6	20.9%	275.4	33.4%	9.05	7.53	-16.8%	7.13	-21.2%	95,350	110,300	15.7%	49.1%
9/11 Attacks in NYC and Washington, DC	September 11, 2001	Islamic terrorists hijacked airplanes and crashed them into World Trade Center and Pentagon; 2,993 killed, 2,000 injured; NYSE closed for one week.	1092.6	1033.8	-5.4%	1168.2	6.9%	909.5	-16.8%	4.84	5.32	9.9%	4.07	-15.9%	190,600	196,400	3.0%	-13.7%
Space Shuttle Columbia Explosion	February 1, 2003	Spacecraft destroyed when re-entering earth's atmosphere. Other Factor: Al-Qaeda War	855.7	829.4	-3.1%	980.0	14.5%	1135.2	32.7%	4.00	4.44	11.0%	4.18	4.5%	205,950	235,800	14.5%	47.2%
		Average		-1.0%					-0.5%			0.9%		-3.5%			9.6%	9.1%

EXTENDED EVENTS	Date	Description (What is it? What did it do?)	Price	1 Week After	% Chg	6 Months After	% Chg	1 Year After	% Chg	Yields	6 Months After	% Chg	1 Year After	% Chg	Prices	1 Year After	% Chg	% Chg
1967 Oil Embargo	June 6 to September 1, 1967	OPEC limits oil supplies to Western countries supporting Israel in Six Day War. Other Factor: Vietnam War	89.79					93.7	4.3%	4.85			5.27	8.7%	24,327	22,270	-8.5%	-4.1%
Nixon Administration Scandals (Watergate)	June 15, 1972 to August 9 1974	Worst political scandal in US history; resignation of both president and vice president in 1 year. Other Factors: Vietnam War, 1973 Oil Embargo	108.4					80.9	-25.4%	6.10			8.03	31.6%	27,779	37,919	36.5%	11.1%
1973 Oil Embargo	October 17, 1973 to March 17, 1974	OPEC halted all oil exports to countries militarily supporting Israel in the Yom Kippur War; oil prices rose from 75 cents to $12 a barrel. Other Factor: Vietnam War	110.2					98.1	-11.0%	6.82			7.23	6.0%	34,303	37,112	8.2%	-2.8%
President Clinton Impeachment Trial	December 19, 1998 to February 12, 1999	Impeached by the House, acquitted by the Senate on charges of perjury and obstruction of justice. Other Factor: Dot-com Bubble	1188.0					1230.1	3.5%	4.58			5.06	10.5%	164,800	175,700	6.6%	10.2%
2000 Presidential Election (Bush and Gore)	November 7 to December 12, 2000	Virtual tie in election required several vote recounts in Florida; Supreme Court stopped recounts and ruled in favor of Bush. Other Factor: Dot-com Bubble	1432.2					1371.2	-4.3%	5.87			5.36	-8.7%	195,700	185,050	-5.4%	-9.7%
		Average							-6.6%				9.6%				7.5%	0.9%

(1) Monthly Prices on Stocks — Best Performance
(2) Year-End Prices on Real Estate — Worst Performance

As the table shows, there have been various market reactions to these disasters. The common pattern is a knee-jerk correction averaging (1.0%), but within six months, stocks and real estate have appreciated well. The sinking of "gold ship" SS *Central America* with its fifteen tons of gold bound for Wall Street triggered the Panic of 1857. Of the presidential tragedies, the McKinley assassination caused the worst short-term damage to the stock market.

> It was considered indispensable by the (Gold Panic of 1869) conspirators, for the consummation of their plans, that President Grant should be got out of the way by some means or other. Fortunately for him, and the honor of the nation, the plan succeeded without the necessity of offering him any violence.
>
> —Henry Clews, *Twenty-Eight Years in Wall Street*, 1887

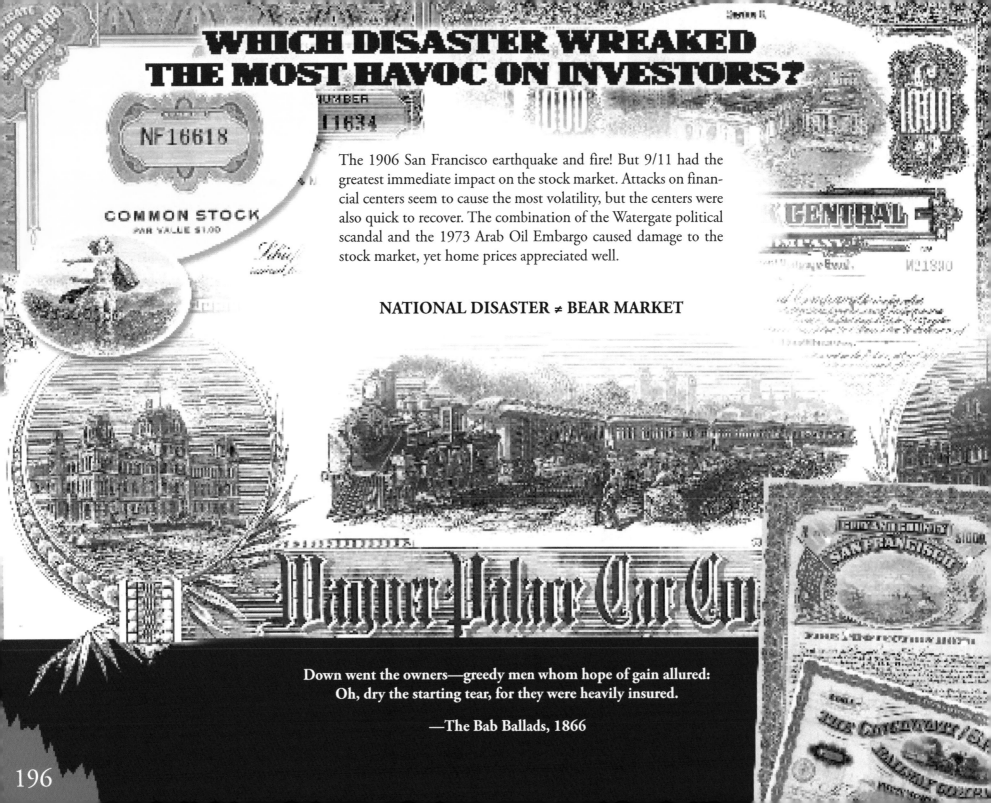

WHICH DISASTER WREAKED THE MOST HAVOC ON INVESTORS?

The 1906 San Francisco earthquake and fire! But 9/11 had the greatest immediate impact on the stock market. Attacks on financial centers seem to cause the most volatility, but the centers were also quick to recover. The combination of the Watergate political scandal and the 1973 Arab Oil Embargo caused damage to the stock market, yet home prices appreciated well.

NATIONAL DISASTER ≠ BEAR MARKET

Down went the owners—greedy men whom hope of gain allured:
Oh, dry the starting tear, for they were heavily insured.

—The Bab Ballads, 1866

AMERICA'S PEACEFUL ACHIEVEMENTS

PANAMA CANAL

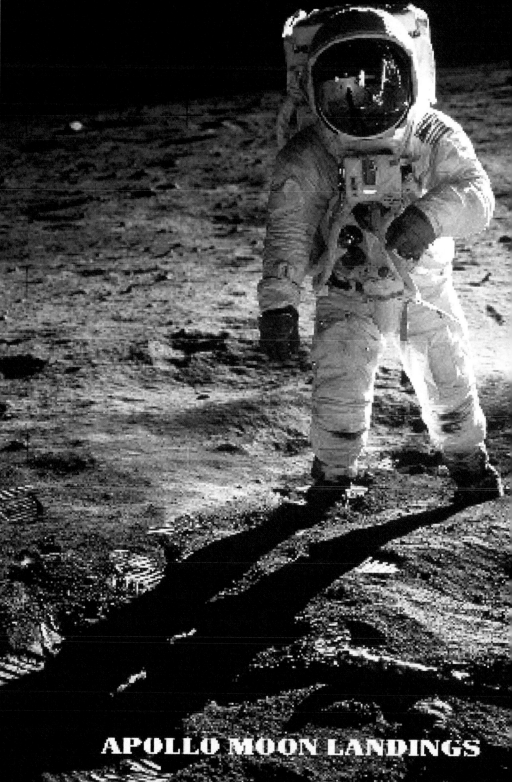

APOLLO MOON LANDINGS

TRANSCONTINENTAL RAILROAD
Completed May 10, 1869

Northern Pacific Railroad certificate
signed by J. P. Morgan (1883)

Railroad certificate signed
by Jay Gould (1869)

> The basis of all the discredit, the embarrassments, the bankruptcies, and the robberies of our railroad system is thus laid at the inception of the enterprises.
>
> —Henry Clews, *Twenty-Eight Years in Wall Street*, 1887

Important Facts

- Considered by many the greatest American technological feat of the nineteenth century, some 1,777 miles of railroad were built through the Rocky Mountains and the Sierra Nevada.
- A national high-speed transportation system was created that accelerated the economic development, population growth, and military security of the American West.
- A scandal surrounded the awarding of $23 million of overbilled work.
- Estimated cost was $106 million (more than $500 billion in today's dollars).
- 38,000 acres of public land granted to Central Pacific and Union Pacific railroads.
- Other event—Fisk-Gould gold market scandal.

Investment Performance

	Price	% Chg 6 months	% Chg 1 year
Common Stocks ($)	$3.66	(6%)	2%
T-Bond Interest Rates (%)	5%	3%	3%
New Homes ($)	$1,380	na	(9%)

US COMMON STOCKS

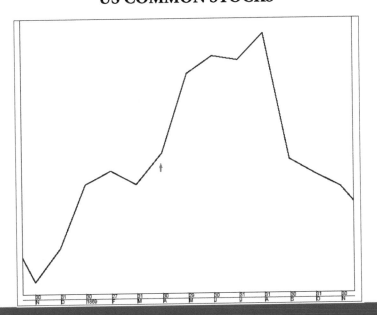

US NEW HOME PRICES

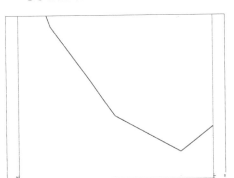

US T-BOND YIELDS

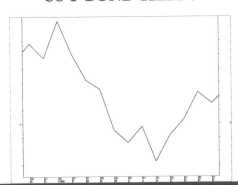

The Crédit Mobilier scam was born out of a simple reality: in the 1860s, the US government wanted a transcontinental railroad more than investors did. While a railroad across the Rockies had a glorious air to it, the project also carried an enormous amount of risk, and risk is generally something investors prefer to avoid.

—*New Yorker* magazine, 2003

PANAMA CANAL—Completed August 15, 1914

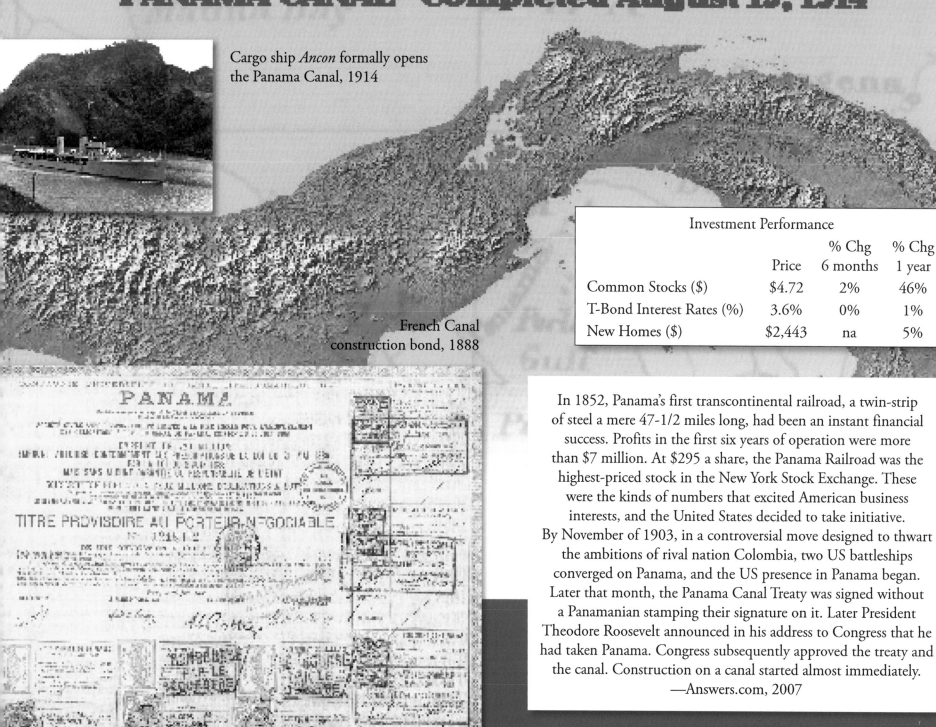

Cargo ship *Ancon* formally opens the Panama Canal, 1914

French Canal construction bond, 1888

Investment Performance			
	Price	% Chg 6 months	% Chg 1 year
Common Stocks ($)	$4.72	2%	46%
T-Bond Interest Rates (%)	3.6%	0%	1%
New Homes ($)	$2,443	na	5%

In 1852, Panama's first transcontinental railroad, a twin-strip of steel a mere 47-1/2 miles long, had been an instant financial success. Profits in the first six years of operation were more than $7 million. At $295 a share, the Panama Railroad was the highest-priced stock in the New York Stock Exchange. These were the kinds of numbers that excited American business interests, and the United States decided to take initiative.

By November of 1903, in a controversial move designed to thwart the ambitions of rival nation Colombia, two US battleships converged on Panama, and the US presence in Panama began. Later that month, the Panama Canal Treaty was signed without a Panamanian stamping their signature on it. Later President Theodore Roosevelt announced in his address to Congress that he had taken Panama. Congress subsequently approved the treaty and the canal. Construction on a canal started almost immediately.

—Answers.com, 2007

US COMMON STOCKS WITH NYSE VOLUME

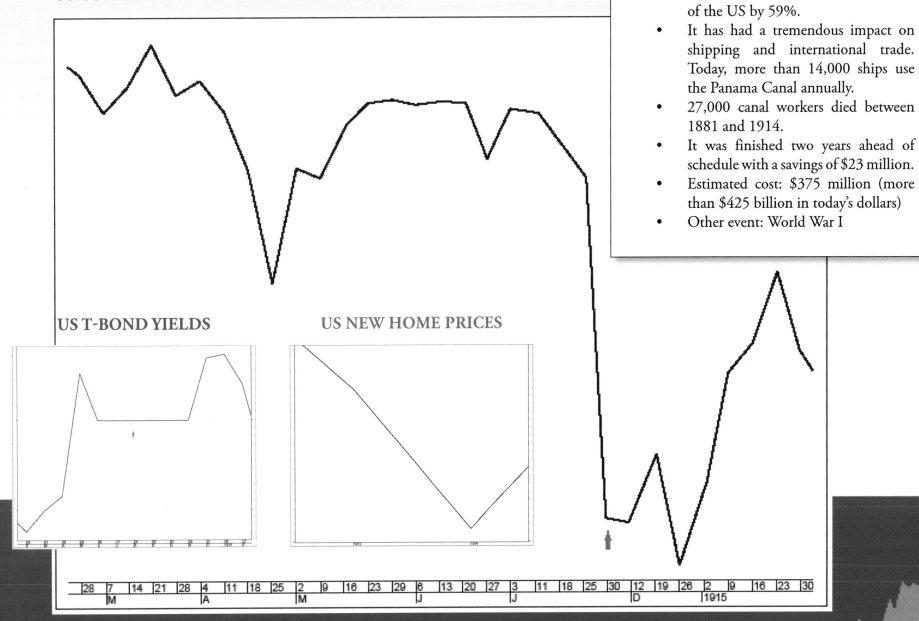

US T-BOND YIELDS

US NEW HOME PRICES

Important Facts

- Called the Big Ditch, this canal connected the Atlantic and Pacific Oceans and cut the distance needed to sail from the East Coast to the West Coast of the US by 59%.
- It has had a tremendous impact on shipping and international trade. Today, more than 14,000 ships use the Panama Canal annually.
- 27,000 canal workers died between 1881 and 1914.
- It was finished two years ahead of schedule with a savings of $23 million.
- Estimated cost: $375 million (more than $425 billion in today's dollars)
- Other event: World War I

28	7	14	21	28	4	11	18	25	2	9	16	23	29	6	13	20	27	3	11	18	25	30	12	19	26	2	9	16	23	30
	M				A				M					J				J					D			1915				

HOOVER DAM — Completed October 26, 1936

When the bills are paid and the turbines begin to produce electricity, the 'Six Companies' group will have turned a profit estimated at $7,000,000 and upward for all their work. This profit, which must be understood as a highly unofficial estimate, is the insurance premium the US pays for efficiency. If the contractors spent all their money, botched the job, and went broke, the government might have to finish the dam to the tune of a great many millions. The US is willing to pay a good profit for a good dam built rapidly.

—*Fortune* magazine, September 1933

US T-BOND YIELDS

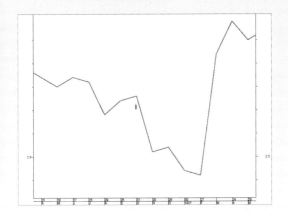

US NEW HOME PRICES

US COMMON STOCKS
with NYSE volume

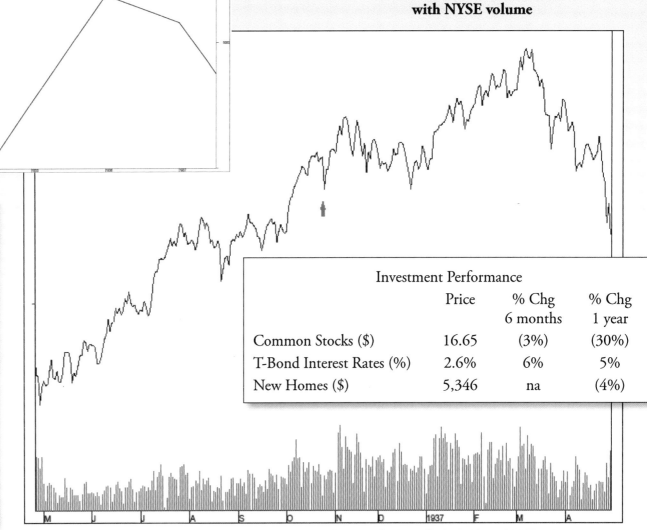

Important Facts

- At 726 feet tall, it was the largest dam in the US of its time. It provides electric power, water storage, and flood control of the Colorado River for the Southwestern states. It provides a significant amount of Southern California's electric needs.
- It was finished two years ahead of schedule.
- Estimated cost: $49 million (more than $676 million in today's dollars)
- Other event: Great Depression

Investment Performance			
	Price	% Chg 6 months	% Chg 1 year
Common Stocks ($)	16.65	(3%)	(30%)
T-Bond Interest Rates (%)	2.6%	6%	5%
New Homes ($)	5,346	na	(4%)

Hoover's response to the stock market crash was to try and temper the effects of the financial panic on other sectors of the economy. This would be done primarily through the cooperation between business and labor, with the assistance of federal and local governments. These efforts were largely based on his experiences with the depression of 1921. In January, Hoover instituted a vigorous public works program which authorized $60 million to begin construction of the Hoover Dam, $75 million for road construction, and $500 million for public buildings.

—Presidentialtimeline.org, 2007

GOLDEN GATE BRIDGE—Opened May 27, 1937

Bond used to pay for
Golden Gate Bridge, 1933

The construction budget at the time of voter approval was $30.1 million. However, the Golden Gate Bridge and Highway District was unable to sell the bonds until 1932, when the founder of San Francisco based Bank of America agreed on behalf of his bank to buy the entire project in order to help the local economy. The last of the construction bonds were retired in 1971, with $35 million and $38 million in interest payments financed only from bridge tolls.

—Wikipedia.com, 2007

US COMMON STOCKS WITH NYSE VOLUME

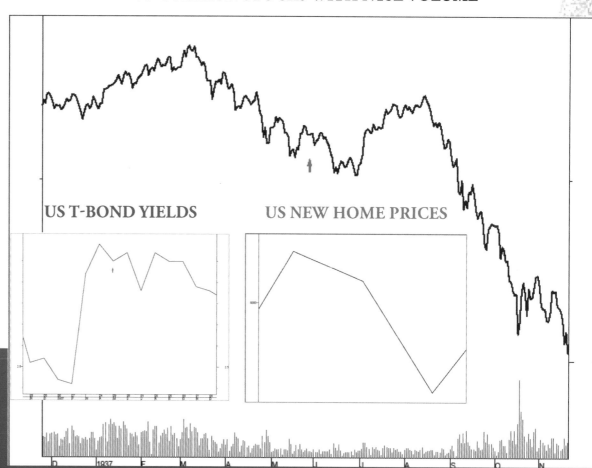

US T-BOND YIELDS   US NEW HOME PRICES

Investment Performance			
	Price	% Chg 6 months	% Chg 1 year
Common Stocks ($)	16.26	(34%)	(43%)
T-Bond Interest Rates (%)	2.8%	(2%)	(9%)
New Homes ($)	5,341	na	(4%)

Important Facts

- The Golden Gate Bridge was the longest suspension bridge of its time.
- With 40 million cars crossing annually, it is an important traffic artery for America's financial center of the West.
- Completed $1.3 million under budget.
- Estimated cost: $35 million (more than $483 million in today's dollars)
- Other event: Great Depression

GOLDEN GATE BRIDGE
MAIN SPAN
4200 FEET

APOLLO 11 MOON LANDING – July 20, 1969

Investment Performance	Price	% Chg 6 months	% Chg 1 year
Common Stocks ($)	93.52	(4%)	(17%)
T-Bond Interest Rates (%)	6.7%	16%	12%
New Homes ($)	27,541	na	(15%)

US T-BOND YIELDS

US NEW HOME PRICES

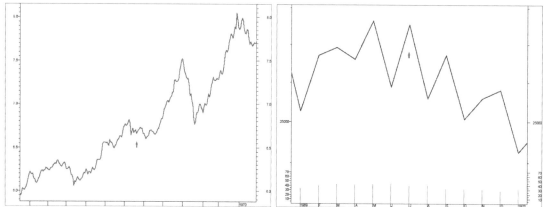

US COMMON STOCKS
with NYSE volume

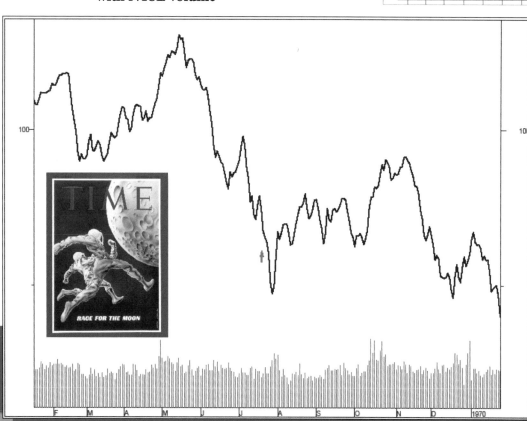

Important Facts

- It was the first of six lunar landings, a record achieved only by the US.
- It helped jump-start a new age of technological innovation. Thousands of products and processes were developed during the Mercury, Gemini, and Apollo space programs.
- NYSE closed on July 21, 1969, for National Day of Participation for Lunar Exploration.
- Kennedy's goal was exceeded with two moon landings by the end of 1969.
- Estimated cost: $25 billion (more than $135 billion in today's dollars)
- Other event: Vietnam War

When John Kennedy first fixed US sights on the moon in 1961, he recognized it as a project of giant technological and economic proportions.

—*Newsweek*, July 7, 1969

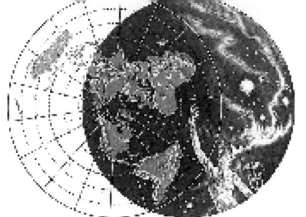

IBM-made computers and components were used on all US spacecraft.

INTERNATIONAL BUSINESS MACHINES CORPORATION

For the past eight days the world has thrilled to the Apollo mission. The moon landing, whatever doubts about it linger, has injected a sense of achievement into a species of late notably bereft of that gift.

—*The Wall Street Journal*, July 26, 1969

COLD WAR ENDED – December 31, 1991

Just days after the dissolution of the Soviet Union, Boris Yeltsin resolved to embark on a program of radical economic reform, with the aim of restructuring Russia's economic system—converting the world's largest socialist planned economy into a market-oriented capitalist one.

—Wikipedia.com, 2007

Important Facts

- The forty-four-year nuclear stand-off between the United States and the USSR ended peacefully with the Soviet Union dissolving into many countries and politically switching to a democratic structure.
- Largest benefits: many military technologies transferred to private sector, large increases in worldwide trade between former adversaries, and the world economy primarily functioning by free-market capitalism.
- Estimated cost: $8 trillion
- Other event: recession

US NEW HOME PRICES

US COMMON STOCKS
with NYSE volume

US T-BOND YIELDS

We didn't win the Cold War, we were just a big bank that bankrupted a smaller bank because we had an arms race that wiped the Russians out.

—Norman Mailer, journalist, 1996

The Cold War was fought at a tremendous cost globally over the course of more than four decades. It cost the US up to $8 trillion in military expenditures, and the lives of nearly 100,000 Americans.

—Wikipedia.com, 2007

Investment Performance			
	Price	% Chg 6 months	% Chg 1 year
Common Stocks ($)	417.1	(2%)	5%
T-Bond Interest Rates (%)	6.7%	6%	0%
New Homes ($)	132,500	na	3%

USSR government bond, early 1980s

Map of Iron Curtain

Berlin Wall, photo by NATO

PEACEFUL ACHIEVEMENTS SUMMARY

The achievements listed below rank among the world's great accomplishments and America's mark on history. Though many of these endeavors were greeted by roaring crowds and ticker tape parades, stocks declined for six months following these events within an environment of raising interest rates and a mixed real estate market.

Sometimes the market's inverted logic is hard to understand. Take the years 1968 and 1969 and how investment markets reacted to them. By any measure, 1968 was a terrible year, with nationwide riots, political assassinations, and the realization that America was going to lose a war for the first time. Editorials of the time expressed the belief that our country was going to rip itself apart. Yet through this turbulence, stocks and real estate increased 8% and 19% that year.

With a new popular president, the first troop withdrawals from Vietnam, and the crowning achievement of exceeding Kennedy's goal of "landing a man on the moon before this decade is out," one would have thought that an improved American mood in 1969 would have translated into investment profits. Not the case! Both stocks and new homes suffered large losses and interest rates increased to 27%.

Investors need to remember that history has repeatedly shown that what makes the cover of a magazine or a website's homepage isn't necessarily important to the financial markets.

EVENTS	DATE	DESCRIPTION (What is it? What did it do?)	Common Stocks										T-Bond						Real Estate		
			Price	1 week After	% Chg	6 months Before	% Chg	6 months After	% Chg	1 Year After	% Chg	% Rates	6 months Before	% Chg	6 months After	% Chg	1 Year After	% Chg	Prices	1 Year After	% Chg
Transcontinental Railroad Completed	5/10/1869	1,777 miles of railroad through West's mountain ranges linked all of the US Considered by many the greatest technological feat of the 19th century. Other Factor: Fisk-Gould gold market scandal	3.66	na		3.26	-11%	3.44	-6%	3.72	2%	4.98	5.29	6%	5.12	3%	5.14	3%	1,380	1,254	-9%
Panama Canal Opens	8/15/1914	A 48-mile canal through Panama connected the Atlantic and Pacific Oceans and reduced the distance needed to travel from the East Coast to the West Coast of the US by 59%. Other Factor: World War I	4.72	na		5.34	-12%	4.81	2%	6.88	46%	3.60	3.61	0%	3.60	0%	3.62	1%	2,443	2,560	5%
Hoover Dam Opens	10/26/1936	One of the largest dams in the US A major factor for electric power, water storage, and flood control of the Colorado River for the fast-growing Southwestern states. Other Factor: Great Depression	16.65	17.17	3%	14.25	-14%	16.16	-3%	11.74	-30%	2.63	2.67	2%	2.79	6%	2.75	5%	5,346	5,144	-4%
Golden Gate Bridge Opens	5/27/1937	This bridge over San Francisco Bay was the longest suspension bridge of its time. It is an important traffic artery for America's financial center of the West. Other Factor: Great Depression	16.26	15.96	-2%	17.34	7%	10.67	-34%	9.28	-43%	2.75	2.51	-9%	2.69	-2%	2.51	-9%	5,341	5,144	-4%
Apollo 11 Moon Landing	7/20/1969	The first of six landings on the moon by human beings. It is widely recognized as one of the defining moments in human history. Other Factor: Vietnam War	93.52	90.21	-4%	101.69	9%	89.83	-4%	77.78	-17%	6.66	5.95	-11%	7.72	16%	7.45	12%	27,541	23,535	-15%
Cold War Ends	12/31/1991	The 44-year nuclear weapons standoff with the USSR ended peacefully with the Communist Soviet Union dissolving and placing most of the world under a free-market economy. Other Factor: Recession	417.10	418.00	0%	371.20	-11%	408.10	-2%	435.71	5%	6.71	8.26	23%	7.14	6%	6.68	-0%	132,500	136,100	3%
HISTORY SUMMARY Best and Worst of Times!	1968 and 1969	1968: Tet Offensive (lost Vietnam War), assassination of Dr. Martin Luther King Jr. and Robert F. Kennedy	96.47							103.86	8%	5.70					6.21	9%	22,784	27,224	20%
		1969: Popular new president, troop withdrawals begin, exceed nation's moon landing goal	103.86							92.06	-11%	6.21					7.88	27%	27,224	25,801	-5%

Best Performance
Worst Performance

TICKER TAPE PARADE ≠ BULL MARKET

INVESTING THE HISTORICAL WAY

My advice to investors who cannot give full time to a study of investments is to seek out some trusted Investment Counselor.

—Bernard Baruch (1870–1965), famous financier and investor

The focus of this book has been on the "big picture" of investing. This section focuses on putting this knowledge to work regardless of differing philosophies of investment selection (fundamental, technical, growth, value, etc.). In other words, the items discussed in the following pages are required for you to be a successful user of investment history, not a victim of it in the future!

Like an iceberg, the tip of investing is simply placing a buy or sell order. The real size and scale of the investment process should be a logical, consistent strategy tailor-made for the individual investor, which governs what, when, and how much to invest under a given set of historical circumstances.

A solid investment strategy requires the following:

Ken Winans, putting history to work in 1997!

SET REALISTIC GOALS and SENSIBLE ASSET ALLOCATIONS

A good investment strategy will likely lead to profitable, long-term results. This requires establishing and adhering to a realistic performance goal based on historical facts. The performance goal should be a verifiable number and is the foundation on which all portfolio decisions will be made in the years to come.

Unfortunately, after the investment goal is established, it is often misunderstood. This target represents a statically relevant path to profitability over a predetermined period of time. It is not a guarantee of financial success each and every year. As a twenty-five-year veteran of money management, I have witnessed impatient people (who call themselves long-term investors) blindly misuse the performance of market indices in quarterly head-to-head comparisons with their investments and then rapidly make portfolio changes like it is some kind of horse race with the market.

Look at table A. It provides average annual returns for seven types of investments through five time periods dating back to 1900. The statistics are compiled from different sources using various calculation methods to insure accuracy.

This data gives a complete picture of investment performance and is important in getting a realistic assessment of future investment performance. The discipline to set realistic investment goals is truly what separates the successful investor from an individual who randomly buys investments based on dinner party tips (yes, people really do this!).

Time Frame Used for Goal Setting—Assuming no major changes in an investor's finances, it is common practice to set investment goals for a five- to ten-year time horizon. Realistically, most investors don't know enough about their future finances to establish a meaningful investment strategy beyond five years. This means that an investor who invests over the next twenty-five years will have five different five-year investment strategies. Like a long journey, where adjustments are made for direction and speed as more information is gathered during the trip, each new goal incorporates the success or failure of the previous investment campaigns.

TABLE A

Performance Summary Table								
Average Annual Returns	**1900**	**1960**	**1990**	**2000**	**2010**	**Average**	**Negative Years**	**Consecutive Negative Years**
Growth Investments								
US Common Stocks	12.0%	11.0%	10.9%	6.8%	13.9%	**10.9%**	**29%**	**8%**
US Homes (100% Owned)	5.2%	5.9%	3.5%	3.9%	5.2%	**4.7%**	**30%**	**13%**
Commodities	2.8%	2.2%	0.8%	1.7%	-2.5%	**1.0%**	**47%**	**22%**
Income Investments								
US Preferred Stocks	7.7%	10.2%	10.3%	9.7%	10.5%	**9.7%**	**23%**	**7%**
US Corporate Bonds	6.2%	7.9%	7.0%	6.1%	4.9%	**6.4%**	**19%**	**4%**
Interest and Inflation Rates								
10-Year T-Bonds	4.6%	6.1%	4.6%	3.6%	2.5%	**4.3%**		
10-Month T-Bills	5.1%	4.8%	2.9%	1.8%	0.3%	**3.0%**		
Inflation Rate	3.0%	3.8%	2.5%	2.2%	1.5%	**2.6%**		

Setting a Performance Goal—One way to establish long-term performance goals is to take an investment's average return from different periods of time. For example, table A shows the total returns of US common stocks over five different time frames. By simply taking the average return, a reasonable five-year benchmark for common stocks would be an average annual return of 10.9% (55% for a five-year total).

Asset Allocation (a.k.a. investment mix or diversification)—Table B shows performance projections based on different percentages of stocks and corporate bonds in three different portfolios. An investor with $500,000 to invest faces several choices.

Growth (100% in common stocks)
- A 92% chance of achieving the 10.9% historical average return
- $52,000 in annual projected profits
  - $42,000 in capital gains
  - $10,000 in dividend income

Balanced (50% stocks and 50% corporate bonds)
- A 94% chance of achieving an 8.6% average annual return
- $42,500 in projected profits
  - $26,200 in capital gains
  - $16,300 in bond interest and dividend income

TABLE B

Five-Year Portfolio Performance Goal Projections

Initial Investment $500,000				Annual Average		Cumulative Average		Success Probabilities		LT Capital Gains Tax	Oridinary Income Tax
Stock Investments				10.9%		52%		92%			
Bond Investments				6.4%		33%		96%		20%	35%
Stock Asset Allocation	Bond Asset Allocation	Stick Amount	Bond Amount	**Pre-Tax Portfolio Goal**	Portfolio Success Probabilities	Average Annual Return $	Capital Gains $	Income $		Capital Gains $	Income $
100%	0%	$500,000	$0	**10.9%**	92%	$52,000	$42,000	$10,000		$33,600	$6,500
50%	50%	$250,000	$250,000	**8.6%**	94%	$42,500	$26,200	$16,300		$20,960	$10,562
0%	100%	$0	$500,000	**6.4%**	96%	$32,500	$0	$32,500		$0	$21,125

Notes:
Investments bought 12/31 of the previous year
Any realized profits qualify for long-term capital gains
Probabilities are based on the % of time consecutive negative years occur since 1900

Income (100% in corporate bonds)
- • A 96% chance of achieving a 6.4% average annual return
- • $32,500 in annual projected profits
  - • $0 in capital gains
  - • $32,500 in bond interest income
- • All bonds purchased at par value and held to maturity

To the novice investor who simply looks at the highest projected return, the choice is simple: invest in 100% common stocks—full speed ahead!

Hold it! Other factors need to be considered to meet *all* of an investor's expectations.

Is greater certainty of return (i.e., lower volatility) wanted? Though it is common for the investment community to set an investor's asset allocation based mainly on age, an investor's personality and temperament have more to do with the investment mix of a portfolio than merely their seniority.

Many people, regardless of their education and background, simply can't handle high investment uncertainty and will panic and abandon a time-tested investment strategy at the first signs of trouble. US common stocks have consecutive negative years (i.e., serious bear markets) 8% of the time, which can devastate a stock portfolio by taking away years of profits. Bond investments (with predetermined interest payments, par values, and maturity dates) offer an attractive long-term investment choice to risk-averse investors. With few consecutive bad years, they have a 96% probability of meeting the investment goal.

What type of portfolio profit is needed? For investors who need to regularly withdraw funds from a portfolio, the type of investment profits is an important consideration.

In a portfolio 100% invested in stocks, most of the expected profits are in the form of capital gains that would require the selling of an investment or borrowing on margin for an investor to access the needed funds. Furthermore, because stocks historically have negative years 29% of the time, there would probably be instances when a stock investor would need to withdraw funds when his/her portfolio is at a temporary low point, thereby selling investments at less-than-opportune times. On the other hand, a bond portfolio's profits are in the form of income that comes in at regular, predictable intervals and can be accessed without changing the portfolio's holdings.

Are investment taxes important? Historically, the government has treated profits generated by investments differently, in that interest income is typically taxed at a higher level than gains realized by selling a profitable investment (as seen in table B).

This might require bonds to be kept in tax-deferred retirement accounts or use some of the time-tested techniques to minimize taxes, such as using municipal bonds, tax loss selling, bond swaps, and amortizing premiums.

Investment strategy and tax planning need to go hand in hand for the best investment results!

Finally, it can be said that there is no such thing as a single best goal and asset allocation! What is important is to set a course of action that the investor can follow with confidence. Without a realistic expectation of performance, there cannot be the discipline required to take profits in an "easy-money" bull market or aggressively purchase bargains during the financial carnage in a bear market.

EXECUTING THE INVESTMENT GAME PLAN

Once the five-year goal and asset allocation have been set, the job of constructing the portfolio begins.

Regardless of investment philosophy, investors must pay attention to the investment environment. This is the job of market analysis.

Buying new investments can be like trying to cross a busy intersection during rush hour in a new car you're not very familiar with: you need to pay real attention to the traffic signals to avoid an accident.

Market analysis has to answer one simple question: *is it a bull or bear market?* When to buy (or sell) can be as important as what to buy (or sell), and market analysis provides insight about the current investing climate and possible economic threats in the near future.

Patience isn't often discussed in the investment process because it doesn't generate fees and commissions. But it's important not to rush the construction of a portfolio when market conditions are not right and investment prices don't meet the investor's buy parameters.

Take corporate income investments. They can vary in availability and valuation, and it can take up to ninety days to finish the portfolio construction process during normal economic conditions.

An analogy I find most useful in describing the first year of owning an income portfolio is building a new apartment building: (1) You have to pay to have the building built before rental income is received (e.g., transaction costs, accrued interest, etc.). (2) It takes time to find good tenants, so the building is usually not 100% occupied when completed (i.e., availability of income investments to purchase). (3) Because tenants will move in at different times, they pay rent at different times and amounts based on type of rental agreement (i.e., income investments pay different amounts of interest and dividends at various times).

Keep in mind that the performance clock starts ticking *after* the portfolio construction phase, so don't start comparing the returns of a new portfolio to a goal until at least one full year after the portfolio is initially built or reconstructed!

Finally, investment discipline separates a truly successful investor from an individual who randomly puts in buy and sell orders based on dinner party tips. Remember that investing doesn't have to be all or nothing, so be fully invested when your market analysis tools give you a green light.

Cartoon, 1995

215

MONITORING AN INVESTMENT PORTFOLIO

Once a portfolio is constructed, it needs to be monitored and periodically evaluated. Reliable information is needed to properly monitor a portfolio. Unfortunately, today's investors have to deal with two significant problems:

- Information overload caused by a continuous stream of data that can be too short-term to be of any real use
- Despite an abundance of timely information on stocks and commodities, there is a lack of such information on various types of bonds, preferred stocks, collectibles, and even real estate.

So to properly monitor the health of a portfolio and evaluate its performance to the goals established, an investor has to obtain an investment report that answers the following questions:

General Issues
- Does it list the portfolio's five-year performance goal and provide the annual and cumulative returns to show whether the portfolio is on track with the established long-term goals?
- Does the report include all accounts the portfolio's assets are held in as well as all annual deposits and withdrawals made by the investor?
- Does it show the targeted asset allocation versus actual investment mix?
- Does it break down diversification by investment type (stocks, bonds, mutual funds), issuer, capitalization and industry, maturity, and agency ratings?
- Does it show position of original buy size versus the current size of each investment in the portfolio to measure individual investment exposure for rebalancing purposes?
- Does it list the total amount of transaction activity (for tax reporting)?

Bonds and Preferred Stocks
- Does it show market value versus maturity value of the bond investments?
- Does it show a schedule of maturity and call dates so that reinvestment of proceeds can be planned?
- Does it show average annual yield or yield to maturity for income estimation?

Leverage, Hedges, and Short Sales
- Does it show the amount of leverage and/or short sales being used and the level of interest being paid on the margin?
- Does it show what percentage of the portfolio's market value is being hedged and when the hedge expires?

Taxes and Costs
- Does it show the investor's annual taxes for income and capital gains?
- Does it show all portfolio-related costs (brokerage, advisory, sales loads, etc.) during the current year?

Remember, monitoring a portfolio involves more than simply checking the market value from a brokerage statement or website, and it is highly recommended that a portfolio be evaluated no more than quarterly and only when the investment markets are not open.

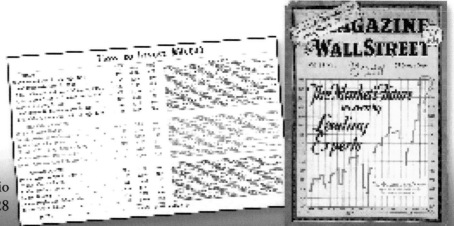

A recommended portfolio in a magazine of Wall Street, 1928

PORTFOLIO REBALANCING

Wall Street roller coaster
This can happen to any investment, anytime!

Investment portfolios are like plants in that they are constantly changing their size and shape. Growth is considered healthy, and there are times when they both need to be pruned to enhance future overall growth and prevent broken limbs from damaging the root system.

In the case of investment portfolios, periodic rebalancing involves selling part of a position that has grown much larger than the average-size investment and reinvesting the proceeds into other investments to restore proper diversification to the portfolio.

If a portfolio is being monitored properly, then the larger positions should be easy to spot on a report. Rebalancing can be done in a logical, systematic fashion. For example, when a stock position becomes twice the size of an average-size position in the portfolio, it is reduced in size by 50%.

The key objective is to keep the portfolio properly diversified and minimize the risk of large positions harming the performance of the overall portfolio. Rotation is also done for tax reasons at year-end. If investors need capital losses to offset capital gains, then investments currently showing a loss are sold, with new investments bought immediately.

Though it is common to identify investments as core holdings, every investment should have a high price in which an investor is willing to realize significant profits by selling a portion of the position. Love your friends and family, but don't love your investments! Does the chart on this page look familiar? We have all witnessed star-performing investments tank in bear markets, in which high levels of profit evaporate quickly. Rebalancing will help to prevent this from happening.

As a final note, the process of creating an investment strategy, executing that strategy, monitoring the portfolio's progress, and rebalancing to keep the portfolio diversified is time-intensive, continuous work. Due to the time and knowledge required, many investors have elected to retain the services of a money manager or investment advisor to oversee the investment process. But the investor still needs to be actively involved in the important process of setting a realistic goal and periodically reviewing the portfolio in light of that goal.

Simply put, investor participation is required to be successful.

FINAL THOUGHTS

This landmark reference book has been designed to help an investor build and maintain a strong foundation based on historical financial facts. An investor can refer to *Investment Atlas II* during a future calamity for clues to investment trends or to find out the performance record of various types of investments (stocks, real estate, bonds, commodities, collectibles, and cash) over the past two hundred years.

This book was broken into five sections:

There's Gold in Them Financial Hills!

This examined the spectacular growth of the US economy and major developments of investing that have allowed investors, big and small, to amass wealth at rates never seen before in world history.

Time-Tested Investments

Here we studied the basic characteristics of six different types of investments since 1800. Unlike many investment books that view only one type of investment in a vacuum, this section included stocks, real estate, bonds, commodities, collectibles, and cash in combined studies. It showed that investors must follow the historical trends to know the advantages and disadvantages of these investments over time.

Market Cycles: From Easy Money to Crash Landings

This section examined major bull and bear markets since 1850 and demonstrated how the tools outlined in the Time-Tested Investments section can provide the reader with early clues as to the market's overall health.

Historical Events: Does Wall Street Care?

We studied the reactions of stocks, housing, and interest rates to various factors and scenarios that have continuously confronted investors throughout history, such as wars, disasters (natural and man-made), and the never-ending government actions (i.e., interest rates, taxes, and regulations) in reaction to these situations.

Investing the Historical Way

This demonstrated ways to practically use historical information in establishing a disciplined investment strategy: (1) Set reasonable goals. (2) Effectively build a portfolio. (3) Use proper ways to monitor an investment portfolio's progress. (4) Use proper investment rebalancing to improve the performance of a portfolio.

As a final thought, this book has demonstrated the power of history and that investors' knowledge of history's trends can help them successfully navigate the investment world over time. But current events and economic cycles have a way of masking their historic roots, and investors suffering from hubris will once again claim that it's different this time during the next bull market. That is another historical fact we can count on!

Be a profitable user of investment history—not a future victim of it!

—Kenneth G. Winans, 2017

APPENDIXES

READERS NOTES

DISCLAIMER

Past performance should not be taken as representative of future results. Kenneth G. Winans will not be liable for any loss or damage caused by readers' reliance on the contents of this book, which is for informational and educational purposes only and should not be considered investment advice.

These investments are not suitable for everyone, and a professional advisor should be consulted about the merits of the investments listed in this book before investing.

The contents in this book were derived from data provided by third parties. While these sources are considered reliable, Kenneth G. Winans does not guarantee or warrant the accuracy, adequacy, or completeness of the data used in this book.

The formulas and calculations used in this book are considered reliable and cannot be guaranteed. Changes can be made without notice.

All tax information provided in this book is for informational purposes only. Anything tax-related should be discussed with your accountant before it is used for tax purposes.

The amounts, percentages, and any reference to individual securities are for illustration purposes only and do not reflect actual performance nor an endorsement of the company by Kenneth G. Winans.

Kenneth G. Winans and/or associates and/or employees may have an interest in the securities herein described and make purchases or sales of these securities without advance notice and at any time.

The opinions expressed in this book are solely of Kenneth G. Winans and not those of Winans Investments.

U.S. Common Stocks (Since 1865)

Year	Total Return	Total Return Index	Inflation Rate	Adjusted Total Return	Adjusted Return Index
		1.00			1.00
1865	-2.4%	0.98	3.7%	-6.1%	0.94
1866	10.4%	1.08	-2.6%	13.0%	1.06
1867	8.0%	1.16	-6.8%	14.8%	1.22
1868	17.3%	1.37	-3.9%	21.3%	1.48
1869	8.3%	1.48	-4.1%	12.4%	1.66
1870	12.2%	1.66	-4.3%	16.5%	1.93
1871	13.2%	1.88	-6.4%	19.5%	2.31
1872	13.0%	2.12	0.0%	13.0%	2.61
1873	-6.2%	1.99	-2.0%	-4.2%	2.50
1874	9.9%	2.19	-4.9%	14.8%	2.87
1875	2.5%	2.24	-3.7%	6.2%	3.05
1876	-11.2%	1.99	-2.3%	-9.0%	2.77
1877	-4.0%	1.91	-2.3%	-1.6%	2.73
1878	11.6%	2.13	-4.8%	16.4%	3.18
1879	48.6%	3.17	0.0%	48.6%	4.72
1880	23.8%	3.92	2.5%	21.3%	5.72
1881	8.2%	4.24	0.0%	8.2%	6.19
1882	2.5%	4.35	0.0%	2.5%	6.34
1883	-2.8%	4.23	-1.6%	-1.2%	6.27
1884	-12.8%	3.69	-2.5%	-10.4%	5.62
1885	25.5%	4.63	-1.7%	27.2%	7.15
1886	12.7%	5.21	-2.6%	15.3%	8.24
1887	-2.1%	5.10	0.9%	-2.9%	8.00
1888	1.8%	5.20	0.0%	1.8%	8.14
1889	7.7%	5.60	-2.6%	10.3%	8.99
1890	-9.4%	5.07	-1.8%	-7.6%	8.30
1891	21.6%	6.17	0.0%	21.6%	10.09
1892	6.2%	6.55	0.0%	6.2%	10.72
1893	-15.5%	5.54	-0.9%	-14.5%	9.16
1894	2.4%	5.67	-4.6%	7.0%	9.81
1895	5.0%	5.95	-1.9%	6.9%	10.49
1896	5.6%	6.28	0.0%	5.5%	11.07
1897	26.4%	7.95	-1.0%	27.4%	14.10
1898	26.6%	10.06	0.0%	26.6%	17.85
1899	12.7%	11.33	0.0%	12.7%	20.11
1900	11.9%	12.68	1.0%	10.9%	22.31
1901	-4.2%	12.15	1.0%	-5.2%	21.15
1902	3.7%	12.60	1.0%	2.7%	21.72
1903	-19.5%	10.14	2.9%	-22.4%	16.85
1904	46.3%	14.84	0.9%	45.4%	24.50
1905	42.1%	21.09	-0.9%	43.0%	35.05
1906	2.2%	21.55	1.9%	0.3%	35.15
1907	-33.1%	14.41	4.6%	-37.8%	21.88
1908	52.4%	21.96	-1.8%	54.2%	33.73
1909	19.9%	26.33	-1.8%	21.7%	41.04
1910	-13.2%	22.86	4.6%	-17.7%	33.76
1911	5.5%	24.12	0.0%	5.5%	35.61
1912	12.9%	27.22	2.6%	10.2%	39.26
1913	-5.1%	25.82	1.7%	-6.9%	36.57
1914	-3.6%	24.91	0.8%	-4.4%	34.96
1915	87.5%	46.69	0.8%	86.6%	65.25
1916	1.8%	47.54	7.4%	-5.6%	61.58
1917	-14.5%	40.64	17.7%	-32.2%	41.75
1918	18.4%	48.12	17.7%	0.8%	42.07
1919	37.3%	66.05	15.0%	22.3%	51.43
1920	-27.1%	48.15	15.9%	-43.0%	29.30
1921	19.2%	57.40	-10.8%	30.0%	38.10
1922	28.7%	73.90	-6.5%	35.3%	51.54
1923	2.7%	75.93	2.0%	0.7%	51.93
1924	32.4%	100.50	0.0%	32.4%	68.72
1925	35.7%	136.38	2.9%	32.8%	91.24
1926	5.8%	144.35	0.5%	5.4%	96.13
1927	34.6%	194.23	-1.4%	36.0%	130.71
1928	42.6%	277.07	-1.4%	44.1%	188.34
1929	-8.0%	254.88	0.0%	-8.0%	173.24
1930	-24.0%	193.75	-2.4%	-21.5%	135.92
1931	-42.0%	112.44	-9.0%	-33.0%	91.11
1932	-9.1%	102.15	-10.4%	1.3%	92.29
1933	52.8%	156.08	-4.9%	57.7%	145.54
1934	-1.6%	153.52	3.2%	-4.9%	138.45
1935	46.5%	224.85	2.5%	44.0%	199.32
1936	33.1%	299.33	1.2%	31.9%	262.91
1937	-34.0%	197.58	3.6%	-37.6%	164.05
1938	29.7%	256.29	-1.7%	31.5%	215.65
1939	-0.5%	255.14	-1.8%	1.3%	218.52
1940	-9.8%	230.16	1.2%	-11.0%	194.50
1941	-11.2%	204.46	4.8%	-15.9%	163.53

Year							Year					
1942	19.0%	243.37	10.8%	8.2%	176.98		1982	20.0%	19,790	6.2%	13.8%	2,386
1943	25.5%	305.54	6.2%	19.4%	211.31		1983	21.7%	24,080	3.2%	18.5%	2,827
1944	19.2%	364.19	1.5%	17.7%	248.81		1984	5.9%	25,501	4.4%	1.5%	2,870
1945	35.6%	493.93	2.4%	33.2%	331.52		1985	29.6%	33,043	3.5%	26.0%	3,617
1946	-8.0%	454.58	8.4%	-16.3%	277.36		1986	18.3%	39,105	1.9%	16.5%	4,214
1947	5.5%	479.58	14.6%	-9.1%	252.15		1987	5.4%	41,228	3.7%	1.8%	4,288
1948	5.6%	506.66	7.9%	-2.2%	246.54		1988	16.0%	47,825	4.1%	11.9%	4,798
1949	17.7%	596.15	-1.0%	18.7%	292.65		1989	30.5%	62,387	4.8%	25.6%	6,028
1950	29.9%	774.27	1.1%	28.8%	377.02		1990	-2.9%	60,604	5.4%	-8.2%	5,531
1951	23.0%	952.06	7.6%	15.3%	434.79		1991	28.7%	78,001	4.2%	24.5%	6,885
1952	17.6%	1,119	2.3%	15.3%	501.40		1992	7.5%	83,823	3.0%	4.5%	7,192
1953	-1.1%	1,107	1.0%	-2.1%	491.00		1993	9.6%	91,833	3.0%	6.6%	7,665
1954	51.1%	1,673	0.3%	50.8%	740.49		1994	1.4%	93,082	2.6%	-1.2%	7,570
1955	31.0%	2,191	-0.3%	31.3%	972.36		1995	36.6%	127,160	2.8%	33.9%	10,132
1956	6.5%	2,334	1.6%	5.0%	1,021		1996	22.4%	155,598	3.0%	19.4%	12,098
1957	-10.4%	2,091	3.4%	-13.8%	880		1997	32.7%	206,489	2.4%	30.4%	15,771
1958	42.3%	2,975	3.0%	39.3%	1,225		1998	28.3%	264,863	1.5%	26.8%	19,991
1959	11.8%	3,325	0.6%	11.2%	1,363		1999	20.4%	318,964	2.2%	18.2%	23,632
1960	0.4%	3,339	1.7%	-1.3%	1,345		2000	-9.6%	288,319	3.4%	-13.0%	20,563
1961	26.5%	4,225	1.1%	25.4%	1,687		2001	-11.8%	254,261	2.9%	-14.7%	17,546
1962	-8.7%	3,857	1.1%	-9.8%	1,521		2002	-21.5%	199,496	1.6%	-23.1%	13,489
1963	22.4%	4,721	1.1%	21.3%	1,845		2003	28.0%	255,337	2.0%	26.0%	16,997
1964	16.3%	5,489	1.4%	14.9%	2,119		2004	10.6%	282,437	3.5%	7.1%	18,203
1965	12.3%	6,162	1.6%	10.6%	2,345		2005	4.8%	295,891	3.5%	1.3%	18,440
1966	-10.0%	5,546	2.9%	-12.9%	2,042		2006	15.4%	341,395	2.0%	13.4%	20,912
1967	23.6%	6,855	2.8%	20.8%	2,466		2007	5.4%	359,728	4.0%	1.4%	21,199
1968	10.9%	7,599	4.3%	6.6%	2,629		2008	-35.3%	232,888	-0.0%	-35.2%	13,729
1969	-8.3%	6,971	5.3%	-13.6%	2,273		2009	26.2%	293,951	2.8%	23.4%	16,942
1970	3.6%	7,221	5.9%	-2.4%	2,219		2010	13.5%	333,575	1.4%	12.0%	18,982
1971	14.1%	8,239	4.3%	9.8%	2,436		2011	2.1%	340,681	3.0%	-0.9%	18,812
1972	18.7%	9,783	3.3%	15.4%	2,812		2012	15.6%	393,827	1.8%	13.8%	21,414
1973	-13.3%	8,485	6.2%	-19.5%	2,265		2013	31.5%	518,040	1.5%	30.0%	27,841
1974	-24.0%	6,446	11.1%	-35.1%	1,469		2014	13.3%	587,043	0.7%	12.6%	31,361
1975	36.2%	8,778	9.0%	27.2%	1,868		2015	1.5%	595,613	0.8%	0.7%	31,576
1976	23.7%	10,862	5.8%	18.0%	2,204		2016	11.5%	664,288	0.6%	10.9%	35,028
1977	-5.8%	10,232	6.6%	-12.4%	1,931		2017	21.2%	805,382	2.1%	19.1%	41,173
1978	7.0%	10,945	7.6%	-0.6%	1,919		**Average**	**11.1%**		**1.9%**	**9.2%**	
1979	18.5%	12,970	11.3%	7.2%	2,057		**Median**	**10.9%**		**1.6%**	**9.8%**	
1980	31.2%	17,012	13.5%	17.7%	2,421		**High**	**87.5%**		**17.7%**	**86.6%**	
1981	-3.0%	16,498	10.4%	-13.4%	2,097		**Low**	**-42.0%**		**-10.8%**	**-43.0%**	

U.S. Preferred Stocks (Since 1900)

Year	Total Return	Total Return Index	Inflation Rate	Adjusted Total Return	Adjustest Return Index
		1.00			1.00
1900	28.8%	1.29	1.0%	27.81%	1.28
1901	31.1%	1.69	1.0%	30.11%	1.66
1902	7.4%	1.81	1.0%	6.38%	1.77
1903	-11.1%	1.61	2.9%	-13.97%	1.52
1904	24.7%	2.01	0.9%	23.76%	1.88
1905	12.0%	2.25	-0.9%	12.93%	2.13
1906	-1.5%	2.22	1.9%	-3.43%	2.05
1907	-22.5%	1.72	4.6%	-27.09%	1.50
1908	37.3%	2.36	-1.8%	39.10%	2.08
1909	13.5%	2.68	-1.8%	15.33%	2.40
1910	-0.4%	2.67	4.6%	-5.04%	2.28
1911	6.7%	2.85	0.0%	6.74%	2.44
1912	5.9%	3.02	2.6%	3.28%	2.52
1913	2.6%	3.10	1.7%	0.94%	2.54
1914	6.8%	3.31	0.8%	5.99%	2.69
1915	12.8%	3.73	0.8%	11.94%	3.01
1916	7.8%	4.02	7.4%	0.41%	3.02
1917	-6.1%	3.78	17.7%	-23.75%	2.31
1918	13.9%	4.31	17.7%	-3.77%	2.22
1919	8.5%	4.67	15.0%	-6.50%	2.08
1920	-2.6%	4.55	15.9%	-18.50%	1.69
1921	15.0%	5.23	-10.8%	25.83%	2.13
1922	14.8%	6.01	-6.5%	21.38%	2.58
1923	3.7%	6.23	2.0%	1.70%	2.63
1924	9.4%	6.82	0.0%	9.42%	2.87
1925	8.3%	7.39	2.9%	5.35%	3.03
1926	9.0%	8.05	0.5%	8.53%	3.29
1927	10.6%	8.91	-1.4%	12.01%	3.68
1928	11.0%	9.89	-1.4%	12.47%	4.14
1929	6.1%	10.49	0.0%	6.12%	4.39
1930	5.6%	11.09	-2.4%	8.08%	4.75
1931	-10.8%	9.88	-9.0%	-1.85%	4.66
1932	8.4%	10.71	-10.4%	18.81%	5.54
1933	6.8%	11.44	-4.9%	11.75%	6.19
1934	22.5%	14.02	3.2%	19.31%	7.38
1935	17.0%	16.40	2.5%	14.47%	8.45
1936	8.1%	17.74	1.2%	6.92%	9.04
1937	0.0%	17.74	3.6%	-3.61%	8.71
1938	11.7%	19.81	-1.7%	13.44%	9.88
1939	5.1%	20.82	-1.8%	6.88%	10.56
1940	8.5%	22.59	1.2%	7.25%	11.33
1941	-1.3%	22.28	4.8%	-6.11%	10.64
1942	3.2%	22.99	10.8%	-7.60%	9.83
1943	6.1%	24.40	6.2%	-0.04%	9.82
1944	11.2%	27.14	1.5%	9.77%	10.78
1945	12.0%	30.39	2.4%	9.63%	11.82
1946	-1.5%	29.93	8.4%	-9.88%	10.65
1947	-4.6%	28.57	14.6%	-19.14%	8.61
1948	3.0%	29.44	7.9%	-4.82%	8.20
1949	11.2%	32.73	-1.0%	12.20%	9.20
1950	3.0%	33.71	1.1%	1.94%	9.38
1951	-6.1%	31.67	7.6%	-13.69%	8.09
1952	9.3%	34.61	2.3%	7.03%	8.66
1953	2.2%	35.36	1.0%	1.22%	8.77
1954	10.8%	39.18	0.3%	10.51%	9.69
1955	0.8%	39.49	-0.3%	1.08%	9.79
1956	-3.9%	37.94	1.6%	-5.47%	9.26
1957	4.5%	39.65	3.4%	1.11%	9.36
1958	0.2%	39.73	3.0%	-2.78%	9.10
1959	-1.2%	39.25	0.6%	-1.77%	8.94

1960	7.0%	42.00	1.7%	5.28%	9.41
1961	8.3%	45.51	1.1%	7.22%	10.09
1962	9.8%	49.98	1.1%	8.71%	10.97
1963	6.1%	53.01	1.1%	4.96%	11.52
1964	7.4%	56.94	1.4%	6.05%	12.21
1965	-2.0%	55.78	1.6%	-3.67%	11.76
1966	-9.8%	50.33	2.9%	-12.69%	10.27
1967	-6.6%	47.01	2.8%	-9.42%	9.30
1968	4.7%	49.24	4.3%	0.47%	9.35
1969	-10.1%	44.28	5.3%	-15.36%	7.91
1970	10.9%	49.11	5.9%	4.96%	8.30
1971	8.7%	53.40	4.3%	4.43%	8.67
1972	4.8%	55.95	3.3%	1.48%	8.80
1973	-5.4%	52.94	6.2%	-11.59%	7.78
1974	-3.0%	51.34	11.1%	-14.12%	6.68
1975	13.2%	58.12	9.0%	4.22%	6.96
1976	21.7%	70.74	5.8%	15.96%	8.07
1977	3.4%	73.14	6.6%	-3.23%	7.81
1978	-3.5%	70.60	7.6%	-11.07%	6.95
1979	-4.5%	67.41	11.3%	-15.80%	5.85
1980	-6.9%	62.73	13.5%	-20.42%	4.66
1981	7.2%	67.26	10.4%	-3.13%	4.51
1982	35.1%	90.84	6.2%	28.90%	5.81
1983	12.3%	102.03	3.2%	9.11%	6.34
1984	15.5%	117.81	4.4%	11.10%	7.05
1985	25.7%	148.08	3.5%	22.15%	8.61
1986	40.9%	208.65	1.9%	39.05%	11.97
1987	-1.9%	204.62	3.7%	-5.59%	11.30
1988	8.8%	222.64	4.1%	4.69%	11.83
1989	19.4%	265.82	4.8%	14.59%	13.56
1990	6.9%	284.21	5.4%	1.53%	13.76

1991	21.5%	345.45	4.2%	17.32%	16.15
1992	12.9%	389.97	3.0%	9.88%	17.74
1993	17.6%	458.46	3.0%	14.58%	20.33
1994	-9.5%	415.07	2.6%	-12.06%	17.88
1995	24.6%	517.33	2.8%	21.88%	21.79
1996	7.4%	555.37	3.0%	4.39%	22.74
1997	22.3%	679.07	2.4%	19.92%	27.28
1998	16.6%	791.54	1.5%	15.05%	31.38
1999	-8.5%	724.16	2.2%	-10.72%	28.02
2000	9.5%	793.24	3.4%	6.16%	29.74
2001	18.9%	943.01	2.9%	16.02%	34.51
2002	13.9%	1073.79	1.6%	12.29%	38.75
2003	16.8%	1253.74	2.0%	14.77%	44.47
2004	11.1%	1392.68	3.5%	7.56%	47.83
2005	2.0%	1420.14	3.5%	-1.49%	47.12
2006	8.6%	1541.90	2.0%	6.60%	50.23
2007	-11.0%	1371.93	4.0%	-15.02%	42.69
2008	-17.4%	1132.78	-0.0%	-17.41%	35.25
2009	38.9%	1573.53	2.8%	36.09%	47.98
2010	29.8%	2041.80	1.4%	28.32%	61.57
2011	6.3%	2170.51	3.0%	3.28%	63.59
2012	16.9%	2537.33	1.8%	15.13%	73.21
2013	-4.4%	2426.19	1.5%	-5.91%	68.88
2014	17.7%	2855.14	0.7%	17.00%	80.59
2015	6.4%	3040.00	0.8%	5.60%	85.19
2016	2.9%	3127.00	0.6%	2.27%	87.13
2017	8.3%	3387.00	2.1%	6.22%	92.55
Average	**7.7%**		**3.0%**	**4.7%**	
Median	**7.4%**		**2.6%**	**5.3%**	
High	**40.9%**		**17.7%**	**39.1%**	
Low	**-22.5%**		**-10.8%**	**-27.1%**	

225

U.S. Homes (Since 1865)

Year	Total Return	Total Return Index	Inflation Rate	Adjusted Total Return	Adjustest Return Index
		1.00			1.00
1865	23.5%	1.23	3.7%	19.76%	1.20
1866	26.3%	1.56	-2.6%	28.88%	1.54
1867	9.3%	1.705	-6.8%	16.11%	1.79
1868	-16.7%	1.42	-3.9%	-12.79%	1.56
1869	-9.1%	1.29	-4.1%	-5.04%	1.48
1870	-3.7%	1.24	-4.3%	0.52%	1.49
1871	5.6%	1.31	-6.4%	11.92%	1.67
1872	-10.4%	1.17	0.0%	-10.37%	1.50
1873	-33.4%	0.78	-2.0%	-31.32%	1.03
1874	23.8%	0.97	-4.9%	28.64%	1.32
1875	14.3%	1.11	-3.7%	17.98%	1.56
1876	5.5%	1.17	-2.3%	7.75%	1.68
1877	-21.2%	0.92	-2.3%	-18.88%	1.36
1878	66.0%	1.53	-4.8%	70.79%	2.33
1879	61.5%	2.47	0.0%	61.50%	3.76
1880	57.3%	3.88	2.5%	54.83%	5.82
1881	-13.4%	3.36	0.0%	-13.41%	5.04
1882	6.9%	3.60	0.0%	6.87%	5.39
1883	-27.4%	2.61	-1.6%	-25.81%	4.00
1884	-11.9%	2.30	-2.5%	-9.43%	3.62
1885	-6.8%	2.14	-1.7%	-5.07%	3.44
1886	14.8%	2.46	-2.6%	17.42%	4.04
1887	-13.5%	2.13	0.9%	-14.34%	3.46
1888	-21.3%	1.68	0.0%	-21.31%	2.72
1889	9.9%	1.84	-2.6%	12.51%	3.06
1890	5.7%	1.95	-1.8%	7.50%	3.29
1891	-6.2%	1.83	0.0%	-6.25%	3.08
1892	0.5%	1.83	0.0%	0.50%	3.10
1893	-1.0%	1.82	-0.9%	-0.03%	3.10
1894	8.7%	1.98	-4.6%	13.35%	3.51
1895	18.1%	2.33	-1.9%	20.01%	4.22
1896	-15.5%	1.97	0.0%	-15.54%	3.56
1897	10.0%	2.17	-1.0%	11.02%	3.95
1898	23.7%	2.68	0.0%	23.67%	4.89
1899	39.3%	3.74	0.0%	39.32%	6.81
1900	-29.4%	2.64	1.0%	-30.44%	4.74
1901	19.7%	3.15	1.0%	18.68%	5.62
1902	-29.1%	2.24	1.0%	-30.07%	3.93
1903	12.8%	2.52	2.9%	9.92%	4.32
1904	21.9%	3.08	0.9%	20.91%	5.23
1905	20.3%	3.70	-0.9%	21.24%	6.34
1906	-19.0%	3.00	1.9%	-20.88%	5.01
1907	-15.5%	2.53	4.6%	-20.11%	4.00
1908	-10.3%	2.27	-1.8%	-8.55%	3.66
1909	29.7%	2.95	-1.8%	31.51%	4.82
1910	-9.0%	2.68	4.6%	-13.60%	4.16
1911	-10.5%	2.40	0.0%	-10.52%	3.72
1912	14.8%	2.75	2.6%	12.12%	4.17
1913	-3.8%	2.65	1.7%	-5.48%	3.95
1914	-5.1%	2.51	0.8%	-5.97%	3.71
1915	4.8%	2.63	0.8%	3.96%	3.86
1916	12.5%	2.96	7.4%	5.02%	4.05
1917	-9.8%	2.67	17.7%	-27.49%	2.94
1918	-8.9%	2.43	17.7%	-26.58%	2.16
1919	36.4%	3.32	15.0%	21.41%	2.62
1920	24.8%	4.14	15.9%	8.89%	2.85
1921	11.5%	4.62	-10.8%	22.30%	3.49
1922	4.9%	4.85	-6.5%	11.49%	3.89
1923	4.9%	5.08	2.0%	2.86%	4.00
1924	-0.3%	5.07	0.0%	-0.29%	3.99
1925	3.1%	5.23	2.9%	0.21%	4.00
1926	20.1%	6.28	0.5%	19.58%	4.78
1927	4.8%	6.58	-1.4%	6.22%	5.07
1928	19.1%	7.83	-1.4%	20.51%	6.12
1929	-3.3%	7.57	0.0%	-3.33%	5.91
1930	-10.9%	6.74	-2.4%	-8.50%	5.41
1931	-10.4%	6.04	-9.0%	-1.36%	5.34
1932	-43.6%	3.41	-10.4%	-33.20%	3.56
1933	66.7%	5.68	-4.9%	71.60%	6.12
1934	-28.6%	4.06	3.2%	-31.80%	4.17
1935	16.7%	4.73	2.5%	14.17%	4.76
1936	16.2%	5.50	1.2%	15.02%	5.48
1937	-3.8%	5.29	3.6%	-7.39%	5.07
1938	-13.5%	4.58	-1.7%	-11.71%	4.48
1939	12.2%	5.14	-1.8%	14.00%	5.10
1940	-10.2%	4.62	1.2%	-11.37%	4.52
1941	-8.7%	4.21	4.8%	-13.49%	3.91

	1892	1893	1894	1895	1896	1897
			.58¾	.61½	.00⅝	.94
					55¾	.71¼
						.87⅝
						.71⅝
						.90¼
						.60⅝
						.97
						.64⅛
						.97⅞
						.08¾
						.83½
						.00⅝
						.79¾
						.68¼

Year					
1942	-1.5%	4.15	10.8%	-12.34%	3.43
1943	-9.4%	3.76	6.2%	-15.55%	2.90
1944	1.3%	3.81	1.5%	-0.19%	2.89
1945	-9.8%	3.43	2.4%	-12.19%	2.54
1946	22.9%	4.22	8.4%	14.52%	2.91
1947	20.7%	5.09	14.6%	6.11%	3.09
1948	26.3%	6.43	7.9%	18.43%	3.65
1949	14.9%	7.39	-1.0%	15.96%	4.24
1950	-13.9%	6.36	1.1%	-14.98%	3.60
1951	38.2%	8.79	7.6%	30.59%	4.71
1952	-5.0%	8.35	2.3%	-7.28%	4.36
1953	13.3%	9.46	1.0%	12.33%	4.90
1954	10.0%	10.41	0.3%	9.73%	5.38
1955	21.8%	12.68	-0.3%	22.09%	6.57
1956	15.9%	14.69	1.6%	14.30%	7.50
1957	8.4%	15.92	3.4%	4.99%	7.88
1958	-9.2%	14.45	3.0%	-12.20%	6.92
1959	2.1%	14.76	0.6%	1.54%	7.02
1960	14.6%	16.91	1.7%	12.84%	7.93
1961	5.8%	17.88	1.1%	4.63%	8.29
1962	7.4%	19.20	1.1%	6.26%	8.81
1963	2.9%	19.76	1.1%	1.79%	8.97
1964	12.3%	22.19	1.4%	10.94%	9.95
1965	-3.4%	21.44	1.6%	-4.99%	9.45
1966	6.9%	22.91	2.9%	3.94%	9.83
1967	2.3%	23.44	2.8%	-0.53%	9.78
1968	19.5%	28.01	4.3%	15.23%	11.26
1969	-5.2%	26.54	5.3%	-10.52%	10.08
1970	-11.2%	23.57	5.9%	-17.13%	8.35
1971	13.6%	26.77	4.3%	9.26%	9.13
1972	17.5%	31.46	3.3%	14.20%	10.42
1973	20.3%	37.85	6.2%	14.12%	11.89
1974	4.8%	39.68	11.1%	-6.29%	11.15
1975	14.1%	45.27	9.0%	5.11%	11.71
1976	9.7%	49.64	5.8%	3.91%	12.17
1977	14.3%	56.74	6.6%	7.68%	13.11
1978	15.4%	65.48	7.6%	7.82%	14.13
1979	5.3%	68.98	11.3%	-5.94%	13.29
1980	10.7%	76.34	13.5%	-2.82%	12.92
1981	1.9%	77.78	10.4%	-8.47%	11.82

Year					
1982	4.8%	81.48	6.2%	-1.40%	11.66
1983	5.8%	86.21	3.2%	2.60%	11.96
1984	4.2%	89.81	4.4%	-0.19%	11.94
1985	11.1%	99.79	3.5%	7.57%	12.84
1986	10.3%	110.03	1.9%	8.40%	13.92
1987	15.9%	127.57	3.7%	12.28%	15.63
1988	8.3%	138.22	4.1%	4.23%	16.29
1989	4.0%	143.78	4.8%	-0.79%	16.16
1990	0.3%	144.24	5.4%	-5.07%	15.34
1991	-5.5%	136.32	4.2%	-9.71%	13.85
1992	2.7%	140.02	3.0%	-0.29%	13.81
1993	-0.3%	139.61	3.0%	-3.27%	13.36
1994	8.5%	151.54	2.6%	5.95%	14.16
1995	3.3%	156.48	2.8%	0.50%	14.23
1996	4.1%	162.91	3.0%	1.15%	14.39
1997	1.6%	165.48	2.4%	-0.77%	14.28
1998	4.4%	172.74	1.5%	2.87%	14.69
1999	9.3%	188.73	2.2%	7.05%	15.73
2000	0.9%	190.38	3.4%	-2.51%	15.33
2001	10.5%	210.34	2.9%	7.62%	16.50
2002	6.5%	223.97	1.6%	4.90%	17.31
2003	3.3%	231.43	2.0%	1.34%	17.54
2004	14.2%	264.35	3.5%	10.71%	19.42
2005	2.9%	272.02	3.5%	-0.56%	19.31
2006	3.4%	281.17	2.0%	1.40%	19.58
2007	-11.0%	250.26	4.0%	-15.00%	16.64
2008	-3.79%	240.78	-0.0%	-3.77%	16.02
2009	-3.94%	231.30	2.8%	-6.75%	14.93
2010	6.39%	246.08	1.4%	4.95%	15.67
2011	-9.65%	222.33	3.0%	-12.68%	13.69
2012	15.78%	257.41	1.8%	14.01%	15.60
2013	7.03%	275.51	1.5%	5.50%	16.46
2014	13.21%	311.89	0.7%	12.53%	18.53
2015	-2.72%	293.34	0.8%	-3.49%	17.28
2016	10.00%	329.20	0.6%	9.40%	18.40
2017	1.58%	333.50	2.1%	-0.52%	18.10
Average	**5.2%**		**1.9%**	**3.3%**	
Median	**4.9%**		**1.6%**	**2.9%**	
High	**66.7%**		**17.7%**	**71.6%**	
Low	**-43.6%**		**-10.8%**	**-33.2%**	

U.S. Corporate Bonds (Since 1865)

Year	Total Return	Total Return Index	Inflation Rate	Adjusted Total Return	Adjustest Return Index
		1.00			1.00
1865	-3.3%	0.97	3.7%	-7.0%	0.93
1866	13.1%	1.09	-2.6%	15.6%	1.08
1867	8.0%	1.18	-6.8%	14.8%	1.23
1868	10.5%	1.30	-3.9%	14.4%	1.41
1869	4.5%	1.36	-4.1%	8.6%	1.53
1870	14.6%	1.56	-4.3%	18.8%	1.82
1871	11.9%	1.75	-6.4%	18.3%	2.16
1872	7.4%	1.88	0.0%	7.4%	2.32
1873	6.1%	1.99	-2.0%	8.2%	2.50
1874	15.0%	2.29	-4.9%	19.9%	3.00
1875	12.2%	2.57	-3.7%	15.8%	3.48
1876	9.3%	2.81	-2.3%	11.6%	3.88
1877	7.1%	3.01	-2.3%	9.4%	4.25
1878	7.2%	3.23	-4.8%	12.0%	4.76
1879	9.9%	3.55	0.0%	9.8%	5.22
1880	10.4%	3.92	2.5%	7.9%	5.64
1881	4.2%	4.08	0.0%	4.2%	5.88
1882	5.3%	4.30	0.0%	5.3%	6.18
1883	6.2%	4.56	-1.6%	7.8%	6.67
1884	4.9%	4.78	-2.5%	7.3%	7.16
1885	17.4%	5.62	-1.7%	19.1%	8.52
1886	8.1%	6.07	-2.6%	10.7%	9.43
1887	0.1%	6.07	0.9%	-0.8%	9.35
1888	7.6%	6.54	0.0%	7.6%	10.07
1889	5.5%	6.90	-2.6%	8.2%	10.89
1890	-1.1%	6.83	-1.8%	0.7%	10.97
1891	10.0%	7.51	0.0%	9.9%	12.06
1892	8.4%	8.13	0.0%	8.4%	13.08
1893	3.9%	8.45	-0.9%	4.8%	13.70
1894	11.0%	9.38	-4.6%	15.6%	15.84
1895	3.5%	9.71	-1.9%	5.5%	16.71
1896	3.2%	10.02	0.0%	3.2%	17.24
1897	10.8%	11.10	-1.0%	11.8%	19.27
1898	12.7%	12.52	0.0%	12.7%	21.73
1899	2.4%	12.82	0.0%	2.4%	22.25
1900	10.8%	14.20	1.0%	9.8%	24.43
1901	9.2%	15.50	1.0%	8.2%	26.42
1902	2.5%	15.89	1.0%	1.5%	26.82
1903	-4.5%	15.17	2.9%	-7.4%	24.83
1904	17.7%	17.85	0.9%	16.7%	28.98
1905	4.4%	18.65	-0.9%	5.4%	30.54
1906	2.3%	19.07	1.9%	0.4%	30.66
1907	-5.1%	18.10	4.6%	-9.7%	27.68
1908	15.3%	20.86	-1.8%	17.0%	32.40
1909	5.3%	21.96	-1.8%	7.1%	34.69
1910	2.7%	22.55	4.6%	-1.9%	34.02

1911	4.9%	23.66	0.0%	4.9%	35.70
1912	2.3%	24.20	2.6%	-0.3%	35.58
1913	-0.2%	24.16	1.7%	-1.9%	34.91
1914	-1.0%	23.92	0.8%	-1.8%	34.27
1915	12.9%	27.01	0.8%	12.1%	38.40
1916	6.1%	28.65	7.4%	-1.4%	37.88
1917	-7.7%	26.43	17.7%	-25.4%	28.25
1918	9.3%	28.88	17.7%	-8.4%	25.88
1919	-2.0%	28.29	15.0%	-17.0%	21.47
1920	0.0%	28.30	15.9%	-15.9%	18.06
1921	17.6%	33.29	-10.8%	28.4%	23.19
1922	11.9%	37.24	-6.5%	18.4%	27.46
1923	2.5%	38.17	2.0%	0.5%	27.60
1924	9.9%	41.95	0.0%	9.9%	30.33
1925	7.8%	45.23	2.9%	4.9%	31.81
1926	8.3%	49.00	0.5%	7.9%	34.31
1927	8.2%	53.00	-1.4%	9.6%	37.60
1928	1.3%	53.68	-1.4%	2.7%	38.62
1929	2.6%	55.05	0.0%	2.5%	39.60
1930	6.6%	58.67	-2.4%	9.0%	43.17
1931	-13.5%	50.76	-9.0%	-4.5%	41.24
1932	7.5%	54.56	-10.4%	17.9%	48.62
1933	17.9%	64.31	-4.9%	22.8%	59.70
1934	19.2%	76.67	3.2%	16.0%	69.25
1935	7.8%	82.66	2.5%	5.3%	72.93
1936	11.5%	92.17	1.2%	10.3%	80.43
1937	-8.0%	84.84	3.6%	-11.6%	71.13
1938	2.5%	86.97	-1.7%	4.3%	74.16
1939	5.1%	91.45	-1.8%	6.9%	79.29
1940	6.6%	97.49	1.2%	5.4%	83.58
1941	2.8%	100.20	4.8%	-2.0%	81.92
1942	8.7%	108.88	10.8%	-2.1%	80.17
1904	17.7%	17.85	0.9%	16.7%	28.98
1905	4.4%	18.65	-0.9%	5.4%	30.54
1906	2.3%	19.07	1.9%	0.4%	30.66
1907	-5.1%	18.10	4.6%	-9.7%	27.68
1908	15.3%	20.86	-1.8%	17.0%	32.40
1909	5.3%	21.96	-1.8%	7.1%	34.69
1910	2.7%	22.55	4.6%	-1.9%	34.02
1911	4.9%	23.66	0.0%	4.9%	35.70
1912	2.3%	24.20	2.6%	-0.3%	35.58
1913	-0.2%	24.16	1.7%	-1.9%	34.91
1914	-1.0%	23.92	0.8%	-1.8%	34.27
1915	12.9%	27.01	0.8%	12.1%	38.40
1916	6.1%	28.65	7.4%	-1.4%	37.88
1917	-7.7%	26.43	17.7%	-25.4%	28.25
1918	9.3%	28.88	17.7%	-8.4%	25.88
1919	-2.0%	28.29	15.0%	-17.0%	21.47
1920	0.0%	28.30	15.9%	-15.9%	18.06
1921	17.6%	33.29	-10.8%	28.4%	23.19

Year						Year					
1922	11.9%	37.24	-6.5%	18.4%	27.46	1972	8.5%	367.16	3.3%	5.2%	101.85
1923	2.5%	38.17	2.0%	0.5%	27.60	1973	2.0%	384.51	6.2%	-4.2%	100.35
1924	9.9%	41.95	0.0%	9.9%	30.33	1974	-2.9%	381.68	11.1%	-14.0%	88.46
1925	7.8%	45.23	2.9%	4.9%	31.81	1975	13.3%	436.43	9.0%	4.3%	93.21
1926	8.3%	49.00	0.5%	7.9%	34.31	1976	18.6%	544.08	5.8%	12.8%	110.84
1927	8.2%	53.00	-1.4%	9.6%	37.60	1977	7.0%	574.42	6.6%	0.4%	109.68
1928	1.3%	53.68	-1.4%	2.7%	38.62	1978	1.2%	581.38	7.6%	-6.4%	102.68
1929	2.6%	55.05	0.0%	2.5%	39.60	1979	0.7%	557.86	11.3%	-10.6%	86.95
1930	6.6%	58.67	-2.4%	9.0%	43.17	1980	-1.5%	545.29	13.5%	-15.0%	73.27
1931	-13.5%	50.76	-9.0%	-4.5%	41.24	1981	3.2%	559.17	10.4%	-7.1%	67.54
1932	7.5%	54.56	-10.4%	17.9%	48.62	1982	32.8%	774.28	6.2%	26.6%	89.36
1933	17.9%	64.31	-4.9%	22.8%	59.70	1983	12.7%	855.76	3.2%	9.5%	95.90
1934	19.2%	76.67	3.2%	16.0%	69.25	1984	15.9%	997.47	4.4%	11.6%	107.59
1935	7.8%	82.66	2.5%	5.3%	72.93	1985	24.0%	1,275	3.5%	20.5%	133.76
1936	11.5%	92.17	1.2%	10.3%	80.43	1986	17.9%	1,557	1.9%	16.1%	160.84
1937	-8.0%	84.84	3.6%	-11.6%	71.13	1987	4.4%	1,590	3.7%	0.8%	158.36
1938	2.5%	86.97	-1.7%	4.3%	74.16	1988	11.3%	1,789	4.1%	7.2%	171.59
1939	5.1%	91.45	-1.8%	6.9%	79.29	1989	15.3%	2,056	4.8%	10.5%	188.95
1940	6.6%	97.49	1.2%	5.4%	83.58	1990	6.8%	2,216	5.4%	1.4%	193.46
1941	2.8%	100.20	4.8%	-2.0%	81.92	1991	20.3%	2,604	4.2%	16.1%	219.22
1942	8.7%	108.88	10.8%	-2.1%	80.17	1992	11.0%	2,956	3.0%	8.0%	242.23
1943	12.2%	122.15	6.2%	6.0%	85.01	1993	14.3%	3,200	3.0%	11.4%	255.03
1944	13.1%	138.10	1.5%	11.6%	94.88	1994	-3.0%	3,065	2.6%	-5.6%	237.65
1945	6.5%	147.03	2.4%	4.1%	98.76	1995	22.2%	3,701	2.8%	19.4%	280.38
1946	-1.2%	145.25	8.4%	-9.6%	89.29	1996	3.8%	3,899	3.0%	0.8%	287.08
1947	-3.3%	140.39	14.6%	-17.9%	73.28	1997	11.7%	4,278	2.4%	9.3%	308.26
1948	6.0%	148.84	7.9%	-1.8%	71.93	1998	8.6%	4,690	1.5%	7.1%	333.30
1949	6.1%	157.95	-1.0%	7.2%	77.07	1999	-3.2%	4,538	2.2%	-5.5%	315.13
1950	5.0%	165.86	1.1%	4.0%	80.12	2000	8.3%	4,964	3.4%	4.9%	334.04
1951	-2.6%	161.51	7.6%	-10.3%	71.90	2001	12.8%	5,493	2.9%	9.9%	360.06
1952	5.8%	170.81	2.3%	3.5%	74.42	2002	15.2%	6,059	1.6%	13.6%	391.47
1953	1.9%	174.04	1.0%	0.9%	75.12	2003	11.9%	6,599	2.0%	9.9%	418.60
1954	7.3%	186.71	0.3%	7.0%	80.36	2004	10.6%	6,928	3.5%	7.1%	424.72
1955	0.4%	187.48	-0.3%	0.7%	80.93	2005	5.1%	6,985	3.5%	1.6%	413.50
1956	-5.2%	177.78	1.6%	-6.7%	75.49	2006	5.3%	7,207	2.0%	3.3%	418.50
1957	2.1%	181.52	3.4%	-1.3%	74.52	2007	6.3%	7,553	4.0%	2.3%	421.88
1958	3.2%	187.40	3.0%	0.3%	74.72	2008	-5.7%	7,491	-0.0%	-5.7%	418.52
1959	-1.5%	184.51	0.6%	-2.1%	73.13	2009	19.1%	8,869	2.8%	16.3%	483.73
1960	7.7%	203.76	1.7%	5.9%	79.50	2010	12.6%	9,487	1.4%	11.2%	510.46
1961	4.7%	211.77	1.1%	3.6%	81.73	2011	15.2%	10,076	3.0%	12.2%	526.71
1962	6.3%	232.76	1.1%	5.1%	88.91	2012	8.1%	11,053	1.8%	6.3%	568.48
1963	3.6%	245.67	1.1%	2.5%	92.87	2013	-3.3%	10,797	1.5%	-4.8%	546.59
1964	4.6%	260.49	1.4%	3.2%	97.20	2014	13.1%	11,576	0.7%	12.4%	582.36
1965	1.4%	264.62	1.6%	-0.2%	97.16	2015	-1.8%	11,522	0.8%	-2.5%	575.12
1966	-3.2%	258.88	2.9%	-6.1%	92.22	2016	7.9%	12,251	0.6%	7.3%	588.20
1967	-2.7%	253.79	2.8%	-5.5%	87.78	2017	8.2%	12,962	2.1%	6.1%	599.80
1968	4.5%	268.32	4.3%	0.3%	89.07	**Average**	**6.7%**		**2.2%**	**4.5%**	
1969	-2.5%	265.62	5.3%	-7.8%	83.46	**Median**	**6.6%**		**1.6%**	**5.4%**	
1970	12.5%	290.11	5.9%	6.6%	86.20	**High**	**32.8%**		**25.2%**	**28.4%**	
1971	13.3%	333.58	4.3%	9.0%	95.40	**Low**	**-13.5%**		**-10.8%**	**-25.4%**	

229

10-Year U.S. Treasury Bond Yields (Since 1865)

Year	Yield	Total Return Index	Inflation Rate	Adjusted Yield	Adjusted Return Index
		1.00			1.00
1865	5.59%	1.06	3.70%	1.89%	1.02
1866	5.38%	1.11	-2.55%	7.93%	1.10
1867	5.35%	1.17	-6.81%	12.16%	1.23
1868	5.24%	1.23	-3.93%	9.17%	1.35
1869	5.07%	1.30	-4.09%	9.16%	1.47
1870	5.30%	1.36	-4.27%	9.57%	1.61
1871	5.10%	1.43	-6.37%	11.47%	1.80
1872	5.39%	1.51	0.01%	5.38%	1.89
1873	5.39%	1.59	-2.04%	7.43%	2.04
1874	5.30%	1.68	-4.86%	10.16%	2.24
1875	5.11%	1.76	-3.65%	8.76%	2.44
1876	5.31%	1.86	-2.27%	7.58%	2.63
1877	5.44%	1.96	-2.33%	7.77%	2.83
1878	3.98%	2.04	-4.76%	8.74%	3.08
1879	3.88%	2.12	0.01%	3.87%	3.19
1880	3.57%	2.19	2.50%	1.07%	3.23
1881	3.39%	2.26	0.01%	3.38%	3.33
1882	3.33%	2.34	0.01%	3.32%	3.44
1883	3.22%	2.42	-1.63%	4.85%	3.61
1884	3.25%	2.49	-2.48%	5.73%	3.81
1885	3.23%	2.57	-1.69%	4.92%	4.00
1886	3.11%	2.65	-2.59%	5.70%	4.23
1887	3.19%	2.74	0.88%	2.31%	4.33
1888	3.12%	2.82	0.01%	3.11%	4.46
1889	3.14%	2.91	-2.63%	5.77%	4.72
1890	3.27%	3.01	-1.80%	5.07%	4.96
1891	3.40%	3.11	0.01%	3.39%	5.12
1892	3.53%	3.22	0.01%	3.52%	5.30
1893	3.49%	3.33	-0.92%	4.41%	5.53
1894	3.47%	3.45	-4.63%	8.10%	5.98
1895	3.33%	3.56	-1.94%	5.27%	6.29
1896	3.34%	3.68	0.01%	3.33%	6.50
1897	3.10%	3.80	-0.99%	4.09%	6.76
1898	3.12%	3.92	0.01%	3.11%	6.97
1899	2.99%	4.03	0.01%	2.98%	7.17
1900	2.95%	4.15	1.00%	1.95%	7.31
1901	2.90%	4.27	0.99%	1.91%	7.45
1902	2.86%	4.39	0.98%	1.88%	7.59
1903	2.95%	4.52	2.91%	0.04%	7.59
1904	2.98%	4.66	0.94%	2.04%	7.74
1905	3.05%	4.80	-0.93%	3.98%	8.05
1906	3.07%	4.95	1.89%	1.18%	8.15
1907	3.06%	5.10	4.63%	-1.57%	8.02
1908	3.38%	5.27	-1.77%	5.15%	8.43
1909	3.28%	5.44	-1.80%	5.08%	8.86
1910	3.45%	5.63	4.59%	-1.14%	8.76
1911	3.46%	5.83	0.01%	3.45%	9.06
1912	3.52%	6.03	2.63%	0.89%	9.14
1913	3.51%	6.24	1.71%	1.80%	9.31
1914	3.58%	6.47	0.84%	2.74%	9.56
1915	3.63%	6.70	0.83%	2.80%	9.83
1916	3.61%	6.95	7.44%	-3.83%	9.45
1917	3.61%	7.20	17.69%	-14.08%	8.12
1918	3.84%	7.47	17.65%	-13.81%	7.00
1919	3.75%	7.75	15.00%	-11.25%	6.21
1920	4.90%	8.13	15.94%	-11.04%	5.53
1921	5.40%	8.57	-10.83%	16.23%	6.42
1922	4.47%	8.95	-6.54%	11.01%	7.13
1923	4.32%	9.34	2.00%	2.32%	7.30
1924	4.35%	9.75	0.01%	4.34%	7.61
1925	3.96%	10.13	2.94%	1.02%	7.69
1926	3.80%	10.52	0.48%	3.32%	7.95
1927	3.56%	10.89	-1.42%	4.98%	8.34
1928	3.17%	11.24	-1.44%	4.61%	8.73
1929	3.45%	11.63	0.01%	3.44%	9.03
1930	3.36%	12.02	-2.44%	5.80%	9.55
1931	3.22%	12.40	-9.00%	12.22%	10.72
1932	3.93%	12.89	-10.44%	14.37%	12.26
1933	3.35%	13.32	-4.91%	8.26%	13.27
1934	3.53%	13.79	3.23%	0.30%	13.31
1935	2.99%	14.21	2.50%	0.49%	13.37
1936	2.82%	14.61	1.22%	1.60%	13.59
1937	2.52%	14.97	3.61%	-1.09%	13.44
1938	2.68%	15.38	-1.74%	4.42%	14.03
1939	2.48%	15.76	-1.78%	4.26%	14.63
1940	2.30%	16.12	1.20%	1.10%	14.79
1941	1.88%	16.42	4.76%	-2.88%	14.37

	1892	1893	1894	1895	1896	1897
			.58¾	.61¼	.00⅞	.94
				55⅜		.71¼
						.87⅞
						.71⅝
						.90¼
						.60⅝
						.97
						.61⅛
						.97⅞
						.68¼
						.89⅛
						.66⅜

1942	2.07%	16.76	10.80%	-8.73%	13.11
1943	2.11%	17.12	6.15%	-4.04%	12.65
1944	2.12%	17.48	1.45%	0.67%	12.74
1945	2.10%	17.85	2.38%	-0.28%	12.70
1946	1.67%	18.14	8.37%	-6.70%	11.85
1947	1.82%	18.47	14.59%	-12.77%	10.34
1948	2.18%	18.88	7.87%	-5.69%	9.75
1949	2.12%	19.28	-1.04%	3.16%	10.06
1950	1.80%	19.62	1.05%	0.75%	10.13
1951	2.18%	20.05	7.64%	-5.46%	9.58
1952	2.51%	20.56	2.26%	0.25%	9.60
1953	2.52%	21.07	0.95%	1.57%	9.75
1954	2.59%	21.62	0.31%	2.28%	9.98
1955	2.51%	22.16	-0.31%	2.82%	10.26
1956	2.96%	22.82	1.56%	1.40%	10.40
1957	3.59%	23.64	3.38%	0.21%	10.42
1958	3.21%	24.40	2.98%	0.23%	10.45
1959	3.86%	25.34	0.58%	3.28%	10.79
1960	4.69%	26.53	1.72%	2.97%	11.11
1961	3.84%	27.54	1.13%	2.71%	11.41
1962	4.06%	28.66	1.12%	2.94%	11.75
1963	3.85%	29.77	1.10%	2.75%	12.07
1964	4.14%	31.00	1.37%	2.77%	12.40
1965	4.21%	32.30	1.62%	2.59%	12.72
1966	4.65%	33.80	2.92%	1.73%	12.95
1967	4.64%	35.37	2.84%	1.80%	13.18
1968	5.70%	37.39	4.26%	1.44%	13.37
1969	6.16%	39.69	5.29%	0.87%	13.48
1970	7.88%	42.82	5.94%	1.94%	13.75
1971	6.50%	45.60	4.31%	2.19%	14.05
1972	5.89%	48.29	3.31%	2.58%	14.41
1973	6.41%	51.39	6.20%	0.21%	14.44
1974	6.90%	54.93	11.11%	-4.21%	13.83
1975	7.40%	59.00	8.98%	-1.58%	13.61
1976	7.76%	63.57	5.75%	2.01%	13.89
1977	6.81%	67.90	6.62%	0.19%	13.91
1978	7.78%	73.19	7.59%	0.19%	13.94
1979	9.15%	79.88	11.28%	-2.13%	13.64
1980	10.33%	88.14	13.48%	-3.15%	13.21
1981	12.43%	99.09	10.36%	2.07%	13.49

1982	13.98%	112.94	6.16%	7.82%	14.54
1983	10.36%	124.64	3.21%	7.15%	15.58
1984	11.82%	139.38	4.37%	7.45%	16.74
1985	11.55%	155.48	3.54%	8.01%	18.08
1986	9.00%	169.47	1.86%	7.14%	19.37
1987	7.23%	181.72	3.66%	3.57%	20.07
1988	8.83%	197.77	4.12%	4.71%	21.01
1989	9.14%	215.84	4.81%	4.33%	21.92
1990	7.93%	232.96	5.39%	2.54%	22.48
1991	8.08%	251.78	4.22%	3.86%	23.34
1992	6.71%	268.68	3.01%	3.70%	24.21
1993	6.70%	286.68	2.98%	3.72%	25.11
1994	5.83%	303.39	2.60%	3.23%	25.92
1995	7.84%	327.18	2.76%	5.08%	27.24
1996	5.58%	345.43	2.96%	2.62%	27.95
1997	6.43%	367.64	2.35%	4.08%	29.09
1998	5.75%	388.78	1.51%	4.24%	30.32
1999	4.65%	406.86	2.21%	2.44%	31.06
2000	6.45%	433.10	3.38%	3.07%	32.02
2001	5.12%	455.28	2.86%	2.26%	32.74
2002	5.07%	478.36	1.58%	3.49%	33.88
2003	3.83%	496.68	1.99%	1.84%	34.51
2004	4.27%	517.89	3.52%	0.75%	34.77
2005	4.24%	539.85	3.46%	0.78%	35.04
2006	4.39%	563.55	1.97%	2.42%	35.88
2007	4.70%	590.04	4.00%	0.70%	36.14
2008	4.03%	613.82	-0.02%	4.05%	37.60
2009	2.21%	627.38	2.81%	-0.60%	37.37
2010	3.83%	651.41	1.44%	2.39%	38.27
2011	3.29%	672.84	3.03%	0.26%	38.37
2012	1.87%	685.42	1.77%	0.10%	38.41
2013	1.71%	697.14	1.53%	0.18%	38.48
2014	2.17%	712.27	0.68%	1.49%	39.05
2015	2.31%	728.73	0.77%	1.54%	39.65
2016	2.45%	746.55	0.60%	1.85%	39.65
2017	2.40%	764.47	2.10%	0.30%	39.65
Average	**4.5%**		**1.93%**	**2.6%**	
Median	**3.7%**		**1.58%**	**2.7%**	
High	**14.0%**		**17.69%**	**16.2%**	
Low	**1.7%**		**-10.83%**	**-14.1%**	

30-Year Fixed Mortgage Rates (Since 1900)

Year	Rate	Total Return Index	Inflation Rate	Adjusted Rate	Adjusted Return Index
		1.00			1
1900	5.11%	1.05	1.0%	4.11%	1.04
1901	5.09%	1.10	1.0%	4.10%	1.08
1902	5.18%	1.16	1.0%	4.20%	1.13
1903	5.35%	1.22	2.9%	2.44%	1.16
1904	5.50%	1.29	0.9%	4.56%	1.21
1905	5.68%	1.36	-0.9%	6.61%	1.29
1906	5.45%	1.44	1.9%	3.56%	1.34
1907	5.60%	1.52	4.6%	0.97%	1.35
1908	5.35%	1.60	-1.8%	7.12%	1.44
1909	5.35%	1.69	-1.8%	7.15%	1.55
1910	5.47%	1.78	4.6%	0.88%	1.56
1911	5.46%	1.88	0.0%	5.45%	1.65
1912	5.50%	1.98	2.6%	2.87%	1.69
1913	5.58%	2.09	1.7%	3.87%	1.76
1914	5.60%	2.21	0.8%	4.76%	1.84
1915	5.50%	2.33	0.8%	4.67%	1.93
1916	5.47%	2.46	7.4%	-1.97%	1.89
1917	5.55%	2.59	17.7%	-12.14%	1.66
1918	5.65%	2.74	17.7%	-12.00%	1.46
1919	5.75%	2.90	15.0%	-9.25%	1.33
1920	5.97%	3.07	15.9%	-9.97%	1.19
1921	5.95%	3.25	-10.8%	16.78%	1.40
1922	5.91%	3.44	-6.5%	12.45%	1.57
1923	5.92%	3.65	2.0%	3.92%	1.63
1924	5.90%	3.86	0.0%	5.89%	1.73
1925	5.89%	4.09	2.9%	2.95%	1.78
1926	5.88%	4.33	0.5%	5.40%	1.87
1927	5.85%	4.58	-1.4%	7.27%	2.01
1928	5.92%	4.85	-1.4%	7.36%	2.16
1929	5.95%	5.14	0.0%	5.94%	2.29
1930	5.75%	5.44	-2.4%	8.19%	2.47
1931	5.77%	5.75	-9.0%	14.77%	2.84
1932	5.60%	6.07	-10.4%	16.04%	3.29
1933	5.45%	6.41	-4.9%	10.36%	3.63
1934	5.26%	6.74	3.2%	2.03%	3.71
1935	5.09%	7.09	2.5%	2.59%	3.80
1936	5.11%	7.45	1.2%	3.89%	3.95
1937	5.00%	7.82	3.6%	1.39%	4.01
1938	5.05%	8.22	-1.7%	6.79%	4.28
1939	5.03%	8.63	-1.8%	6.81%	4.57
1940	4.90%	9.05	1.2%	3.70%	4.74
1941	4.98%	9.50	4.8%	0.22%	4.75
1942	4.77%	9.96	10.8%	-6.03%	4.46
1943	4.71%	10.42	6.2%	-1.44%	4.40
1944	4.70%	10.91	1.5%	3.25%	4.54
1945	4.74%	11.43	2.4%	2.36%	4.65
1946	4.80%	11.98	8.4%	-3.57%	4.48
1947	4.91%	12.57	14.6%	-9.68%	4.05
1948	4.93%	13.19	7.9%	-2.94%	3.93
1949	4.95%	13.84	-1.0%	5.99%	4.17
1950	4.93%	14.52	1.1%	3.88%	4.33
1951	5.03%	15.25	7.6%	-2.61%	4.21
1952	5.09%	16.03	2.3%	2.83%	4.33
1953	5.15%	16.86	1.0%	4.20%	4.52
1954	5.18%	17.73	0.3%	4.87%	4.74
1955	5.19%	18.65	-0.3%	5.50%	5.00
1956	5.79%	19.73	1.6%	4.23%	5.21
1957	5.75%	20.86	3.4%	2.37%	5.33

1958	5.92%	22.10	3.0%	2.94%	5.49
1959	5.98%	23.42	0.6%	5.40%	5.78
1960	5.93%	24.81	1.7%	4.21%	6.03
1961	5.81%	26.25	1.1%	4.68%	6.31
1962	5.89%	27.80	1.1%	4.77%	6.61
1963	5.83%	29.42	1.1%	4.73%	6.92
1964	5.81%	31.13	1.4%	4.44%	7.23
1965	6.25%	33.07	1.6%	4.63%	7.56
1966	6.46%	35.21	2.9%	3.54%	7.83
1967	6.97%	37.66	2.8%	4.13%	8.16
1968	7.81%	40.60	4.3%	3.55%	8.45
1969	8.45%	44.04	5.3%	3.16%	8.71
1970	7.48%	47.33	5.9%	1.54%	8.85
1971	7.44%	50.85	4.3%	3.13%	9.12
1972	8.54%	55.19	3.3%	5.23%	9.60
1973	9.62%	60.50	6.2%	3.42%	9.93
1974	9.10%	66.01	11.1%	-2.01%	9.73
1975	8.79%	71.81	9.0%	-0.19%	9.71
1976	8.96%	78.25	5.8%	3.21%	10.02
1977	10.35%	86.34	6.6%	3.73%	10.40
1978	12.90%	97.48	7.6%	5.31%	10.95
1979	14.79%	111.90	11.3%	3.51%	11.33
1980	16.92%	130.83	13.5%	3.44%	11.72
1981	13.62%	148.65	10.4%	3.26%	12.10
1982	13.42%	168.60	6.2%	7.26%	12.98
1983	13.18%	190.82	3.2%	9.97%	14.28
1984	11.26%	212.31	4.4%	6.89%	15.26
1985	9.31%	232.08	3.5%	5.77%	16.14
1986	10.65%	256.79	1.9%	8.79%	17.56
1987	10.61%	284.04	3.7%	6.95%	18.78
1988	9.74%	311.70	4.1%	5.62%	19.84
1989	9.67%	341.84	4.8%	4.86%	20.80

1990	8.50%	370.90	5.4%	3.11%	21.45
1991	8.22%	401.39	4.2%	4.00%	22.31
1992	7.17%	430.17	3.0%	4.16%	23.23
1993	9.20%	469.74	3.0%	6.22%	24.68
1994	7.20%	503.57	2.6%	4.60%	25.81
1995	7.60%	541.84	2.8%	4.84%	27.06
1996	7.10%	580.31	3.0%	4.14%	28.18
1997	6.72%	619.30	2.4%	4.37%	29.42
1998	7.91%	668.29	1.5%	6.40%	31.30
1999	7.38%	717.61	2.2%	5.17%	32.92
2000	7.07%	768.35	3.4%	3.69%	34.13
2001	6.05%	814.83	2.9%	3.19%	35.22
2002	5.88%	862.74	1.6%	4.30%	36.74
2003	5.75%	912.35	2.0%	3.76%	38.12
2004	6.27%	969.56	3.5%	2.75%	39.16
2005	6.14%	1,029	3.5%	2.68%	40.21
2006	6.10%	1,092	2.0%	4.13%	41.87
2007	5.33%	1,150	4.0%	1.33%	42.43
2008	4.93%	1,207	-0.0%	4.95%	44.53
2009	4.71%	1,264	2.8%	1.90%	45.38
2010	3.96%	1,314	1.4%	2.52%	46.52
2011	3.35%	1,358	3.0%	0.32%	46.67
2012	4.46%	1,418	1.8%	2.69%	47.93
2013	3.87%	1,473	1.5%	2.34%	49.05
2014	4.01%	1,532	0.7%	3.33%	50.69
2015	3.93%	1,513	0.8%	3.16%	52.29
2016	4.32%	1,568	0.6%	3.73%	52.89
2017	3.99%	1,527	2.1%	1.89%	52.10
Average	**6.58%**		**3.0%**	**3.57%**	
Median	**5.80%**		**2.6%**	**3.96%**	
High	**16.92%**		**17.7%**	**16.78%**	
Low	**3.35%**		**-10.8%**	**-12.14%**	

233

U.S. GOVERNMENT ACTIONS and INVESTMENTS

Beginning of Year	President	House Speaker	Individual Income Tax	% Change	Capital Gains Tax	% Change	Fed Chairman	Fed Funds Rate %	% Change	Common Stocks	Homes	Corporate Bonds
1913	Wilson (D)	Clark (D)	15		7		Hamlin	3.00		-5.14%	-3.72%	-0.65%
1914	Wilson (D)	Clark (D)	15	0%	7	0%	Hamlin	3.00	0%	-3.58%	-5.18%	-1.18%
1915	Wilson (D)	Clark (D)	15	0%	7	0%	Hamlin	3.00	0%	87.46%	4.81%	11.78%
1916	Wilson (D)	Clark (D)	15	0%	7	0%	Harding	3.00	0%	1.81%	12.49%	4.65%
1917	Wilson (D)	Clark (D)	67	347%	7	0%	Harding	3.00	0%	-14.51%	-9.82%	-7.75%
1918	Harding (R)	Clark (D)	77	15%	7	0%	Harding	4.00	33%	18.41%	-8.90%	9.26%
1919	Harding (R)	Clark (D)	73	-5%	7	0%	Harding	4.75	19%	37.25%	36.38%	-2.03%
1920	Harding (R)	Gillett (R)	73	0%	7	0%	Harding	7.00	47%	-27.10%	24.82%	0.05%
1921	Harding (R)	Gillett (R)	73	0%	12.5	79%	Harding	4.50	-36%	19.22%	11.45%	17.60%
1922	Harding (R)	Gillett (R)	58	-21%	12.5	0%	Harding	4.00	-11%	28.74%	4.97%	11.87%
1923	Harding (R)	Gillett (R)	44	-24%	12.5	0%	Crissinger	4.50	13%	2.75%	4.84%	2.52%
1924	Harding (R)	Gillett (R)	46	5%	12.5	0%	Crissinger	3.00	-33%	32.36%	-0.26%	9.90%
1925	Coolidge (R)	Gillett (R)	25	-46%	12.5	0%	Crissinger	3.50	17%	35.70%	3.13%	7.82%
1926	Coolidge (R)	Longworth (R)	25	0%	12.5	0%	Crissinger	4.00	14%	5.84%	20.05%	8.33%
1927	Coolidge (R)	Longworth (R)	25	0%	12.5	0%	Crissinger	4.00	0%	34.55%	4.80%	8.18%
1928	Coolidge (R)	Longworth (R)	25	0%	12.5	0%	Young	5.00	25%	42.65%	19.07%	1.28%
1929	Hoover (R)	Longworth (R)	24	-4%	12.5	0%	Young	4.50	-10%	-8.01%	-3.34%	2.56%
1930	Hoover (R)	Longworth (R)	25	4%	12.5	0%	Young	2.00	-56%	-23.98%	-10.94%	6.58%
1931	Hoover (R)	Longworth (R)	25	0%	12.5	0%	Meyer	3.50	75%	-41.97%	-10.35%	-13.48%
1932	Hoover (R)	Garner (D)	63	152%	12.5	0%	Meyer	2.50	-29%	-9.15%	-43.64%	7.47%
1933	F. Roosevelt (D)	Garner (D)	63	0%	12.5	0%	Meyer	2.00	-20%	52.79%	66.70%	17.87%
1934	F. Roosevelt (D)	Rainey (D)	63	0%	32	156%	Eccles	1.50	-25%	-1.64%	-28.57%	19.22%
1935	F. Roosevelt (D)	Byrns (D)	63	0%	32	0%	Eccles	1.50	0%	46.47%	16.65%	7.82%
1936	F. Roosevelt (D)	Byrns (D)	78	24%	39	22%	Eccles	1.50	0%	33.12%	16.24%	11.50%
1937	F. Roosevelt (D)	Bankhead (D)	78	0%	39	0%	Eccles	1.00	-33%	-33.99%	-3.78%	-7.96%
1938	F. Roosevelt (D)	Bankhead (D)	78	0%	30	-23%	Eccles	1.00	0%	29.71%	-13.44%	2.52%
1939	F. Roosevelt (D)	Bankhead (D)	78	0%	30	0%	Eccles	1.00	0%	-0.45%	12.21%	5.14%
1940	F. Roosevelt (D)	Bankhead (D)	78	0%	30	0%	Eccles	1.00	0%	-9.79%	-10.17%	6.61%
1941	F. Roosevelt (D)	Rayburn (D)	80	3%	30	0%	Eccles	1.00	0%	-11.16%	-8.74%	2.78%
1942	F. Roosevelt (D)	Rayburn (D)	88	10%	25	-17%	Eccles	0.50	-50%	19.03%	-1.53%	8.66%
1943	F. Roosevelt (D)	Rayburn (D)	88	0%	25	0%	Eccles	0.50	0%	25.55%	-9.39%	12.19%
1944	F. Roosevelt (D)	Rayburn (D)	94	7%	25	0%	Eccles	0.50	0%	19.20%	1.25%	13.06%
1945	F. Roosevelt (D)	Rayburn (D)	94	0%	25	0%	Eccles	0.50	0%	35.62%	-9.83%	6.47%
1946	Truman (D)	Rayburn (D)	86	-9%	25	0%	Eccles	0.50	0%	-7.97%	22.90%	-1.21%
1947	Truman (D)	Rayburn (D)	86	0%	25	0%	Eccles	1.00	100%	5.50%	20.72%	-3.35%
1948	Truman (D)	Martin (R)	82	-5%	25	0%	Eccles	1.50	50%	5.65%	26.30%	6.02%
1949	Truman (D)	Martin (R)	82	0%	25	0%	McCabe	1.50	0%	17.66%	14.93%	6.12%
1950	Truman (D)	Rayburn (D)	84	2%	25	0%	McCabe	1.75	17%	29.88%	-13.93%	5.01%
1951	Truman (D)	Rayburn (D)	91	8%	25	0%	McCabe	1.75	0%	22.96%	38.22%	-2.62%
1952	Truman (D)	Rayburn (D)	91	0%	25	0%	Martin	1.75	0%	17.58%	-5.02%	5.76%
1953	Eisenhower (R)	Rayburn (D)	91	0%	25	0%	Martin	2.00	14%	-1.12%	13.27%	1.89%
1954	Eisenhower (R)	Martin (R)	91	0%	25	0%	Martin	1.28	-36%	51.12%	10.04%	7.28%
1955	Eisenhower (R)	Martin (R)	91	0%	25	0%	Martin	2.48	94%	31.00%	21.78%	0.41%
1956	Eisenhower (R)	Rayburn (D)	91	0%	25	0%	Martin	2.94	19%	6.52%	15.86%	-5.17%
1957	Eisenhower (R)	Rayburn (D)	91	0%	25	0%	Martin	2.98	1%	-10.41%	8.36%	2.10%
1958	Eisenhower (R)	Rayburn (D)	91	0%	25	0%	Martin	2.42	-19%	42.26%	-9.22%	3.24%
1959	Eisenhower (R)	Rayburn (D)	91	0%	25	0%	Martin	3.99	65%	11.78%	2.12%	-1.54%
1960	Eisenhower (R)	Rayburn (D)	91	0%	25	0%	Martin	1.98	-50%	0.43%	14.56%	7.62%
1961	Kennedy (D)	Rayburn (D)	91	0%	25	0%	Martin	2.33	18%	26.53%	5.76%	4.70%
1962	Kennedy (D)	McCormack (D)	91	0%	25	0%	Martin	2.93	26%	-8.71%	7.38%	6.25%
1963	Kennedy (D)	McCormack (D)	91	0%	25	0%	Martin	3.38	15%	22.39%	2.89%	3.58%
1964	Johnson (D)	McCormack (D)	91	0%	25	0%	Martin	3.85	14%	16.27%	12.30%	4.58%
1965	Johnson (D)	McCormack (D)	70	-23%	25	0%	Martin	4.32	12%	12.26%	-3.33%	1.44%

1892 1893 1894 1895 1896 1897

.94
.71¼
.87⅞
.71⅞
.90¼
.60⅝
.97
.64⅛
.97⅞
.68⅜
.83¼
.60⅜

Year	President	Speaker	Top	%Chg	CG	%Chg	Fed	Rate	%Chg	Ret1	Ret2	Ret3
1966	Johnson (D)	McCormack (D)	70	0%	25	0%	Martin	5.40	25%	-9.99%	6.90%	-3.15%
1967	Johnson (D)	McCormack (D)	70	0%	25	0%	Martin	4.51	-16%	23.59%	2.30%	-2.70%
1968	Johnson (D)	McCormack (D)	75	7%	26.9	8%	Martin	6.02	33%	10.86%	19.37%	4.52%
1969	Nixon (R)	McCormack (D)	77	3%	27.5	2%	Martin	8.97	49%	-8.26%	-5.28%	-2.52%
1970	Nixon (R)	McCormack (D)	70	-9%	32.3	17%	Martin	4.90	-45%	3.59%	-11.16%	12.50%
1971	Nixon (R)	Albery (D)	70	0%	31.3	-3%	Burns	4.14	-16%	14.09%	13.45%	13.30%
1972	Nixon (R)	Albery (D)	70	0%	36.5	17%	Burns	5.33	29%	18.74%	17.39%	8.49%
1973	Nixon (R)	Albery (D)	70	0%	36.5	0%	Burns	9.95	87%	-13.27%	20.20%	2.03%
1974	Ford (R)	Albery (D)	70	0%	36.5	0%	Burns	8.86	-11%	-24.03%	4.76%	-2.90%
1975	Ford (R)	Albery (D)	70	0%	36.5	0%	Burns	5.50	-38%	36.17%	14.12%	13.29%
1976	Ford (R)	Albery (D)	70	0%	39.9	9%	Burns	4.75	-14%	23.75%	9.66%	18.59%
1977	Carter (D)	Albery (D)	70	0%	39.9	0%	Burns	6.48	36%	-5.80%	14.30%	7.00%
1978	Carter (D)	O'Neill (D)	70	0%	39	-2%	Burns	10.00	54%	6.96%	15.41%	1.23%
1979	Carter (D)	O'Neill (D)	70	0%	39	0%	Miller	13.75	38%	18.51%	5.34%	0.72%
1980	Carter (D)	O'Neill (D)	70	0%	28	-28%	Volcker	20.00	45%	31.16%	10.66%	-1.51%
1981	Reagan	O'Neill (D)	70	0%	23.7	-15%	Volcker	12.50	-38%	-3.02%	1.89%	3.24%
1982	Reagan (R)	O'Neill (D)	50	-29%	20	-16%	Volcker	8.98	-28%	19.95%	4.76%	32.80%
1983	Reagan (R)	O'Neill (D)	50	0%	20	0%	Volcker	8.98	0%	21.68%	5.81%	12.68%
1984	Reagan (R)	O'Neill (D)	50	0%	20	0%	Volcker	8.98	0%	5.90%	4.18%	15.92%
1985	Reagan (R)	O'Neill (D)	50	0%	20	0%	Volcker	8.23	-8%	29.57%	11.11%	24.00%
1986	Reagan (R)	O'Neill (D)	50	0%	20	0%	Volcker	7.00	-15%	18.35%	10.26%	17.94%
1987	Reagan (R)	O'Neill (D)	38.5	-23%	28	40%	Volcker	6.75	-4%	5.43%	15.94%	4.40%
1988	Reagan (R)	Wright (D)	33	-14%	28	0%	Greenspan	8.75	30%	16.00%	8.35%	11.29%
1989	GH Bush (R)	Wright (D)	33	0%	28	0%	Greenspan	8.55	-2%	30.45%	4.02%	15.34%
1990	GH Bush (R)	Foley (D)	33	0%	28	0%	Greenspan	6.50	-24%	-2.86%	0.32%	6.80%
1991	GH Bush (R)	Foley (D)	31	-6%	28	0%	Greenspan	3.50	-46%	28.71%	-5.49%	20.31%
1992	GH Bush (R)	Foley (D)	31	0%	28	0%	Greenspan	2.50	-29%	7.46%	2.72%	10.97%
1993	Clinton (D)	Foley (D)	39.6	28%	28	0%	Greenspan	3.38	35%	9.56%	-0.29%	14.34%
1994	Clinton (D)	Foley (D)	39.6	0%	28	0%	Greenspan	5.50	63%	1.36%	8.55%	-2.99%
1995	Clinton (D)	Foley (D)	39.6	0%	28	0%	Greenspan	5.50	0%	36.61%	3.26%	22.20%
1996	Clinton (D)	Gingrich (R)	39.6	0%	28	0%	Greenspan	6.00	9%	22.36%	4.11%	3.76%
1997	Clinton (D)	Gingrich (R)	39.6	0%	20	-29%	Greenspan	6.00	0%	32.71%	1.58%	11.69%
1998	Clinton (D)	Gingrich (R)	39.6	0%	20	0%	Greenspan	4.00	-33%	28.27%	4.38%	8.59%
1999	Clinton (D)	Gingrich (R)	39.6	0%	20	0%	Greenspan	5.75	44%	20.43%	9.26%	-3.24%
2000	Clinton (D)	Hastert (R)	39.6	0%	20	0%	Greenspan	6.25	9%	-9.61%	0.87%	8.26%
2001	GW Bush (R)	Hastert (R)	39.1	-1%	20	0%	Greenspan	1.63	-74%	-11.81%	10.48%	12.79%
2002	GW Bush (R)	Hastert (R)	38.6	-1%	20	0%	Greenspan	1.19	-27%	-21.54%	6.48%	15.22%
2003	GW Bush (R)	Hastert (R)	35	-9%	18	-10%	Greenspan	0.93	-22%	27.99%	3.33%	11.93%
2004	GW Bush (R)	Hastert (R)	35	0%	15	-17%	Greenspan	2.24	141%	10.61%	14.23%	10.62%
2005	GW Bush (R)	Hastert (R)	35	0%	15	0%	Greenspan	4.18	87%	4.76%	2.90%	5.08%
2006	GW Bush (R)	Hastert (R)	35	0%	15	0%	Greenspan	5.25	26%	15.38%	3.37%	5.28%
2007	GW Bush (R)	Pelosi (D)	35	0%	15	0%	Bernake	4.01	-24%	5.37%	-6.31%	6.30%
2008	GW Bush (R)	Pelosi (D)	35	0%	15	0%	Bernake	0.09	-98%	-35.26%	-3.79%	-5.74%
2009	Obama (D)	Pelosi (D)	35	0%	15	0%	Bernake	0.11	22%	26.22%	-3.94%	19.12%
2010	Obama (D)	Pelosi (D)	35	0%	15	0%	Bernake	0.19	73%	13.48%	6.39%	12.59%
2011	Obama (D)	Boehner (R)	35	0%	15	0%	Bernake	0.09	-53%	2.13%	-9.65%	15.18%
2012	Obama (D)	Boehner (R)	35	0%	15	0%	Bernake	0.11	22%	15.60%	15.78%	8.07%
2013	Obama (D)	Boehner (R)	39.6	13%	20	33%	Bernake	0.10	-9%	31.54%	7.03%	-3.32%
2014	Obama (D)	Boehner (R)	39.6	0%	20	0%	Yellen	0.11	10%	13.32%	13.21%	13.05%
2015	Obama (D)	Boehner (R)	39.6	0%	20	0%	Yellen	0.35	218%	1.46%	-5.95%	-1.77%
2016	Obama (D)	Ryan (R)	39.6	0%	20	0%	Yellen	0.75	114%	11.53%	10.00%	7.94%
2017	Trump (R)	Ryan (R)	32	-19%	20	0%	Yellen	1.50	100%	21.24%	1.58%	8.21%
Average			**58.6**		**22.5**			**4.0**		**12.4%**	**5.6%**	**6.5%**
High			**94.0**	**347%**	**39.9**	**156%**		**20.0**	**218%**	**87%**	**67%**	**38%**
Low			**15.0**	**-46%**	**7.0**	**-29%**		**0.1**	**-74%**	**-42%**	**-44%**	**-13%**

Large Tax Rate Decreases
Large Tax Rate Increasses
Large Rate Decreases
Large Rate Increases
Severe Bear Markets

TAXATION and INVESTMENTS

Year	Corporate Tax	% Chg	Individual Tax	% Chg	Capital Gains Tax	% Chg	Common Stocks	Real Estate	Corporate Bonds
1913	1		15		7		-5.1%	-3.7%	-0.7%
1914	1	0%	15	0%	7	0%	-3.6%	-5.2%	-1.2%
1915	1	0%	15	0%	7	0%	87.5%	4.8%	11.8%
1916	2	100%	15	0%	7	0%	1.8%	12.5%	4.7%
1917	6	200%	67	347%	7	0%	-14.5%	-9.8%	-7.7%
1918	12	100%	77	15%	7	0%	18.4%	-8.9%	9.3%
1919	10	-17%	73	-5%	7	0%	37.3%	36.4%	-2.0%
1920	10	0%	73	0%	7	0%	-27.1%	24.8%	0.1%
1921	10	0%	73	0%	12.5	79%	19.2%	11.5%	17.6%
1922	12.5	25%	58	-21%	12.5	0%	28.7%	5.0%	11.9%
1923	12.5	0%	44	-24%	12.5	0%	2.7%	4.8%	2.5%
1924	12.5	0%	46	5%	12.5	0%	32.4%	-0.3%	9.9%
1925	13	4%	25	-46%	12.5	0%	35.7%	3.1%	7.8%
1926	13.5	4%	25	0%	12.5	0%	5.8%	20.1%	8.3%
1927	13.5	0%	25	0%	12.5	0%	34.6%	4.8%	8.2%
1928	12	-11%	25	0%	12.5	0%	42.6%	19.1%	1.3%
1929	11	-8%	24	-4%	12.5	0%	-8.0%	-3.3%	2.6%
1930	12	9%	25	4%	12.5	0%	-24.0%	-10.9%	6.6%
1931	12	0%	25	0%	12.5	0%	-42.0%	-10.4%	-13.5%
1932	13.75	15%	63	152%	12.5	0%	-9.1%	-43.6%	7.5%
1933	13.75	0%	63	0%	12.5	0%	52.8%	66.7%	17.9%
1934	13.75	0%	63	0%	32	156%	-1.6%	-28.6%	19.2%
1935	13.75	0%	63	0%	32	0%	46.5%	16.6%	7.8%
1936	15	9%	78	24%	39	22%	33.1%	16.2%	11.5%
1937	15	0%	78	0%	39	0%	-34.0%	-3.8%	-8.0%
1938	19	27%	78	0%	30	-23%	29.7%	-13.4%	2.5%
1939	19	0%	78	0%	30	0%	-0.5%	12.2%	5.1%
1940	24	26%	78	0%	30	0%	-9.8%	-10.2%	6.6%
1941	31	29%	80	3%	30	0%	-11.2%	-8.7%	2.8%
1942	40	29%	88	10%	25	-17%	19.0%	-1.5%	8.7%
1943	40	0%	88	0%	25	0%	25.5%	-9.4%	12.2%
1944	40	0%	94	7%	25	0%	19.2%	1.3%	13.1%
1945	40	0%	94	0%	25	0%	35.6%	-9.8%	6.5%
1946	38	-5%	86	-9%	25	0%	-8.0%	22.9%	-1.2%
1947	38	0%	86	0%	25	0%	5.5%	20.7%	-3.4%
1948	38	0%	82	-5%	25	0%	5.6%	26.3%	6.0%
1949	38	0%	82	0%	25	0%	17.7%	14.9%	6.1%
1950	42	11%	84	2%	25	0%	29.9%	-13.9%	5.0%
1951	50.75	21%	91	8%	25	0%	23.0%	38.2%	-2.6%
1952	52	2%	91	0%	25	0%	17.6%	-5.0%	5.8%
1953	52	0%	91	0%	25	0%	-1.1%	13.3%	1.9%
1954	52	0%	91	0%	25	0%	51.1%	10.0%	7.3%
1955	52	0%	91	0%	25	0%	31.0%	21.8%	0.4%
1956	52	0%	91	0%	25	0%	6.5%	15.9%	-5.2%
1957	52	0%	91	0%	25	0%	-10.4%	8.4%	2.1%
1958	52	0%	91	0%	25	0%	42.3%	-9.2%	3.2%
1959	52	0%	91	0%	25	0%	11.8%	2.1%	-1.5%
1960	52	0%	91	0%	25	0%	0.4%	14.6%	10.4%
1961	52	0%	91	0%	25	0%	26.5%	5.8%	3.9%
1962	52	0%	91	0%	25	0%	-8.7%	7.4%	9.9%
1963	52	0%	91	0%	25	0%	22.4%	2.9%	5.6%
1964	50	-4%	91	0%	25	0%	16.3%	12.3%	6.0%
1965	48	-4%	70	-23%	25	0%	12.3%	-3.3%	1.6%
1966	48	0%	70	0%	25	0%	-10.0%	6.9%	-2.2%
1967	48	0%	70	0%	25	0%	23.6%	2.3%	-2.0%
1968	52.8	10%	75	7%	26.9	8%	10.9%	19.4%	5.7%
1969	52.8	0%	77	3%	27.5	2%	-8.3%	-5.3%	-1.0%
1970	49.2	-7%	70	-9%	32.3	17%	3.6%	-11.2%	9.2%
1971	48	-2%	70	0%	31.3	-3%	14.1%	13.5%	15.0%
1972	48	0%	70	0%	36.5	17%	18.7%	17.4%	10.1%
1973	48	0%	70	0%	36.5	0%	-13.3%	20.2%	4.7%
1974	48	0%	70	0%	36.5	0%	-24.0%	4.8%	-0.7%
1975	48	0%	70	0%	36.5	0%	36.2%	14.1%	14.3%
1976	48	0%	70	0%	39.9	9%	23.7%	9.7%	24.7%
1977	48	0%	70	0%	39.9	0%	-5.8%	14.3%	5.6%
1978	48	0%	70	0%	39	-2%	7.0%	15.4%	1.2%
1979	46	-4%	70	0%	39	0%	18.5%	5.3%	-4.1%
1980	46	0%	70	0%	28	-28%	31.2%	10.7%	-2.3%
1981	46	0%	70	0%	23.7	-15%	-3.0%	1.9%	2.6%
1982	46	0%	50	-29%	20	-16%	20.0%	4.8%	38.5%
1983	46	0%	50	0%	20	0%	21.7%	5.8%	10.5%
1984	46	0%	50	0%	20	0%	5.9%	4.2%	16.6%
1985	46	0%	50	0%	20	0%	29.6%	11.1%	27.9%
1986	46	0%	50	0%	20	0%	18.3%	10.3%	22.1%
1987	40	-13%	38.5	-23%	28	40%	5.4%	15.9%	2.1%
1988	34	-15%	33	-14%	28	0%	16.0%	8.3%	12.5%
1989	34	0%	33	0%	28	0%	30.5%	4.0%	14.9%
1990	34	0%	33	0%	28	0%	-2.9%	0.3%	7.8%
1991	34	0%	31	-6%	28	0%	28.7%	-5.5%	17.5%
1992	34	0%	31	0%	28	0%	7.5%	2.7%	13.5%
1993	35	3%	39.6	28%	28	0%	9.6%	-0.3%	8.3%
1994	35	0%	39.6	0%	28	0%	1.4%	8.5%	-4.2%
1995	35	0%	39.6	0%	28	0%	36.6%	3.3%	20.7%
1996	35	0%	39.6	0%	28	0%	22.4%	4.1%	5.4%
1997	35	0%	39.6	0%	20	-29%	32.7%	1.6%	9.7%
1998	35	0%	39.6	0%	20	0%	28.3%	4.4%	9.6%
1999	35	0%	39.6	0%	20	0%	20.4%	9.3%	-3.2%
2000	35	0%	39.6	0%	20	0%	-9.6%	0.9%	9.4%
2001	35	0%	39.1	-1%	20	0%	-11.8%	10.5%	10.7%
2002	34	-3%	38.6	-1%	20	0%	-21.5%	6.5%	10.3%
2003	34	0%	35	-9%	18	-10%	28.0%	3.3%	8.0%
2004	34	0%	35	0%	15	-17%	10.6%	14.2%	4.8%
2005	34	0%	35	0%	15	0%	4.8%	2.9%	0.3%
2006	34	0%	35	0%	15	0%	15.4%	3.4%	3.4%
2007	34	0%	35	0%	15	0%	5.4%	-6.3%	6.4%
2008	34	0%	35	0%	15	0%	-35.3%	-3.8%	-0.8%
2009	34	0%	35	0%	15	0%	26.2%	-3.9%	18.4%
2010	34	0%	35	0%	15	0%	13.5%	6.4%	7.0%
2011	34	0%	35	0%	15	0%	2.1%	-9.7%	6.2%
2012	34	0%	35	0%	15	0%	15.6%	15.8%	9.7%
2013	36	6%	39.6	13%	20	33%	31.5%	7.0%	-2.3%
2014	36	0%	39.6	0%	20	0%	13.3%	13.2%	7.2%
2015	36	0%	39.6	0%	20	0%	1.5%	-6.0%	-0.5%
2016	36	0%	39.6	0%	20	0%	11.5%	10.0%	7.9%
2017	21	-41%	32	-19%	20	0%	21.2%	1.6%	8.2%
Average	33.9	5%	58.6	4%	22.5	2%	12.4%	5.6%	6.5%
High	52.8	200%	94.0	347%	39.9	156%	87.5%	66.7%	38.5%
Low	1.0	-17%	15.0	-46%	7.0	-29%	-42.0%	-43.6%	-13.5%

Large Tax Rate Decreases

Large Tax Rate Increases

Severe Market Declines

SOURCES and CREDITS

Charts	All charts were created in MetaStock from Equis International by Kenneth G. Winans, CMT.
Tables	All tables were created by Kenneth G. Winans, CMT.
Historical Facts	All historical references were obtained from Wikipedia.com and *The Almanac of American History*, 2004

Page	Name or Calculation Method	Dates	Data Source
All Sections	US Common Stocks, S&P 500 Index™ combined with percentage changes of Dow Jones Industrial Average™ Cowles Commission Studies and Smith & Cole Studies	1927–2017 1871–1886 1800–1870	Global Financial Data, National Bureau of Economic Research, Dial Data
	US New Homes, Winans International Real Estate Index WIREI™		Winans International patent pending: 11670914
	US Interest Rates, Ten-year Treasury Bond Constant Maturity		Global Financial Data, Federal Reserve, Dial Data
Cover	S&P 500 Index™		Global Financial Data, Dial Data
4	Winans US Preferred Stock Index WIPSI	1980–2017	Winans International, Global Financial Data
5	Winans International Preferred Stock Index	1980–2017	Winans International, Global Financial Data
10	US Gross Domestic Product	1800–2017	Global Financial Data, Economic History Services
10	Economic Expansions and Recessions	1800–2017	National Bureau of Economic Research
11	US Inflation Rate	1800–2017	Dial Data, Economic History Services
12	NYSE Share Volume	1874–2017	Global Financial Data, NYSE, National Bureau of Economic Research
12	NYSE Corporate Bond Volume	1900–2017	New York Stock Exchange
12	New Home Sales	1964–2017	US Census Bureau
13	Individual Retirement Accounts	1962–2017	Federal Reserve
13	Mutual Fund Assets and Number of Mutual Funds	1940–2017	Institute of Investment Companies
20	US Common Stock Prices with Dividend Yields	1800–2017	Global Financial Data, National Bureau of Economic Research, NYSE
20	US Common Stocks Total Return with Inflation Adjusted Return	1850–2017	Winans International
21	US Large-Cap Stocks	1927–2017	Global Financial Data, S&P 500 Index
21	US Midcap Stocks S&P 400 Midcap Index combined with percentage changes of Ibbotson studies	1927–2017 1981–2017 1980–1915	Global Financial Data, Morningstar
21	US Small-Cap Stocks Russell 2000 Index combined with Ibbotson studies	1927–2017 1978–2017 1978–2017	Global Financial Data, Morningstar

21	US Common Stocks Total Return by Market Capitalization	1927–2017	Winans International
22	NYSE Margin Use	1918–2017	Global Financial Data, New York Stock Exchange
22	CBOE Stock Call Options	1989–2017	Global Financial Data
23	NYSE Short Selling Short Interest Sales	1931–2017	Global Financial Data
23	CBOE Stock Put Options	1931–2017	Global Financial Data
26	Global Stock Transactions	1958–2017	New York Stock Exchange
26	Foreign Stocks Versus US Stocks	1958–2017	Reuters
27	Common Stocks Total Return Table	1958–2017	Winans International
28	Winans International Preferred Stock Index WIPSI	1980–2017	Winans International, Global Financial Data
29	Winans US Preferred Stock Index WIPSI	1980–2017	Winans International, Global Financial Data
31	NYSE Advancing Volume/Declining Volume	1970–2017	Global Financial Data, Reuters
32	NYSE Advancing/Declining Stock Price Line	1970–2017	Global Financial Data, Reuters
32	NYSE Twelve-Month New High/New Low Price Line	1970–2017	Global Financial Data, Reuters
33	Winans Legacy Stock Index	1970–2017	Global Financial Data, New York Stock Exchange
36	US New Home Prices	1830–2017	Winans International
37	Regional Home Prices Total Return	1974–2017	Winans International
38	Standard and Poors Homebuilders Index	1965–2017	Global Financial Data
38	Winans International REIT Composite	1975 –2017	Winans International/Global Financial Data
39	Winans-GFD International Housing Index	1970–2017	Winans International/Global Financial Data
40	Thirty-Year Fixed Rate Mortgages	1990–2017	Federal Reserve
40	First Trust Deed Yields	1990–2017	Edward Brown and Mark Hanf
41	US Home Prices Adjusted for Size	1974–2017	US Census Bureau
42	US New Home Listings and Sales	1963–2017	US Census Bureau
43	US Mortgage Rates Thirty30-Yyear Conventional	1900–2017	Federal Reserve
43	US Mortgage Rates One1-Yyear Adjustable	1983–2017	Global Financial Data
46	US Corporate Bond Prices	1862–2017	Global Financial Data
46	US Corporate Bond Yields	1862–2017	Global Financial Data, National Bureau of Economic Research
46	US Corporate Bond Total Return and Inflation Adjusted Table	1862–2017	Winans International
47	High-Quality Corporate Bond Yields	1900–2017	Global Financial Data, National Bureau of Economic Research
47	Low-Quality Corporate Bond Yields	1900–2017	Global Financial Data, National Bureau of Economic Research
50	Ten-Year US Treasury Bond Yields	1800–2017	Global Financial Data, National Bureau of Economic Research / Federal Reserve

51	Three-Month US Treasury Bill	1820–2017	Global Financial Data, National Bureau of Economic Research / Federal Reserve
52	US Municipal Bond Yields	1800–2017	Global Financial Data, National Bureau of Economic Research
55	Foreign Bonds Total Return	1923–2017	Global Financial Data
57	Yield Spreads	1800–2017	Winans International
60	Gold and Silver Bullion (in British Pounds)	since 1257	Global Financial Data
61	Gold and Silver per Ounce	1800–2017	Global Financial Data, National Bureau of Economic Research
62	Commodities Spot Index	1800–2017	Global Financial Data, National Bureau of Economic Research
63	Crude Oil Spot Price	1860–2017	National Bureau of Economic Research
65	British Pound	1800–2017	Global Financial Data
66	Commodity Table	1900–2017	Source: Winans International / Lind Waldock
68	Morgan Silver Dollar	1883–1921	US-Coin-Values-Advisor.com
69	Morgan Silver Dollar	1950–2017	US-Coin-Values-Advisors.com
71	Cabernet Sauvignon Wine	1960–2012	Beaulieu Vineyards, Wine-Searcher.com
72	Apollo 11 Crew Autographed Portrait	1992–2017	Reynolds, Winans Apollo Collection Index; Ken Winans, Mike Reynolds
73	Apollo 11 Crew Autographed Items	1992–2017	Reynolds, Winans Apollo Collection Index; Ken Winans, Mike Reynolds
76	US Money 1800–2007 US Dollar Index	1973–2017 1800–1974	Global Financial Data, National Bureau of Economic Research, Economic History Services
77	Ninety-Day T-Bill Yields	1820–2017	Global Financial Data, National Bureau of Economic Research, / Federal Reserve
77	Three-Month Commercial Paper	1830–2017	Global Financial Data
78	Treasury Maturity Yield Spread	1800–2017	Winans International
81	Performance Summery Table		Winans International
84	US Common Stocks: Longest Bull Markets		Winans International
85	US Homes: Longest Bull Markets		Winans International
90	US Common Stocks: Longest Bear Markets		Winans International
91	US Homes: Longest Bear Markets		Winans International
96	Worst Financial Panics		Ken Winans, Museum of American Finance
100	Shareholder Dilution		Winans International, Valueline
104	Presidents and Investments		Winans International

106	The GOP		Winans International
107	The Dems		Winans International
109	US Gross Domestic Product		Global Financial Data, Economic History Services
110	US Inflation Rate		Dial Data, Economic History Services
113	Taxation Spread		Winans International, Internal Revenue Service, Global Financial Data
115	AT&T		Global Financial Data, Dial Data
115	Microsoft		Global Financial Data, Dial Data
118	Government Actions and Investments		Winans International
123	British Stocks		Global Financial Data
124	British Bonds		Global Financial Data
127	Mexican Bonds		Global Financial Data
131	Confederate Cotton Bond		Global Financial Data
138	Spanish Interest Rates		Global Financial Data
141	German Common Stocks		Global Financial Data
142	German Interest Rates		Global Financial Data
145	Japanese Common Stocks		Global Financial Data
145	German Common Stocks		Global Financial Data
146	Japanese Bonds		Global Financial Data
146	German Bonds		Global Financial Data
151	South Korea Interest Rates		Global Financial Data
155	South Vietnam Interest Rates		Global Financial Data
159	Iraq Interest Rates		Global Financial Data
161	Wartime Investments Summary		Winans International
176	Natural Disasters Summary		Winans International
178	Oil Prices Spot		Global Financial Data, National Bureau of Economic Research
195	Man-Made Disasters Summary		Winans International
210	Peaceful Achievements Summary		Winans International
212	Performance Summery Table		Winans International
213	Five-Year Portfolio Performance Goal and Asset Allocation Projections		Winans International
217	Bear Sterns Common Stock	2003–2007	Dial Data

ARTIFACT and CHART PAGE REFERENCES

ABOUT THE AUTHOR

Kenneth Grant Winans is a successful investment management entrepreneur, an award-winning author, astute collector, and an active philanthropist.

Over a long career, he has conducted landmark investment research and designed creative investment strategies while serving as a portfolio manager, investment analyst, and financial writer. He is a regular guest on TV and radio shows nationwide and has had much of his investment research published as headline articles by leading websites, magazines, and newspapers.

Unique in the financial services industry, Mr. Winans has documented "track records" as a market strategist and a portfolio manager in equity and fixed income.

Mr. Winans pioneered the development of several important investment indexes and technical indicators. In fact, The Winans Preferred Stock Index (WIPSI)™ and the Winans Real Estate Index™ are used by major financial and academic institutions in market research studies. This research has aided Mr. Winans in making timely market forecasts in a variety of economic conditions since 1991.

As one of today's most astute market historians, his four investment history books have won thirty-two honors in international competitions: *Investment Atlas II: Using History as a Financial Tool* (2016), *Preferred Stocks: The Art of Profitable Income Investing* (2010), *Investment Atlas: Financial Maps to Investment Success* (2008), and *Preferreds: Wall Street's Best-Kept Income Secret* (2005).

A true entrepreneur, Mr. Winans left a promising career with Merrill Lynch and started Winans International in 1992 with only seven clients. Today, Winans Investments manages equity and fixed income investments for its expanding clientele based on a solid performance record. Since 2012, WI is among the Best of Best financial advisors attending Barron's Winner's Circle Top Independent Advisors Summit.

Mr. Winans holds a masters in finance from the University of San Francisco and a BA in business economics from the University of San Diego. As a chartered market technician (CMT), he was the founding president of the San Francisco Chapter of the Market Technician Association. He is also a senior member of the CFA Institute and has served on several committees for its San Francisco Chapter.

Ken is the cofounder and president of the Space Station Museum (Novato, CA) and serves as a trustee for several other nonprofit organizations: W Foundation (Novato), USS Hornet Museum (Alameda, CA), the Society of California Pioneers (San Francisco) and the Holland Society of New York. He served board terms for the Museum of American Finance (New York City), San Francisco Fleet Week Association, Chabot Space and Science Center (Oakland), University of San Francisco Alumni Association, and the Institute of Ecolonomics (Ridgway, CO).

Ken and his wife, Debbie, are long-time residents of the San Francisco area. In his spare time, Ken travels internationally, rides motorcycles, scuba dives, and ski races. He enjoys researching his family history and is a renowned collector of artifacts from space exploration and rare financial documents.

More information can be found at www.KenWinans.com.

WINANS FINANCIAL INVENTIONS

Kenneth G. Winans pioneered the development of six investment indexes (with thirty-nine subindices) and a technical trend indicator. These indexes have been featured in lead articles on media websites and used by researchers in major financial and academic institutions. The charts and data can be purchased through Global Financial Data, MetaStock, and Securities Research Company (SRC) on a subscription basis. Mr. Winans' books are available on Amazon.

STOCK AND BOND INDICES AND INDICATORS

Winans Legacy Stock Index (Symbol: WILSI)
Developed in 2013, Winans Legacy Stock Index is an unweighted composite of 251 senior common stocks from diverse industry sectors that comprise the historical leadership of the US economy. Most of the companies have been in continuous operation since 1897 (on average), and most have been continuously traded on the New York Stock Exchange (NYSE) since 1970.

Since the WILSI's underlying components remain unchanged, this provides a baseline to compare today's financial conditions to past stock market cycles using the exact same securities. The WILSI provides an alternative means to evaluate stock market activity (past and present), and it eliminates many of the statistical flaws inherent in conventional stock market indices (such as S&P 500 Index and Dow Jones Industrial Average) due to their frequent changes in underlying components and data weighting methods.

Subindices: WILSI includes price, dividend yield, total return, volume, fifty-two-week high/low line, advance/decline line, price to sales ratio, price to earnings ratio, and industry sector breakdowns.

Winans Legacy Bond Index (Symbol: WILBI)
Developed in 2017, Winans Legacy Bond Index is an unweighted composite of 251 senior corporate bonds from diverse industry sectors that comprise the historical leadership of the US economy. Most of the companies have been in continuous operation since 1897 (on average), and most have been continuously traded on the New York Bond Exchange (NYSE) since 1970.

Since the WILBI's underlying components remain unchanged, this provides a baseline to compare today's financial conditions to past bond market cycles using the exact same securities. The WILBI provides an alternative means to evaluate bond market activity (past and present), and it eliminates many of the statistical flaws inherent in conventional bond market indices due to their frequent changes in underlying components and data weighting methods.

Subindices: WILBI includes price, yield, total return, volume, and industry sector breakdowns.

Winans Preferred Stock Index® (Symbol: WIPSI®)
Developed in 2005, the WIPSI was the first modern index to track these long-established equities. It is an even-weighted index that consists of eighty-five traditional preferred stocks of US companies that have consistently issued listed preferred stocks on the NYSE since 1980. As of December 2017, the industry breakdown was 58% financial services, 22% real estate investment trusts, 12% utilities, and 8% industrials. The issuers' average revenue is $24 billion. Mr. Winans' 2010 book, *Preferred Stocks: The Art of Profitable Income Investing* provides comprehensive analysis of preferred stocks using the WIPSI.

Subindices: WIPSI includes price, dividend yield, total return, volume, and inflation adjustments since 1890.

Winans Trend Indicator (Symbol: WITI) (Pat. Pend.)
Developed in the early 1990s, the Winans Trend Indicator is used in determining significant trend changes in a US stock market average. Based on the analysis of hundreds of years of investment data, it was discovered that a simple moving average works better for long-term trend analysis. The 200-day moving average was found to be most effective as a selling indicator while the 125-day moving average was better as a buying indicator. Further studies showed that percentage adjustments used as filters on each moving average significantly improved the indicator's effectiveness (Patent Pending 11/767,880).

REAL ESTATE INDICES

Winans Real Estate Index ™ (Symbol: WIREI™) (Pat. Pend.)

Developed in 2007, the WIREI (Patent Pending 11/670,914) tracks new US home prices since 1830. Its unique approach rescaled and combined several well-known government studies of US new home prices into a continuous data set without the gapping and time lag problems found in other housing indices (such as the Case Shiller Real Estate Indices.)

Subindices: WIREI includes price and inflation adjustment since 1830; sales, listings, and inventory figures since 1962; and geographic regions and home size figures since 1973.

Winans / GFD International Real Estate Index (Symbol: WITIRE)

Developed in 2011, the Winans / GFD International Real Estate Index is the first benchmark to track new homes prices from forty-four different countries since 1970: Australia, Austria, Belgium, Canada, Chile, China, Colombia, Czech Republic, Denmark, Finland, France Germany, Greece, Hong Kong, Hungary, Indonesia, Ireland, Israel, Italy, Japan, Korea, Malaysia, Mexico, Morocco, Netherlands, New Zealand, Norway, Peru, Philippines, Poland, Portugal, Romania, Russia, Singapore, Slovakia, South Africa, Spain, Sweden, Switzerland, Thailand, Turkey, UK, and USA (WIREI). In order to combine studies with different scales, the median and average calculations from individual indices' annual percentage change are averaged. The index is even-weighted.

Subindices: The WITIRE has been adjusted for by currency, country GDP, and ex-US housing market.

More information can be found at www.KenWinans.com.

Preferred Stocks
The Art of Profitable
Income Investing

Kenneth G. Winans